IDEAS AND INFLUENCE

PETER SAUNDERS has been the Director of the Social Policy Research Centre at the University of New South Wales since 1987. His research interests include poverty and income distribution, household needs and living standards, social security reform and comparative social policy. His most recent book is *The Poverty Wars: Reconnecting Research with Reality* (UNSW Press 2005). He is currently an Australian Research Council Professorial Fellow working on the concepts and measurement of poverty and inequality. He was elected a Fellow of the Academy of the Social Sciences in 1995.

JAMES WALTER has published in the areas of political biography, institutions, leadership and political ideas. His last book was *The Citizens' Bargain* (UNSW Press 2002). He is professor of politics at Monash University, and has previously held chairs in Australian Studies at Griffith University (where he is Emeritus Professor) and the University of London. He was elected a Fellow of the Academy of Social Sciences in Australia in 1997.

IDEAS AND INFLUENCE

SOCIAL SCIENCE AND
PUBLIC POLICY
IN AUSTRALIA

Edited by
PETER SAUNDERS
and
JAMES WALTER

UNSW PRESS

A UNSW Press book

Published by
University of New South Wales Press Ltd
University of New South Wales
Sydney NSW 2052
AUSTRALIA
www.unswpress.com.au

National Library of Australia
Cataloguing-in-Publication entry

    Saunders, Peter.
    Ideas and influence: social science and public policy in
    Australia.

    Bibliography.
    Includes index.
    ISBN 0 86840 914 6.

    1. Social policy - Research. 2. Social policy - Public
    opinion. 3. Public opinion - Australia. 4. Australia -
    Social policy. I. Walter, James, 1949- . II. Title.

361.994

Design Di Quick
Print Southwood Press

MONASH
Institute for the Study of Global Movements

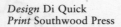

CONTENTS

ACKNOWLEDGEMENTS

The original idea for this project came from John Nieuwenhuysen, Director of the Institute for the Study of Global Movements at Monash University, without whose foresight and persistence this book would not exist. After a series of discussions at the Academy of the Social Sciences, the kernel of the idea of a book about the contribution of social science to Australian public policy began to take shape in late 2003. A meeting between the editors and John Nieuwenhuysen took place some months later, at which the Institute agreed to provide financial support for the project. Crucial inputs to the development of its scope were provided in this early stage by Graeme Davison from Monash and by John Beaton, Executive Director of the Academy, and its Research Director, John Robertson.

After that, we were on our own! We were able to convince a group of leading social scientists that the project was worth adding yet another commitment to their growing list, not only as authors, but as members of a project committee that provided oversight of progress on behalf of the Academy. An initial workshop was held at the Academy of the Social Sciences in Canberra in August 2004 to discuss the scope of the project and initial chapter outlines, followed by a second workshop in March 2005 to discuss draft chapters. This model has been developed over recent years by the Academy as an effective way of encouraging cross-disciplinary interaction while working towards coherence in content and consistency of style. The assistance of the Academy secretariat was integral to the success of these workshops.

The project committee consisted of Bruce Chapman, Meredith Edwards, Mike Keating, Stuart Macintyre and Marian Sawer, while Andrew Leigh attended a final workshop as an additional discussant. All gave valuable comments on a number of draft chapters. Without the support, guidance and comments of the project committee, the task would have been far harder and less enjoyable, and we thank them for their contribution.

Phillipa McGuinness at UNSW Press was enthusiastic about the proposal and gave us sound advice while persuading her colleagues to endorse publication. Edward Caruso and Heather Cam provided efficient support that was critical in keeping us on a tight deadline and we thank them all for their efforts.

CONTRIBUTORS

JON ALTMAN is Director of the Centre for Aboriginal Economic Policy Research at the Australian National University, where he has been since appointed foundation director in 1990. He was originally trained as an economist at the University of Auckland and then as an anthropologist at the ANU. His research interests include Indigenous economic development, natural and cultural resource management, and Indigenous public policy. He has published widely in these areas and was elected a Fellow of the Academy of the Social Sciences in 2003. His current research focuses on the development potential of the Indigenous 'hybrid' economy using a model that incorporates the customary sector.

CHILLA BULBECK is Professor of Women's Studies in the School of Social Sciences, Faculty of Humanities and Social Sciences, University of Adelaide, where she teaches gender studies and social science courses. Her current research extends her interest in gender in cross-cultural perspectives (for example, see *Reorienting Western Feminisms* 1998) to compare young people's attitudes to gender and social issues in ten countries in the Asia-Pacific region. The book is provisionally titled 'Crafting Gender Identities in a Globalising World: An Asia-Pacific Comparison'. Her latest book is something completely different: *Facing the Wild: Ecotourism, Conservation and Animal Encounters* (Earthscan, London 2005).

RICHARD ECKERSLEY is a Fellow at the National Centre for Epidemiology and Population Health at the Australian National

University, Canberra, where he is exploring progress and well-being, and whether or not life is getting better. His research includes measures of progress; the relationships between economic growth, quality of life and environmental sustainability; the social and cultural determinants of health and happiness; and visions of the future. Richard's work has been brought together in a book, *Well & Good: Morality, Meaning and Happiness* (Text 2004 and 2005). He is the co-author of a national index of subjective well-being, the first of its kind in the world; a member of the board of Families Australia, a peak national body representing families; a member of the ACT Government's Community Inclusion Board; and a director of Australia 21, a non-profit company established to promote interdisciplinary and cross-institutional networks on important challenges facing Australia this century.

RUTH FINCHER is presently Dean of the Faculty of Architecture, Building and Planning at the University of Melbourne, and since 1997 she has been Professor of Urban Planning and Adjunct Professor of Geography there. An urban geographer, she was elected a Fellow of the Academy of Social Sciences in 2002. Her research interests are in spatial expressions of inequality, urban and social policy; and the urban experiences of immigrants and women in labour markets, housing and community services.

BRIAN HEAD is Professor of Governance at Griffith University. He has held senior positions in both the governmental sector and in university research centres. He has written or edited ten books on public management, as well as numerous government reports. He is currently researching collaboration, inter-governmental policy relations, community consultation, and new partnership and network models.

JENNY HOCKING is Australian Research Council QEII Research Fellow with the National Centre for Australian Studies at Monash University. Her first book, *Beyond Terrorism: The Development of the Australian Security State* (Allen & Unwin

1993) was an early examination of contemporary counter-terrorism developments in Australia. She is the author of the best-selling biography *Lionel Murphy: A Political Biography* (Cambridge University Press 1997, 2000). In 2002 she gave evidence to both the Legal and Constitutional Legislation Committee and the Parliamentary Joint Committee on the government's proposed security legislation. Her recent book on Australia's counter-terrorism developments post-September 11, *Terror Laws: ASIO, Counter-terrorism and the Threat to Democracy* was published by UNSW Press in 2004, and her biography of Australian author Frank Hardy, will be published in November 2005.

SIMON MARGINSON is an Australian Professorial Fellow in Education at Monash University. He works mainly on higher education, and comparative and international education, in the context of globalisation. He has held a Monash Personal Chair and been a Fellow of ASSA since 2000, and is an active commentator on public policy. His most recent book was *The Enterprise University* (2000) with Mark Considine; he is preparing 'Going Global: The Internationalisation of Australian Universities' (with Fazal Rizvi) and a monograph on the future of the research university.

IAN MARSH is a Professor in the Graduate School of Government, University of Sydney, and Director of Research for the Committee for the Economic Development of Australia. Recent publications include (with David Yencken) *Into the Future: The Neglect of the Long Term in Australian Politics* (Black Inc. 2004); and two edited studies: *Democratisation, Governance and Regionalism in East and Southeast Asia* (Routledge 2005) and *Australia's Parties and Party System in an Era of Globalisation* (Federation Press 2006).

BARBARA POCOCK is a Queen Elizabeth II Research Fellow in Social Sciences at the University of Adelaide. She was initially trained as an economist, but now considers herself a social scientist. She has been investigating work, broadly defined, for over two decades, studying Australia in particular. She has held many jobs and published widely (details are available at: www.barbarapocock.com.au). Her most recent book is *The Work/Life Collision* (Federation Press 2003). Her next book (2006) is provisionally titled *The Market Ate My Babies! How Markets Contradict Care.*

JOHN QUIGGIN is a Federation Fellow in Economics and Political Science at the University of Queensland. Professor Quiggin is prominent both as a research economist and as a commentator on Australian economic policy. He has published over 700 research articles, books and reports in fields including environmental economics, risk analysis, production economics, and the theory of economic growth. He has also written on policy topics, including unemployment policy, microeconomic reform, privatisation, competitive tendering and the management of the Murray–Darling river system.

TIM ROWSE is in the History Program in the Research School of Social Sciences, ANU. Since 1981, he has been researching the past and contemporary forms of the colonial relationships between Indigenous and non-Indigenous Australians. In particular, he has worked on the history and health problems of Central Australian Aborigines (*Traditions for Health* 1996, *White Flour White Power* 1998). As well, Tim has written a number of critical syntheses within Australian Indigenous studies (*Remote possibilities* 1992, *After Mabo* 1993, and *Indigenous Futures* 2002). His two-book study of the career of Dr H C Coombs came out in 2000 and 2002. His current research interests include Indigenous autobiographies and the comparative study of settler-colonial nations' Indigenous statistical archives. He is a Fellow of the Australian Academy of the Humanities, and in 2003–04 he held the Australian Studies Chair at Harvard University.

PETER SAUNDERS has been the Director of the Social Policy Research Centre at the University of New South Wales since 1987. His research interests include poverty and income distribution, household needs and living standards, social security reform, and comparative social policy. He has published widely in these and related areas, and was elected a Fellow of the Academy of the Social Sciences in Australia in 1995. He is currently an Australian Research Council Professorial Fellow working on the concepts and measurement of poverty and inequality.

PETER TRAVERS has written extensively on living standards in Australia and New Zealand. With Sue Richardson, he is co-author of *Living Decently: Material Well Being in Australia* (Oxford University Press 1993). He was President of ACOSS from 1977 to 1979, and later studied in Oxford. He joined the staff of the School of Social Administration and Social Work at Flinders University in 1981, and was Head of School from 1999 to 2003.

JAMES WALTER has published in the areas of political biography, institutions, leadership and political ideas. His last book was *The Citizens' Bargain* (UNSWP 2002); his next is provisionally titled *The Ideology Makers: Ideas and Activists in Australian Politics* (2006). He is professor of politics at Monash University, and has previously held chairs in Australian Studies at Griffith University (where he is Emeritus Professor) and the University of London. He was elected a Fellow of the Academy of Social Sciences in Australia in 1997.

1

INTRODUCTION:
RECONSIDERING THE
POLICY SCIENCES

Peter Saunders and James Walter

A day rarely passes without reminders that our collective well-being depends on successfully adapting our behaviour to new challenges: 'the instruments of influence are words, spoken or written; if the influence is to be for the good, it must rest on knowledge' (Beveridge 1955: 3). We know the sorts of questions that frame such debate. If prosperity depends on a skilled population, how should education be organised to achieve that end? If the means of living well depend upon success in a world market, who is responsible for the infrastructure that delivers our exports to that market? If my life within the community brings benefits (services, facilities and social support) what should I be obliged to pay to sustain that community and how should the obligation be distributed between the more and the less affluent? Such a list could be endless. The point is that living together entails the solution of such collective problems, and our attempts to prescribe solutions are encapsulated in public policy.

This book is about the intermediary stage between a problem and a public policy response – the analysis that should draw on expert knowledge. Specifically, it deals with the relations between social science research, the facilitation of informed public opinion and the policy community, and it's intended to show that expert knowledge can shape better futures. Our method is to highlight a range of policy issues, asking where the ideas that provide solutions come from and identifying potential sources of new approaches in the social sciences. Our purpose is not a general review, but a targeted analysis of some of the policy problems of the moment that will reveal the capacities of the social sciences to assist in addressing these. Our broader aim is to demonstrate that a better understanding of the complementary relations between researchers and policymakers will help to release those capacities productively. Inevitably, this involves paying attention to the international movement of ideas, since the practices of social science, and the conversations about the problems of contemporary societies, transcend national boundaries. Yet, as the cases discussed below will show, while some of the most influential ideas driving current policy derive from elsewhere, Australians not only adapt such currents in particular ways, but also have initiated approaches that lead innovation abroad.

When it comes to those collective decisions that determine how we will live together, we rely on leadership – from politicians, business gurus and community figures – to define the problems, filter the options and suggest solutions. This generates public policy: prescribed ways of acting intended to address specific problems or to achieve stated outcomes. Yet in fashioning policy, our leaders and policy activists must make sense of the welter of information, the clamour of expert voices on every side. Political objectives might filter their options, but those options must draw on the work of those who inquire into the nature of things, whose research is reliable and whose analysis promises realistic responses to our problems. Sensible policy will emerge from an effective partnership between policy practitioners and socially responsive yet scientifically rigorous researchers. We must begin by acknowledging that such a partnership will be inherently uneasy.

AN UNEASY RELATIONSHIP

The relationship between researchers and policy practitioners is an uneasy fit between complementary but divergent interests, making for a creative but unpredictable dynamic. Although seemingly sharing many common interests, attempts to base policy on this relationship can be a source of frustration for both parties: for the researcher because of the lack of attention accorded to the subtleties and qualifications of the findings; and for the policy-maker because of the emphasis given to theory, to situating the issue within a broader context, and to a lack of timeliness (of both content and delivery). Some have argued that these factors imply that the partnership, though important, will always be a limited one (Weiss 1986), yet the relationship continues because its part-ners share a desire to understand and influence the course of events. And with the increasing complexity of modern societies, this interface is becoming increasingly important. From a research perspective, the increasing ease of communication, access to infor-mation and availability of social data have combined to make policy research not only more feasible, but also more challenging intellectually. From a policy perspective, increased pressure on public resources impels demands that all initiatives pass an 'effec-tiveness test' that has focused attention on understanding the impact of policy, generating an evidence base of new ideas and a better understandings of old ones.

These developments have driven social science and public policy closer, but in a climate often characterised by mistrust and suspicion. Researchers fear that those driving policy are seeking to justify actions already decided by 'cherry-picking' from among the available evidence with little regard for the robustness or validity of the material selected. Policy advisers see social researchers as pursuing their own political agendas under the guise of scholar-ship. The enlightened findings of the social scientist often spell trouble for the minister!

The essence of scientific inquiry is an open approach that

explores the relevance of all possibilities, whereas the policy agenda is often closed to particular ideas or concepts by political determination. Topics that diverge sharply from prevailing ideological proclivities frequently fail to make it on to the radar screen of policy. A current example: reference to poverty has been effectively banned from official discourse despite its ongoing salience to public concerns. Thus, while the Department of Family and Community Services (FaCS) notes at the beginning of its submission to the recent Senate Inquiry into *Poverty and Financial Hardship* that 'good policy needs a good definition of the problem' (FaCS 2003: 3), and the Submission is critical of a number of existing approaches, it does not propose a quantifiable definition of poverty – presumably because its political masters do not want to see the topic on the policy agenda.

Even while acknowledging that the context within which inquiry is carried out will be decisively shaped by public and political climates, with concomitant effects on the questions asked and the solutions proposed, the social sciences have observed shared protocols of knowledge validation (such as disciplinary ethics, the demand for high levels of professional accreditation, a self-reflexive critique of assumptions and values, and rigorous peer review). The framing of agendas determines which issues are subject to policy determination, and which are ignored. Can social science influence this framing? Should it? At the very least, it is important to recognise that those who set policy have 'busy minds [and] ... strong views about how things are and ought to be', so that 'findings do not fall on blank minds that get made up as a result' (Marmot 2004: 906).

POLITICAL CLIMATES AND THE POLICY SCIENCES

The work of social scientists does not occur in a vacuum. Not only is their curiosity and hence the projects they generate driven by personal values, but the public and political climates in which they operate shape the possibilities of their research. For instance, the definition of policy options and the interplay between experts and policymakers in the period 1945–1975 assumed a more active role for the State than has been common since. Most Western economies then were protectionist; Keynes provided the template for (limited) intervention in the economy; the Beveridge reports significantly influenced social policy; and there was deference to expert opinion – scientific rationality, it was thought, would solve our collective problems. Technocratic management and 'brains trusts' were as popular in market economies (for example, the United States) as in those experimenting with the expansion of welfare (for example, the United Kingdom) (Fischer 1990). In Australia, the characteristic policy pronouncements of the period – the Labor government's white paper on full employment, as well as the Institute of Public Affairs' (IPA) rejoinder *Looking Forward,* the Commonwealth's funding of tertiary education, the heavy public subsidy for industrial sectors and tariff protection – all drew on 'expert' advice and assumed a partnership between the public and private sectors: that is, an active role for the State.

The outcome of this project would be social change and a new policy climate, as John Quiggin shows below. The success of post-war economic restructuring within nations meant that eventually business, finance and investment would become trans-national, international competitors would emerge to challenge national heavyweights, new technologies would enormously increase the circulation of capital, and increasing demands for global invest-ment opportunities would outstrip the capacity of governments to control what was happening. This was behind the tectonic changes from the late 1970s on, when the role of the State came into ques-tion, market provision (and the outsourcing of both services and knowledge production to private providers) was seen as the path to providing individuals with choice, and policy questions tended to be framed in relation to how market mechanisms and 'user pays' could best serve community needs. Thus, approaches taken for granted by both policy actors and researchers in the post-war period became 'unthinkable' in the 1980s and 1990s when market paradigms dominated. Most of the contributors to this book reflect upon the efficacy of policy initiatives within this latter political climate, and some argue the necessity of new approaches: how, for instance, would a change from 'efficiency' to 'sustainability' as the measure of economic success influence contemporary policymaking, asks Richard Eckersley?

By the mid-twentieth century, leading practitioners attempted to encapsulate the potential of the social sciences collectively to address social problems by identifying them as 'the policy sciences'. They wished to link what they saw as advances in social scientific methods with political decisions (Lasswell 1951). Their faith in systematic planning, and productive links between the research community and the policy community in the joint endeavour of responding to 'the intelligence needs of the time', should still be the kernel of the policy sciences. Yet, while recovering the notion of the policy sciences usefully focuses attention on the point at issue in this book, we need to explore the relations between the research community and the policy community anew, for three reasons. First, the 'policy sciences' enterprise was shaped by the technocratic assumptions of its times. Second, that the producers of expert knowledge and policy activists will have complementary objectives should not be too readily assumed. While the Keynesian consensus of the post-war period produced conditions where knowledge producers and policy actors were 'on the same page' (Walter 2004), the very conditions that led thereafter to the 'end of certainty' (Kelly 1992) have generated a much more contested relationship (Sawer 2004a; 2004b), and the easy fit assumed by the policy scientists no longer prevails. Third, and by extension, the advocates of the policy sciences approach assumed that their problem orientation overcame disciplinary fragmentation, yet contemporary developments have seen a diversification and reconfiguration of knowledge production that further complicates this assumption. This latter point deserves elaboration.

COMPETITION IN 'KNOWLEDGE' PRODUCTION

In the post-war period, as Simon Marginson argues in Chapter 4, many countries encouraged higher education to facilitate economic development. The expanding cohorts of the tertiary educated augmented university research (with a substantial increase in conventional social science) and boosted professional occupations and management. Increasing numbers also worked as knowledge producers in government, corporations, consultancies, think tanks and private practice. Knowledge produced in those contexts, in different ways (not necessarily observing the conventions of validation characteristic of the social sciences) and for different social purposes, now competes vigorously for influence in the field of policy determination.

What this means can best be illustrated by observing the distinction between social science practice and the processes of think tanks, which have become significant sources of ideas in contemporary policy debate. Early think tanks, even if established with a specific agenda (like the Institute of Public Affairs in 1943), tended to pursue traditional policy research (Kemp 1988: 328–9, 331, 347–8). In the past 20 years, however, think tank research has become secondary to the purpose of influencing public opinion and public policy. We have seen the emergence of advocacy think tanks – explicitly ideological and aggressive in promulgating partisan approaches to public issues (Abelson and Carberry 1997; Denham and Garnett 1999).

Think tank activists are usually trained social scientists, but they are policy entrepreneurs rather than researchers, eschewing scholarly objectivity by prioritising a particular political philosophy and seeking only initiatives that will serve that position. Arguably, they have filled a policy void. As Ian Marsh notes in Chapter 12, academics have sometimes been reluctant to marry social inquiry to policy needs, or to respond to problems of the moment in a timely fashion, and political parties have declined as a channel for policy ideas. The public service has been increasingly obliged to outsource research functions, generating opportunities for consultancies and think tanks.

More attuned to public opinion and media dissemination than academic researchers have cared to be, think tanks have arguably stimulated necessary public debate and enlightenment. The very process of generating competing options to which they contribute facilitates the vigorous contest between alternatives that is generally regarded as a prerequisite for good policy outcomes (Preston and 't Hart 1999). On the other hand, the appearance of bringing practicality and timeliness to the resolution of options and offering the comfort of a shared political framework to relevant political actors may give think tanks leverage over better based sources of advice. When political preferences restrict options – as in the suppression of poverty as a policy issue mentioned above – think tanks will more comfortably accommodate to the brief than will social science researchers. But we should not ignore the downside: that advocacy think tanks will not review all options limits policy development. Their entrepreneurial bent is more attuned to winning the war of ideas than to considering how their proposals might play out in practice.

THE SCHOLARSHIP POLICY INTERFACE

In a context of vigorous competition over ideas and the production of knowledge, we are making a claim for the importance of social science expertise. This book assumes that not all knowledge is of equal value: that which is most significant in the sphere of public policy is governed by widely shared principles of social science. At the same time, we enjoin social scientists to recognise the constraints within which the policy community must work. While the research community can afford to be driven by curiosity (and relatively expansive time horizons), the policy community must be driven by the need to develop realistic solutions to practical problems within feasible time lines. The nature of the tasks demanded of the policy community has been clearly analysed elsewhere (see Colebatch 1998; Bridgman and Davis 2000; Edwards 2001; Davis and Keating 2000; Yeatman 1998). Social scientists must draw on this research to develop awareness of the practical, institutional and political constraints within which policy activists operate.

The fact that almost everyone has an opinion about many of the topics addressed by social science – the changing nature of work and family, the benefits of deregulation, the factors contributing to crime and social upheaval – fuels the perception that there is no clear demarcation between social science research and general knowledge or common sense. Paradoxically, this is exacerbated by the complex nature of many social problems and the consequences of this for attempts to understand them. Because all social issues involve a human dimension, there is a degree of uncertainly surrounding their understanding that sits uncomfortably with the certainties sought by policy analysts. Rather than having a body of 'given' scientific knowledge that develops incrementally, social scientists are continuously reviewing what is known in the light of new theories, data or evidence, and debating the nature of observed or presumed relationships and lines of causality. The appearance that things are never straightforward can encourage the misapprehension that conclusions are unduly driven by personal proclivities. Hence, with the possible exception of (some) economists, many social scientists are regarded with suspicion in policy circles for seeming to let their values influence what they study, how they go about it, what findings they highlight and what implications they draw from them.

These factors clash with the role of politicians, whose job it is to balance competing views and make informed judgments about action by choosing between competing objectives. In consequence, the social scientist's role as 'expert', providing the knowledge or evidence base that supports policy choices, is undermined, because the evidence presented is often perceived as tainted. Malcolm Gillies' recent contrast between media portrayals of the scientific researcher shown working 'at the bench of activity' and the presentation of social scientists as commentators 'with the implication that they are just peddling opinions in some personal capacity' captures this mindset evocatively (Gillies 2005).

In addition, the self-reflexive critical stance adopted by social scientists – the driving force behind intellectual innovation – creates tensions between those who study social problems and those in government who are responsible for the policies that address them. Government ministers and the advisers and policy analysts who surround them thus frequently respond to the criticisms of social scientists aggressively, before they give rise to political consequences – an opportunity that Opposition members are all too keen to exploit. Scholarly criticism thus becomes portrayed as political criticism, and since it is always possible to criticise any policy from some perspective, it is not difficult to generate legitimate differences that further undermines the status of the social scientist as 'expert'.

Finally, the ivory tower location of much social research reinforces the idea that its contributors are poorly placed to offer solutions to 'real world' problems. The recent proliferation of 'public intellectuals' – some of them academics, and indeed social scientists – prepared through their commentary to provide a bridge between specialist research and public concerns, might seem to ameliorate such perceptions. Yet they, too, have institutional niches and careers to defend, and their adversarial tactics and claims to moral authority can mobilise oppositional groupings while occluding more open inquiry (see Carter 2004; McCredden 2004).

One response to such impediments is to argue that social scientists should attempt to make their voice heard before policy is set – an approach favoured by those like Meredith Edwards (2001; 2004) who have worked at the coalface of policy development. However, this raises issues about how the social scientist can gain a hearing in a policymaking environment that is generally (and understandably) shrouded in secrecy. This *can* happen – as several contributors to this book note – but it has often been more the result of personal contact or sheer accident, than a deliberately engineered outcome. As Barbara Pocock argues in Chapter 7, regular contact between social scientists and policy actors can and should be engineered rather than left to chance. A similar point has been made in the United Kingdom by politician David Blunkett, who has argued that:

> For researchers to maximise the potential impact of their work, they must ensure that politicians and civil servants are aware of their findings. This means learning how to communicate effectively with government, and discovering the entry points into the policy-making process (Blunkett 2000).

If the complementarity between the research and policy communities is to be re-established, there must be acute awareness among policy activists of what social science can offer, as well as its limitations. Data are critical in this context, since they are the lifeblood of empirical research, but their availability is constrained by the willingness of governments to fund their collection. All too often the key questions cannot be answered because of a lack of data, yet too little thought is put into planning data needs so that the situation does not recur. Many social scientists generate their own data and others analyse existing data sets, but there are many gaps that prevent research from contributing to policy in key areas. More attention needs to be paid to how to overcome these gaps by interacting directly with agencies like the Australian Bureau of statistics (ABS) and otherwise exerting pressure to gather new data.

BUILDING BRIDGES

In general, there are three ways in which social science can seek to use what Blunkett called 'entry points' to exert an influence on policy. The first involves influencing *professional opinion* by publishing research in peer-reviewed journals and using other forms of dissemination to influence the development of social science knowledge. The new ideas, concepts, theories and empirics that result from this core activity can be extremely influential – but usually only if they coincide or overlap with the inclinations of those setting the policy agenda. Nonetheless, as Weber argued, new ideas can help create new world images that 'fundamentally reshape the terms of struggle among interests' (Davis 1998: 36). Social science can help in this way to shape the policy debate by 'framing the problem' and influencing the discourse and ideas that surround it.

The second approach involves influencing *public opinion* by disseminating research findings or implications in the media in order to exert pressure on policymakers to change policy. Where public imagination is captured by the messages from researchers – the inequalities exposed by second-wave feminists (see Chilla Bulbeck, in Chapter 8), the threat of global warming, the nature and impact of overseas welfare reforms (see Peter Travers, in Chapter 5) – policy agendas must respond. This can have important effects, although the risks involved are considerable as the media may distort the message in ways that undermine the legitimacy of the research and the status of the researcher (Haslam and Bryman 1994; Davis 1998). Few social scientists are trained in dealing with the media, yet they play a crucial role in linking research with society.

The third approach – one discussed by Meredith Edwards (2001) and many other public policy analysts – involves influencing *policy opinion* directly by engaging with policy practitioners in ways that affect their thinking and ideas. Barbara Pocock provides an illuminating discussion of 'transmission mechanisms for research' in her chapter, arguing that social scientists must take the initiative in their engagements with policymakers. This also requires its own skills and a level of expertise and ability to communicate that is relatively rare. In many cases, it will depend on personal contact with those involved in policy ('the Canberra premium') and often results from research published under the first approach described above: the pervading influence of 'pure' theories and concepts is stronger than generally acknowledged – ideas do matter!

Although the status attached to each of these three approaches differs widely, affecting the incentives to engage in each, Australian social scientists have contributed in all three spheres. Economists in particular have influenced public opinion in ways that have assisted the reform process and the adaptations it has necessitated, as Keating (1993) has argued. But while the first approach is the 'bread and butter' of scholarship, the other two require specific skills and, above all, time, combined with a willingness to be at the beck and call of others. Even if it were possible to develop structures that allow social science to have a seat at the policy table, many social scientists would find it very uncomfortable to be there. The need to make quick decisions, to push the evidence further than is academically justified, or to choose between widely different outcomes for different groups, are not competences for which most academic social scientists have any training, or inclination. What they are trained in is to be critical of *all* the evidence – including their own – and the idea that their research may have an impact on people's lives is a prospect that some would regard with fear, bordering on horror.

The fault does not lie entirely with the social scientist. Those involved in policy development often have little idea of how or where existing research can contribute, or what is needed to help resolve outstanding issues. Asking policy advisers what it is they need to know often produces either a blank stare or a relatively trivial question that can be answered easily – although often not immediately. Those working in the policy domain also fail to appreciate the motivations and constraints that face academic social scientists: research that has an impact is a highly valued performance indicator, but it is very difficult to demonstrate the link so that, in practice, involvement in policy development may require other professional sacrifices. In this context, it is ironic that the incentive structures being built into higher education funding rarely give sufficient recognition to those activities (such as being awarded a grant or publishing a report commissioned by government) that link academics most closely with policy.

There are thus many barriers to be overcome before we can build effective structures that encourage interaction between social scientists and those involved in policy. The divide between scholarship and policy is not very wide – many social scientists are committed to 'making the world a better place' and increasing numbers of policy analysts have been trained in the social sciences – but it is deep and ways must be found of crossing it that are 'capable of carrying the weight of traffic in both directions' (Young, Ashby, Boaz and Grayson 2002: 223).

This imperative is not new. When the Australian Research Council asked the Academy of the Social Sciences in Australia (ASSA) to commission its various disciplines to reflect on their future and develop research strategies, several recommendations addressed the need to bridge the gaps between researchers in the social sciences and humanities and the beneficiaries of that research (ASSA 1998). One recommendation was that ASSA should meet with other relevant bodies 'to examine the contribution of social science research to public policy, and ways of enhancing their mutual relationships'. Almost a decade on, little has changed. In compiling this volume, we have been acutely aware of the difficulties involved in this seemingly straightforward task.

FUNDING POLICY RESEARCH: AN EXAMPLE OF BUILDING BRIDGES

One example of the third approach indicated above – directly engaging with policymakers – illustrates its possibilities and its limitations. In 2000, the Commonwealth Department of Family and Community Services (FaCS) issued a tender for independent research organisations to supply it with a package of social policy research services (SPRS), generally in the form of research projects, under a contractual arrangement that would provide guaranteed (indexed) funding for four (now five) years. One aim of the new SPRS agreements was to bring the policy focus of the successful tenderers closer to the research and policy interests of FaCS. One advantage has been to engage FaCS staff more directly in project development, increasing their ownership of the research. Many of the projects would not have been possible without the very close relationship between researchers and bureaucrats that has developed under the new arrangements – for example, those that have utilised information extracted from administrative records, or conducted interviews with FaCS clients accessed through the department. Increased availability of data generated or funded by FaCS has been important, not only as the basis for the research, but also because the SPRS arrangements can be used to ensure that the data is used to support policy, thereby building political support for the data collections themselves. The Household Income and Labour Dynamics in Australia (HILDA) survey is an important example.

Not surprisingly, there have been some sensitivities over publication – although there is provision in the form of a sunset clause that allows publication one year after completion of a project if this has not already occurred. However, even when publication is agreed, it is difficult to persuade professional journals to accept papers that are often narrow in scope and of immediate interest, while publication by FaCS does not always enjoy the same status as other forms of academic publication. This has made it harder for emerging researchers working on SPRS projects to build their professional profiles in ways that will assist them to establish a research career. A consequence has been that it has become harder to maintain the interest of promising younger scholars, undermining the longer term research capacity of participating bodies.

There is also a tendency to focus the research on issues that align with prevailing policy priorities, neglecting the 'big' issues, or issues that have fallen off the agenda. Such research can impact on policy – and often does – but only at the margins in very small, almost invisible (and thus impossible to document) ways. Another major problem relates to the tendency at times for FaCS to want to specify not only the *content* of the research but also its *methodology*. While more open lines of communication can help to resolve this issue, the problem of restricting the scope of the research presents a formidable longer term challenge. One of the key ingredients of successful and influential research is independence and these kinds of arrangements have the potential to compromise this in ways that can only be harmful to the longer term interests of research *and* policy. There is thus a danger that such processes will produce future generations of social scientists who are extremely able at conducting research that addresses specific policy interests in narrow areas, but who will be unable to develop the more generic skills and expertise that are the ultimate lifeblood of policy-relevant social science.

OVERVIEW

The developments and arguments set out above were the primary motivations that led to a need to take stock of where the 'uneasy relationship' between the social sciences and public policy now stands. Our main goal has been to explore how social science can contribute to public policy, to identify if and why it has not done so, and to chart ways in which it might contribute more usefully in the future. This task has inevitably involved examining not only the international movement of ideas in the social sciences but also the avenues through which ideas infiltrate the public consciousness and mindsets of those driving policy.

The two opening chapters in this collection deal not with policy specifics, but with the frameworks within which policies are conceived and developed. John Quiggin outlines the broad history of what has become the dominant economic paradigm since the 1970s, not only assessing its success against objectives, but also the impact of its assumptions on other policy domains. This pointedly raises the issue of the constraints within which social scientists are obliged to operate: it also provokes the question of what social scientists might do to shift such 'discursive frames' when they fail to deliver – a topic that arises repeatedly in later chapters. In contrast, Brian Head shows that options and possibilities are influenced as much by practices of governance as by ways of thinking. Indeed, sophisticated institutional responses – more integrated governance, adaptive management, the building of learning networks linking researchers with governmental, industry and community users of knowledge – can engender innovative policy, despite the limitations of initial assumptions. Mutual learning might be triggered by critique, but can only prosper with the encouragement of institutional and sociological literacy, on all sides.

Discussions of six discrete policy sectors then follow. These chapters review current ideas, their international origins and local adaptations, their applications and lacunae – in each case attending to institutional contexts. Simon Marginson analyses educational policy to show that, despite achievements, it has lost coherence and autonomy in the face of economic meta-policy. Social science might address the obstacles by developing a theorisation that could comprehend, monitor and augment the complete range of educational costs and benefits, and thus identify resource allocations that would most efficiently address society's needs – and the full potential of human capital development. Peter Travers discusses welfare regimes within an international comparative perspective, mapping outcomes and citizen expectations. The 'message effect' of radical reform (as in the United States) can significantly dampen such expectations, but political culture appears still to have an influence. While Australia has adopted a system of 'mutual obligation', with welfare dependency an evil to be avoided, the entrenchment of poverty lines has been an incentive for policymakers to ensure that social security recipients are not living in poverty. The cost of a system that is both generous and targeted towards the worst off is very high effective marginal tax rates, but we lack evidence on their behavioural consequences, leaving an opening for ideological assertion rather than evidence-based reasoning.

Ruth Fincher addresses spatial policies – those relating to territorial or jurisdictional containers of populations and infrastructure. Policies to redress locational disadvantage by infrastructure investment are seen to have profound effects. Attempts to achieve 'social mix' (melding diverse ethnicities, socioeconomic categories and so on) within bounded areas have been unsuccessful. Research on creating learning regions of economic innovation is little developed and promises a productive nexus between government and social scientists. Barbara Pocock asks what are the appropriate institutional, labour market and household forms to ease the interactions between work and family? The answers demand good, publicly engaged research – and Pocock gives particular attention to the nature of public engagement and the need for 'transmission mechanisms' (between communities, researchers and policymakers) to influence policy decisions. Hers is an applied case study of the learning networks mooted by Head, and of the obligations upon social scientists within such networks.

Chilla Bulbeck's discussion of gender policies shows that, despite the achievements of the women's movement, gendered patterns of advantage and disadvantage persist and the current climate is not propitious for further progress. She asks whether a framing of gender equity issues in terms of economic efficiency, costs savings, the restoration of 'at risk' individuals, and strengthening families and communities can capture the imagination of the policy community. Jon Altman and Tim Rowse explore the history of Indigenous policy. This is a domain where the incommensurate assumptions of social scientists have had extraordinary impact on policy outcomes: anthropology, for instance, presuming social difference to be a good, with the implication that Aborigines should go their own ways; economics dwelling on indicators of inequality and encouraging Aborigines towards integration as economic actors. This is a good example of where social scientists have pressured successfully for new data that have shed light on the extent of the problems faced by the Indigenous population. The quandary for social scientists – between acknowledging difference and aspiring for greater parity in measures of wellbeing – will not be resolved unless social science more adequately attends to human agency in these outcomes.

The final three chapters raise broader political questions. Jenny Hocking, while writing on security and counter-terrorism as 'the policy domain of the moment', raises the disturbing question of the potential for a 'post-democratic' regime arising from the supposed urgency, the lack of transparency and the difficulty of accountability inherent in this field. Have crisis measures obscured the erosion of civil rights? Will closed and secretive decision-making be translated into other policy fields? How can social science recover and reinforce democratic imperatives? Richard Eckersley highlights questions of wellbeing and sustainability, as opposed to growth and efficiency, asking what would happen if the paradigm underlying policy debate – as outlined by Quiggin – were radically transformed? Ian Marsh shows that parties and parliament – the familiar channels for dramatising options, for opinion aggregation and for policy debate – are failing. The ways of getting issues on to the agenda, of registering and responding to public concerns – the whole theatre of opinion, rejoinder and political negotiation – must be rethought.

It is not feasible to cover every policy problem of the day in one book: coverage here, of course, has been selective. We hope, nonetheless, that the cases discussed below not only suggest productive potential in specific policy areas, but also highlight more overarching issues: the need to draw on international comparisons and currents of ideas (while remaining alert to and sceptical about international fads); the capacities to rethink the very frameworks within which policy is conceived; the contribution of evidence-based research; the significance of understanding the relations between the policy and the research communities (which will entail sociological literacy on one side and institutional literacy on the other); the need for public engagement; and, above all, the potential in building mutual learning networks.

2

Economic Liberalism: Fall, Revival and Resistance
John Quiggin[1]

Until the last quarter of the twentieth century, it seemed reasonable to interpret modern political history in terms of the fairly steady advance of socialist and social democratic political ideas and policies. From the mid-1970s onwards, however, this trend was halted and at least partially reversed. Socialist and social democratic ideas, previously dominant in policy debate, were displaced by market-oriented ideologies variously referred to as Thatcherism, economic rationalism, neo-liberalism and the Washington consensus.

As usual with dominant ideologies, these labels are most commonly used in a pejorative sense, by opponents of the dominant view. Supporters of the dominant viewpoint have commonly preferred to avoid any ideological label, and to treat their policy approach as self-evident 'common sense'. Perhaps the most popular term used in favourable descriptions of the free-market approach has been 'economic liberalism', and, because this term is also reasonably accurate as a description, it will be used in this chapter.

There are differing views on the extent and significance of the re-emergence of economic liberalism. Henderson (1995; 1998) sees economic liberalism as the 'hero of the story' of policy reform since the 1970s, and presents Australia, during the 1980s, as one of the leaders in the adoption of economic liberalism, though somewhat behind the United Kingdom and New Zealand. By contrast, Keating (2004) downplays the influence of economic liberalism, particularly in Australia, and argues that the adoption of market-based policy instruments is a pragmatic political response to the combination of limited state capacity and steadily growing demands for state services.

There are elements of truth in both views. It will be argued, however, that the influence of economic liberalism has passed its peak and that the more pragmatic approach described by Keating is increasingly dominant.

The chapter is organised as follows. The first section is a historical survey of the fluctuating fortunes of economic liberalism from its eclipse after 1914, to its resurgence in the 1990s, and ending with evidence that economic liberalism has lost ground since the late 1990s, particularly in the English-speaking countries. The second section describes the ideology and rhetoric of economic liberalism. The third, fourth and fifth sections deal with specific aspects of the policy framework of economic liberalism. The final section provides a brief assessment of the outcomes generated by economic liberalism. Finally, some concluding comments are offered.

HISTORY

THE FALL OF NINETEENTH-CENTURY ECONOMIC LIBERALISM

The world economy in the period before 1914 was one of untrammelled global capitalism. Politically, this was the golden age of classical liberal capitalism, which was the dominant ideology of the era, especially in Britain. By 1914, however, the global economy of liberal capitalism faced external and internal stresses, which seemed likely to result in major structural changes. The rising economic powers, Germany and the United States, pursued protectionist trade policies, providing an apparent counter-example to the liberal belief in the optimality of free trade.

A more fundamental challenge arose from the socialist move-ment. Although initially allied with liberals in struggles for democ-racy and against various forms of arbitrary power, socialists generally favoured large-scale government intervention, particu-larly as the extension of voting rights raised the prospect that the working class would be able to elect governments that would serve its interests.

The result was a split within liberalism, reflected in the differ-ent usages of the term in, for example, Australia and the United States. Some liberals maintained their alliance with socialists and social democrats on economic issues, distinguishing themselves by a greater focus on questions of civil liberty. Others joined the conservatives they had previously opposed (Dangerfield 1935).

Australia was an early example of the shift away from classi-cal liberalism, towards a set of interventions variously charac-terised as 'socialism without doctrines' (Metin 1977), the 'Australian settlement' (Kelly 1992) and 'the wage-earners welfare state' (Castles 1994). Key features of the Australian model in the early twentieth century included the Arbitration system, tariff protection and substantial reliance on public enterprise. All of these policies were adopted in the early years of Federation and remained in place until the neo-liberal reforms that began in the 1980s.

THE RISE OF KEYNESIAN SOCIAL DEMOCRACY

The question of whether the global economic system could have survived these stresses was rendered academic by the failure of the political system to prevent the outbreak of the Great War in Europe, which led to the abandonment of the gold standard and a collapse in world trade. The Great Depression, which followed the stock market crash of 1929, ended hopes of a return to the nineteenth-century system. More than this, the Depression discredited liberal capitalism, seemingly forever.

The most effective theoretical challenge to the free-market system was Keynes' (1936) analysis, which showed how unemployment could remain high indefinitely because of inadequate demand. The most effective practical challenge was Roosevelt's New Deal, which showed that government intervention could yield substantial benefits. Support for Keynesianism and for more extensive systems of economic planning was greatly enhanced by the experience of wartime planning between 1939 and 1945.

In terms of economic policy, the crucial new element after 1945 was a commitment to full employment. Confidence in the feasibility of this goal was boosted by the comparison between the success of economic planning during the war, and the failure of orthodox free-market policies during the Depression, a point stressed in the White Paper *Full Employment in Australia* (Commonwealth of Australia 1945).

The achievement of full employment was the basis of a broader consensus. All parties agreed on the need for comprehensive systems of social welfare, and on the need for government intervention in the economy, including, in most countries, public ownership of basic infrastructure (roads, electricity, telecommunications and so on) and public provision of human services (health, education and other community services). Although socialist parties formally advocated complete nationalisation of industry, in practice they accepted private ownership of primary industry, manufacturing, and wholesale and retail trade.

The result was referred to as the 'mixed economy', and was put forward as a 'third way' (Giddens 1999; Pierson and Castles 2001) in the debate between the polar alternatives of laissez-faire and a Soviet-style command economy.

The adoption of Keynesian economic management in Australia and the associated expansion of the welfare state was overlaid on the existing policies of the Federation period. The result was a policy framework in which the older elements like tariff protection played, at most, a supporting role. Advocates of economic liberalisation, such as Kelly (1992), have commonly ignored this, and argued as if the policies they criticised were uniquely Australian. However, as Smyth (1998) and others have argued, it was the Keynesian–social democratic settlement, and not the residual elements of Federation, that was crucial in guiding policy during the decades of post-war prosperity.

THE CRISIS OF KEYNESIANISM IN THE 1970S

For the developed countries, the period from 1945 to 1970 was unparalleled in the history of capitalism as one of full employment, rapid economic growth, and increasing equality of opportunity and outcomes. By 1970, however, the strains that would lead to the breakdown of Keynesian social democracy were already evident.

The crucial problem was the failure of Keynesian economic management to control the combination of high inflation and high unemployment referred to as stagflation. The crucial event was the collapse of the Bretton Woods system of fixed exchange rates between 1970 and 1972, in the face of inflationary pressures driven by rising wages and US budget deficits.

The collapse of the Bretton Woods system began a process of international financial deregulation, which created intense pressure for deregulation of domestic capital markets. (Contrary to the claims made by many writers on globalisation in the 1990s, it was this process of policy change, rather than technical developments in telecommunications and computing, that was responsible for the growth of international financial markets.) This was accompanied by the abandonment of Keynesian macroeconomic policies, and their replacement by the monetarist ideas of Friedman (1968), and his 'new classical' successors.

Monetarism proved little more successful than Keynesianism as a response to stagflation, and policies of monetary targeting were abandoned by the early 1980s. By the 1990s, macroeconomic policy was based on an eclectic mixture of ideas, predominantly Keynesian as regards the short run, and classical or monetarist as regards the long run.

By contrast with the relatively transient reign of monetarism, Friedman's (1962) microeconomic policy program, which was a restatement of nineteenth-century economic liberalism, was far more successful, and formed the basis of market-oriented reforms adopted throughout the world in the 1980s and 1990s.

Although it is usually a mistake to overestimate the intellectual influence of any single person, and the theories of classical liberalism provided an obvious alternative to Keynesian social democracy, there is no doubt that Friedman was among the most persuasive advocates of economic liberalism, being both more insightful and less dogmatic in tone and content than other leading figures in the free-market camp. Friedman's visit to Australia in 1976 marked a turning point in the Australian policy debate: from this point on, economic liberalism was the dominant position in both microeconomic and macroeconomic policy debates.

THE RESURGENCE OF ECONOMIC LIBERALISM 1975–1990

Although the breakdown of the Bretton Woods system was the starting point for an international resurgence of economic liberalism, this was not a uniform global process. The shift away from social democracy and towards free-market policies occurred in different ways and at different times in different countries, as did the subsequent popular reaction against economic liberalism.

In the space limitations of this chapter, it is impossible to describe the national variations in detail, and attention will therefore be focused on the Australian experience. Some international comparisons will be presented later.

The resurgence of economic liberalism in Australia began with the re-opening of the tariff debate. Tariffs were the most prominent example of the regulatory state that emerged after Federation in 1901. Over the course of the 1970s and 1980s, the critics of tariffs broadened their views into a general critique of government intervention. The case for free trade merged with arguments for deregulation, largely derived from the United States (where airline deregulation was generally seen as a major success) and for privatisation (largely derived from the Thatcher government in the United Kingdom).

The resurgence of liberal economic ideas was confined, almost exclusively, to economic and policy elite groups. Influential advocates of economic liberalism included government agencies such as the Industries Assistance Commission (later the Industry Commission and now the Productivity Commission), private-sector think tanks such as the Centre for Independent Studies, and financial and political journalists, including Paul Kelly and Gerard Henderson.

Liberal economic reform proceeded slowly under the Fraser Liberal–National government from 1975 to 1983. In 1983, the Hawke Labor government, was elected on a fairly traditional interventionist platform but soon adopted much of the resurgent liberal ideology. The crucial event in this process was the decision in December 1983 to float the Australian dollar. The broader microeconomic reform agenda of financial deregulation, privatisation, free trade and reductions in public expenditure and taxation followed inevitably, frequently justified by the perceived need to maintain the goodwill of international currency markets.

There were, however, important countervailing policies, most importantly the Prices and Incomes Accord between the government and the Australian Council of Trade Unions, under which unions accepted reductions in real wages in return for influence over government policy in social services and other areas. This agreement encouraged other interventions such as the reintroduction of Medicare, a public health insurance scheme. Nevertheless, there were important respects in which the policies of the Hawke–Keating government foreshadowed those of the Blair government in the United Kingdom and of other advocates of 'modernised' or 'reformed' social democracy.

Even at the high point of the reform era in the late 1980s, few microeconomic reform initiatives gained strong popular support. Nevertheless, the popular mood in the 1980s was one of acquiescence. After the crises of the 1970s and the 1982–83 recession, there was general acceptance that 'There's got to be a better way' (Douglas 1980). Moreover, the economic recovery seemed to validate many of the claims made by reformers regarding the benefits of a more flexible, liberalised economy.

Adverse popular reaction began with the recession of 1990 and crystallised around the term 'economic rationalism' (Pusey 1991; see also Quiggin 1997). The strongest expression of this reaction was the election of 1993, in which the key issue was Fightback! (Hewson and Fischer 1992), a radical package of free-market reforms, put forward by the Liberal Opposition, under the leadership of economist John Hewson. The unpopularity of the Keating Labor government, due both to poor macroeconomic management and to Keating's own position as the leading proponent of free-market reform during the 1980s, was such that the election was widely described as 'unlosable'. Nevertheless, the Liberals lost, and voters waited until 1996 to vent their anger at Keating and the Labor government.

It was clear by this point that microeconomic reform was highly unpopular with the electorate. Even on issues like privatisation, where there was no clear consensus in the 1980s, opposition to reform hardened steadily (Kelley and Sikora 2002). Support for tariff protection, initially strong, become somewhat stronger, though Norton (2004) argues that public attitudes on this topic are more flexible than is commonly supposed. Most notably, the tax revolt of the 1970s and 1980s faded away, with steadily increasing proportions of respondents to public opinion surveys preferring improvements in public services to tax cuts (Wilson and Breusch 2003).

The initial response to what was called 'reform fatigue' was not to slow the pace of reform, but to seek top-down devices that would impose reform without requiring public debate on an issue-by-issue basis. The most notable instance of this process was the National Competition Policy Agreement, reached at a meeting of state and federal leaders in 1994, and involving commitments to comprehensive microeconomic reform, subject to a set of financial incentives and penalties applicable a decade or more into the future.

National Competition Policy contributed to a more virulent popular reaction in the form of Pauline Hanson's One Nation Party, which combined hostility to Asian immigration and multiculturalism with violent opposition to microeconomic reform, and particularly to National Competition Policy.

INTERNATIONAL COMPARISONS

The Australian experience of economic liberalism was broadly similar to that of other English-speaking countries, which followed the lead of the United Kingdom. As in Australia, economic liberalism lost popular support during the late 1990s. In the United Kingdom and New Zealand, and to a lesser extent in Canada, centre-left governments elected in the 1990s have moved away from the radical economic liberalism of their predecessors in favour of policies variously described as 'Third Way' or 'modernised social democracy'. In practice this has meant accepting most of the policy changes introduced in the period of economic liberalism, such as privatisation, though some of the more egregious failures have been reversed (for example, the re-nationalisation of Air New Zealand and Railtrack, the UK rail system operator). However, the central role of the State in the funding and provision of health and education services has been maintained and expenditure on these services has increased relative to national income.

In the developing world, and particularly in Latin America, the policy agenda of economic liberalism is commonly referred to as the 'Washington consensus', a phrase coined by Williamson (1990) with reference to its Washington-based proponents, the World Bank, the International Monetary Fund and the US Treasury.

A third element of the push towards economic liberalisation arose from the collapse of the Soviet bloc. Many, though not all, formerly communist countries in Europe embraced policies of 'shock therapy', involving large-scale privatisation and a radically reduced role for government, compared not only to the central planning of the past but to the social democratic systems of Europe.

After dominating policy developments throughout Latin America in the 1990s, the Washington Consensus is now, to a large extent, discredited. In part, this is due to severe economic crises in countries that adopted the Washington consensus approach. The most severe of these crises affected Argentina, the country that had gone furthest along the path set out by the Washington consensus, to the extent of establishing a currency board with the task of maintaining a fixed exchange rate with the US dollar and thereby fighting inflation. When foreign investors lost faith in Argentina, the ensuing crisis produced a depression in which output and national income declined by 20 per cent.

More generally, the adoption of liberal economic policies has not produced the promised results in Latin America (with the partial exception of Chile) or in other poor countries. Economic growth has been weak, and the distribution of income has become more unequal, leaving the poor worse off than when the reforms began. As a result, movements towards privatisation and other reforms advocated by economic liberals have stalled and, in some cases, been reversed. Similar tendencies have been apparent in a number of Eastern European countries, and particularly in Russia, where many of the 'oligarchs' who benefited from privatisations under the Yeltsin government have been expropriated by the Putin administration.

The core members of the European Union (EU) have been most resistant to economic liberalism. As a result, economic liberalism is still advancing in the eurozone at a time when it has passed its peak in most other countries. Most EU member countries still faced unresolved fiscal problems associated with unfunded retirement income systems, and adjustments to resolve these problems will inevitably involve significant reductions in benefits, and probably increased reliance on private provision of retirement income. Nevertheless, the basic structures of social democracy have remained unchallenged and have, in many respects, been strengthened by the creation of common EU institutions.

THE IDEOLOGY AND RHETORIC OF ECONOMIC LIBERALISM

As has been noted, the shift from social democracy towards economic liberalism occurred in different ways and at different times in different countries, as did the subsequent popular reaction. This is reflected in the many different names that have been attached to the process, including 'Thatcherism', 'economic rationalism', 'the Washington consensus', and, most commonly in critical discussion, 'neo-liberalism'.

As both names imply, economic liberalism or neo-liberalism is a descendant of classical liberalism. Its defining features are the fact that it is a reaction against social democracy (a point captured in part by the 'neo' in neo-liberalism) and the fact that the primary focus is on economic policy.

In considering the relationship of economic liberalism to classical liberalism, it is important to observe that social democracy also draws heavily on the liberal tradition, and has, arguably, inherited the bulk of the political support that once sustained nineteenth-century liberalism. The US use of 'liberal' to mean 'social democrat' reflects this point.

Economic liberalism places more weight on economic freedom

than on personal freedom or civil liberties, reversing the emphasis of classical liberalism. Indeed, it is fair to say that on matters of personal freedom, economic liberalism is basically agnostic, encompassing a range of views from repressive traditionalism to libertarianism. The shift in emphasis is clear in the work of Hayek, the leading representative of economic liberalism as a philosophical viewpoint. Both in his theoretical writing, notably Hayek (1960), and in his support for the Pinochet regime in Chile, viewed as a transitional dictatorship necessary for the restoration of economic liberalism (Quiggin 2005), Hayek placed little emphasis on freedom of speech and thought as compared to freedom of economic action.

In terms of economic policy, economic liberalism is constrained by the need to compete with the achievements of social democracy. Hence, it is inconsistent with the kind of dogmatic libertarianism that would leave the poor to starvation or private charity, and would leave education to parents. Economic liberalism seeks to cut back the role of the State as much as possible, while maintaining public guarantees of access to basic health, education and income security.

The core objectives of economic liberalism are:

1   to remove the State altogether from 'non-core' functions such as the provision of infrastructure services

2   to minimise the role of the State in core functions (health, education, income security) through contracting out, voucher schemes and so on

3   to remove regulation of economic activity, or, where this proves impossible, to adopt 'light-handed' and market-friendly approaches to regulation

4   to reject redistribution of income except in so far as it is implied by the provision of a basic 'safety net'.

RHETORIC OF ECONOMIC LIBERALISM

Just as the successes of Keynesian macroeconomic management during and after World War 2 increased the credibility of the case for government intervention in the economy, the decline of Keynesianism in the 1970s was accompanied by more general disillusionment with the role of government. Initially, the reaction was confined, in large measure, to the English-speaking countries, and much of the associated rhetoric focused on what were seen as specific national failings: the 'British disease', the 'Australian settlement' and so on. However, similar arguments were made with respect to economies as diverse as those of Sweden (Lindbeck 1997) and the East Asian 'tiger economies', in both cases following economic crises that cast doubt on previously successful models.

A common theme in discussions of this kind was a focus on international comparisons, almost invariably to the detriment of the country in which the comparison was being made. The general theme was that, because of its excessively interventionist institutions, the country in question was being left behind by competitors. This trend could only be reversed by the introduction of free-market policies, typically in the form of a 'short sharp shock'. In Australia, claims about relative decline focused on the idea that, in the absence of economic reform, Australians would become the 'poor white trash of Asia' (Scutt 1985), a claim criticised by Quiggin (1987). Although arguments of this kind were sometimes used to promote interventionist industry policies, based on models such as that of the Japanese Ministry of International Trade and Industry (MITI), the dominant trend was towards free-market policies.

Another striking feature of the rhetoric of economic liberalism is its generally negative tone. Although some advocates of economic liberalism point to the positive benefits to be expected from a free-market economy, the dominant tone is that of stern necessity, epitomised by Thatcher's dictum 'there is no alternative'.

Even if the policies of economic liberalism do not produce desirable outcomes, proponents of globalisation argue that any country that rejects them will be crushed by the 'thundering herd' of global financial markets (Friedman 1999).

ECONOMIC LIBERALISM AND THE STATE

Economic liberalism is defined, above all, by a critical view of state involvement in economic activity. The most obvious manifestations of state involvement in the economy are, in qualitative terms, the range of goods and services directly provided or funded by the State and, in quantitative terms, the share of national income absorbed in taxation and redistributed as public spending. A central objective of economic liberalism has been to reverse the qualitative and quantitative expansion of state economic activity that characterised the first 75 years of the twentieth century.

GROWTH IN GOVERNMENT DURING THE TWENTIETH CENTURY

The growth of the State over the twentieth century resulted from a combination of qualitative expansion of the functions undertaken by it (mainly before 1950) and of structural change leading to growth in the share of income devoted to publicly provided services such as health, education and risk management (mainly from 1950 onwards). Although the role of government did not change much in qualitative terms between the 1950s and the 1970s, quantitative measures of the size of the public sector, such as the ratio of public expenditure to GDP, increased steadily.

A number of factors contributed to the growth of the public sector. The most important was the growth in the human services sector, encompassing 'social infrastructure' services such as health, education, police and welfare services. The demand for human services tends to rise with income, and to increase as a proportion of total demand as income rises. On the other hand, productivity growth in the human services sector has been limited. The growth of the services sector was first analysed in these terms by Baumol (1967), who argued that labour productivity grew more slowly in the services sector than in other sectors such as manufacturing. Hence, to maintain output in the services sector at least as a constant proportion of total output, it was necessary that resources should be progressively transferred towards this sector.

THE FISCAL CRISIS AND THE TAX REVOLT

By the early 1970s, the combination of growing demands for government expenditure and increasing difficulty in raising tax revenue produced what O'Connor (1973) described as 'the fiscal crisis of the state'. This reflected an over-extension of commitments during the 1960s, exacerbated by the slowdown in economic growth from the 1970s onwards.

The tax revolt was the name for, and symbolised by, the Proposition 13 referendum campaign in California in 1978. Proposition 13 was a citizen-initiated referendum that required the government to make substantial cuts in property taxes (the main source of funding for public schools and other local services), and to freeze tax rates thereafter. Substantial cuts in public expenditure followed, notably in relation to education, and California's state and local governments have suffered periodic financial crises ever since, most recently resulting in the recall of governor Gray Davis in 2004, and the election of Arnold Schwarzenegger to replace him.

Although attempts to reproduce the tax revolt in Australia and elsewhere were only moderately successful in mobilising popular opposition to taxes, there was no doubt about the strength of resistance to further increases in taxation. Concern about higher taxes was the biggest single source of popular support for economic liberalism. The most notable success of the Australian tax revolt was the abolition of inheritance taxes, beginning in Queensland, and then extending to other states and the Commonwealth.

In qualitative terms, economic liberals have been moderately successful in cutting back state activities. In many countries, the State has withdrawn from large areas of economic activity through privatisation and the withdrawal of public services. The change has been most notable in relation to infrastructure industries, such as energy and telecommunications. In addition, many special services originally established to meet needs that were not being adequately met by the private sector have been scrapped or absorbed into larger agencies as part of a process of cost-cutting and rationalisation.

Despite these successes, the ratio of public expenditure to GDP has increased in most developed countries, though the rate of increase has been greatly reduced. Except in relatively peripheral areas such as public ownership of utilities, economic liberals were unable to produce coherent and politically saleable alternatives to public provision and funding of services. The growth in demand for core public services more than offset the contraction of the State achieved through privatisation and withdrawal of peripheral services. As a result, despite dominating the policy process for 20 years, economic liberals mostly failed to reduce the relative size of the public sector.

STATE CAPACITY

The fiscal crisis of the State and the attempts of economic liberals to reverse its growth may usefully be understood in terms of the idea of 'state capacity' (Mann 1988). The State retains a substantial capacity to intervene effectively in the economy (Weiss 1998). However, that capacity has not grown in line with the demands implied by the range of responsibilities taken on by governments in the post-war period.

The crisis of the 1970s, then, may be seen as a result of states overreaching their capacity, producing a corresponding over-reaction in the 1980s and 1990s. The resurgence of economic liberalism was, in part, an over-reaction to this crisis. Economic liberals saw the crisis as evidence that the State needed to be cut back substantially. The rhetorical dominance of economic liberalism was enhanced by the fact that realistic supporters of the social democratic settlement recognised the need for retrenchment and rearrangement of priorities.

In Australia, economic liberals and modernising social democrats cooperated in the market-oriented reforms. This cooperation concealed divergent ends. Economic liberals saw state intervention as harmful, and sought to reduce the capacity of the State to override the market. By contrast, modernising social democrats sought to improve the effective capacity of the State through the adoption of new methods of public-sector management (discussed in Chapter 3), and to economise on the use of scarce state capacity through a more rigorous approach to the setting of priorities. The conflict between the two groups became more evident in the 1990s, as economic liberals sought to cut back core areas of the welfare state.

In some respects, market-oriented reforms have enhanced state capacity. While claims of a reinvention of government (Osborne and Gaebler 1992) are overstated, the attempt to make governments more market-oriented has, in many cases, increased the capacity of the public sector to provide services efficiently and with lower budgetary costs.

MICROECONOMIC REFORM

State economic activity need not involve direct government provision of goods and services. Governments can and do influence and constrain private economic activity through a range of measures including tariffs, taxes and regulations. In one form or another, these interventions modify the prices faced by private economic actors and therefore provide them with different incentives than those that would arise in a market equilibrium. In the rhetoric of economic liberalism, these differences in incentives are regarded as 'distortions', to be minimised wherever possible.

The general label 'microeconomic reform' has been used to describe a wide range of initiatives aimed at minimising the distortions imposed on private firms, and also at making public enterprises behave more like private firms.

TARIFFS AND THE REGULATORY STATE

In the early phases of microeconomic reform, much attention was focused on 'getting prices right', and, in particular, on eliminating policies that unnecessarily 'distorted' the production and consumption decisions of private firms and households. The paradigmatic example of a 'distorting' policy was tariff protection. The case for tariff reform was bolstered by the argument that, if a government wished to assist particular industries it should do so through subsidies, which did not distort the prices faced by consumers.

The first big instance of deregulation in Australia was the deregulation of financial markets in the 1980s, following the recommendations of the Campbell (1981) and Martin (1984) Committees of Inquiry and the decision to float the Australian dollar in 1983. Deregulation of the airline industry, and the abandonment of the longstanding two-airlines policy, followed in 1990.

MICROECONOMIC REFORM AND GOVERNMENT BUSINESS ENTERPRISES

A second strand of microeconomic reform focused on improving the efficiency of government business enterprises. One of the first, and most successful, instances was the creation of the statutory authorities Australia Post and Telecom Australia from the former Postmaster-General's Department, a public-service department under direct ministerial control. More generally, the reform of government provision of marketed services may be seen in terms of a spectrum (Productivity Commission 1998). At one end is the traditional departmental structure of national, state and local governments. At the other end is a privatised firm, subject only to normal commercial regulation. The points on the spectrum include:

- full cost pricing
- competitive tendering
- commercialisation
- corporatisation
- privatisation.

Each step along the reform spectrum involves an increase in reliance on profit as the primary guide to management decisions, and a reduction in direct public accountability. These two changes are directly linked: increases in profitability arise precisely because managers are not subject to constraints imposed through public accountability, and are therefore free to manage enterprises so as to increase revenues and reduce costs.

From the perspective of advocates of microeconomic reform, the object of reform has been to move as far towards privatisation as possible, subject to constraints arising from potential market failures or political restrictions. Under National Competition Policy, traditional arrangements are considered, prima facie, to be anti-competitive, and governments are required to consider options such as commercialisation and corporatisation.

THE NEW ERA OF REGULATION

For much of the 1980s and 1990s, it seemed that movement along the reform spectrum led inexorably to full privatisation. By the late 1990s, however, political resistance to privatisation had hardened, and the process of privatisation had largely drawn to a halt. At the same time, the hope that privatisation would lead to the emergence of robust competitive markets had proved overoptimistic in many cases. The result was a shift back towards regulation, with the distinctive feature that the objective was to mimic, as far as possible, the outcomes that would prevail in a competitive market.

Although privatisation was advocated for a variety of reasons, economic liberals saw it as being inextricably linked to a movement towards greater competition. Most favoured a short-lived period of light-handed regulation of privatised monopolies, in the expectation that the removal of barriers to entry would lead rapidly to full competition. In fact, monopoly power has remained strong, and the scope of regulation has steadily expanded. State and national regulators – the Australian Competition and Consumer Commission, the National Competition Council, the Essential Services Commissions and so on – now play a larger role in the economy than at any previous time.

Reforms to telecommunications and energy markets in the 1990s are also commonly referred to as 'deregulation'. In these cases, where a politicised regulatory regime, based on publicly owned statutory monopolies subject to direct ministerial control, has been replaced by a complex set of price controls and access undertakings, administered by independent regulators and designed to facilitate competition, 'reregulation' might be a more appropriate term. Continued use of the term 'deregulation' reflects, in part, the idea that the new regulatory structures are interim measures, paving the way for the emergence of a fully competitive market.

CONCLUSION

Economic liberals commonly claim that their domestic and international policy package is a proven success. During the 1980s and early 1990s they contrasted the supposed success of radical free-market reforms in English-speaking countries including New Zealand, Australia, the United Kingdom and the United States with the supposedly sclerotic performance of the European social democracies.

In fact, the example of New Zealand provides no support for the laissez faire model. Following disappointing economic performance for most of the period since World War 2, successive New Zealand governments imposed radical economic reforms after 1984. Although the reforms won the admiration of neo-liberals around the world, New Zealand's economic performance deteriorated. Growth in New Zealand since 1984 has been well below the OECD average, and also slower than in Australia, which faced broadly similar conditions, but which adopted less radical reforms (Quiggin 1998).

More generally, claims for the success of economic liberalism made in the 1980s (the period of the 'Thatcher miracle' in the United Kingdom and Rogernomics in New Zealand), proved premature, as early gains were wiped out by recessions around 1990, common to all the English-speaking countries, but particularly severe in Australia, the United Kingdom and New Zealand.

Since the early 1990s, however, the United Kingdom and Australia have enjoyed sustained economic expansion, and the United States has had generally strong economic performance, interrupted only by the relatively mild recession of 2001. However, this strong performance has been accompanied by the growth of large deficits on trade and current accounts.

On traditional views regarding trade and the macroeconomy, current account deficits in excess of 5 per cent, and low or negative rates of national saving, evident in all the English-speaking countries, would be seen as evidence of an unsustainable consumption boom, driven by excessively expansionary monetary policy. Economic liberals, however, take a more positive view of such tendencies, focusing on the fact that a current account deficit is the necessary counterpart of a capital account surplus. The willingness of overseas investors to lend at low rates of interest is seen as a sign of confidence in future strong growth.

Although current account deficits can, in principle, be sustained indefinitely, exports and imports must balance in the long run (Quiggin 2005). One way or another, the trade deficits observed in the English-speaking countries, including Australia, must return to balance fairly soon. The success or failure of economic liberalism may be judged, in large measure, by observing whether this adjustment takes the form of increased exports, driven by higher productivity, or of reduced imports driven by a contraction in economic activity.

Economic liberalism has dominated policy debates in Australia and elsewhere since the 1970s. In large measure, the goal of economic liberalism has been to reverse the achievements of Keynesian social democrats in building up a mixed-economy welfare state, particularly in the period after 1945.

Viewed in this light, economic liberalism must be seen to have failed. Of the major social welfare systems introduced in the era of social democracy, from universal public education to national health systems to old age and disability pensions, hardly any have been scrapped altogether (the nearest approach has been the radical reforms to the Temporary Assistance to Needy Families welfare program in the United States) and many have expanded. Government enterprises have been privatised in many countries, but, in most cases, they have been replaced by private monopolies that require regulation almost as intrusive as outright public ownership.

The possibility remains open that economic liberals will make more progress in coming years. On the whole, however, this appears unlikely. Radical versions of free-market reform, from Rogernomics in New Zealand and economic rationalism in Australia to the Washington consensus in Latin America, have fallen from favour with the public, and even, to some extent with former supporters among the political and economic elite. Most obviously, the wave of privatisation appears to have run its course in many countries and even to be ebbing in some.

However, no clear alternative has emerged to replace economic liberalism. For the moment, governments appear to be 'muddling through', dealing as best they can with the problems posed by unbounded demands for public services and a strictly limited willingness to pay for such services through higher taxes.

ENDNOTE

1   This research was supported by an Australian Research Council Federation Fellowship. I thank Michael Keating, Andrew Leigh, Andrew Norton, Stuart Macintyre and Nancy Wallace for helpful comments and criticism.

3

GOVERNANCE
Brian Head

This chapter considers the changing institutional patterns that shape and constrain public policy in Australia, and in particular, the recent debates on governance arrangements, their impact on policy development, and the ways in which the social sciences contribute to understanding, analysing and influencing public policy governance. 'Governance', for this purpose, means the institutional arrangements for debating, considering, deciding, prioritising, resourcing, implementing and evaluating public policy. Governance is broader than simply the activities of governmental authorities, especially as reflected in laws and in the formal functions of the executive, parliamentary and judicial branches of government. Governance includes relationships and networks between the public, private and not-for-profit sectors; it includes formal and informal means of policy persuasion; and the creation and use of policy-relevant knowledge. The focus is on examples of productive relationships and innovation, rather than providing a comprehensive overview.

INSTITUTIONAL CHANGE AND GOVERNANCE

Australia, along with other advanced societies (for example, member states of the OECD), has undergone a series of paradigm shifts in recent decades. The regulated welfare state of the 1960s and early 1970s, with its protectionist economic policies, came under attack for engendering low productivity, governmental rigidity, a crisis of public debt, and the impact of 'big government' on standards of living. From the mid-1970s, one response to the 'crisis of productivity' was 'neo-corporatism': a system of elite bargaining, involving trade-offs negotiated between government, business and labour unions, to protect social benefits while promoting economic productivity, efficiency, restructuring and re-skilling (Head 1997). An alternative, increasingly strong response, during the 1980s was the neo-liberal agenda of 'small government' and deregulation. State roles were restructured through competition and contracting-out in service delivery, reduction in direct services provision by the State, attempts to cut 'red tape' and to 'deregulate' business activities, and extensive commercialisation or privatisation of state service agencies (Bell and Head 1994). Dramatic structural change (as in the United Kingdom and New Zealand) was sometimes preferred to gradualism and incrementalism.

Overlaying other trends since the 1980s is the rise of 'new public management' (NPM) and 'responsive government'. NPM focused on identifying and achieving measurable service outcomes. Central steering (that is, setting frameworks, objectives and targets) was favoured over 'rowing' the ship of state (that is, direct provision of services by the public-sector workforce). While productivity and financial reform were the underlying drivers, service delivery improvement and increased 'responsiveness' by the bureaucracy were widely advanced as major objectives of reform. 'Responsiveness' thus had two faces – outwards to citizens/customers (improved quality and relevance of services) and inwards to the political executive (tighter controls by ministers over the bureaucracy). Australia is a leading exemplar of NPM approaches to public-sector management, although the 'small government' rhetoric of earlier decades has become more subdued owing to the long incumbency of a conservative government that has allowed public revenue and expenditure to grow substantially.

The contracting-out of service provision, and use of market-based instruments, encouraged regulatory experimentation, and many opportunities for social science to provide evaluation and advice. As noted by Keating (2004), much of the new challenge for governance is the creation or better management of markets. Governments do not necessarily lose control of policy settings when more competition is introduced into infrastructure, social services and economic services; for example, in employment services, public housing, education and health care. Governments may retain significant controls through conditional funding, and through providing material incentives to influence behaviour. Governments may manage markets to protect consumers, workers, and investors, rather than just the interests of producers. There is a much greater use of 'new economic instruments', which are regarded as a 'light-handed' means of guiding behaviour through incentives, competition, taxes and price signals rather than through traditional models of prescriptive regulation. These are favoured by advocates of lean government and new public management because they are seen as flexible and require lower enforcement costs. The Productivity Commission argues that 'economic instruments offer great promise of achieving better regulatory outcomes at lower cost' (Banks 2003: 18).

PERFORMANCE-BASED REFORM AGENDAS

National policymaking proceeds differently through the institutions. In some policy areas, such as defence, immigration and social security, the Commonwealth exercises its constitutional powers to create a uniform legislative regime. In other policy areas, with overlapping jurisdiction between federal and state levels, there has been a broad trend towards expanding the number of policy domains in which a more consistent national approach is negotiated. There has been a continuous expansion in power by the federal government during the last 35 years. The scope of its powers has been extended through funding specific-purpose programs, and through its constitutional control over trade, foreign affairs and treaties, corporations, and federal territories. Unlike countries such as the United Kingdom, where there has been some genuine devolution of power to regional assemblies, in Australia there has been a steady process of continuing centralisation, regardless of the political colours of the incumbent government.

Several institutional devices, usually chaired by the Commonwealth, have been developed to facilitate the discussion and bargaining required to achieve national frameworks. These mechanisms include the Council of Australian Governments (COAG), Ministerial Councils, and other inter-jurisdictional forums, some of which have a lengthy history. This elite bargaining process is sometimes termed 'executive federalism'.

The early 1990s saw remarkably energetic negotiation of national frameworks in new areas through the COAG process, most notably in competition policy and 'micro-economic reform' (Painter 1998), but also in environmental policy and other areas. The microeconomic regulatory reform programs, together with the NPM reforms of the public sector, represent one of the most intensive periods in public policy reform in Australia. This was also a period when social policy and human services programs were thoroughly recast by the Commonwealth, using its tied funding powers, with the objective of improving performance measures, accountability for service outcomes, and value-for-money. Thus, many non-economic policy areas were influenced by broader trends in NPM, microeconomic reform and business regulation. In recent years, the COAG process has returned to key aspects of sustainable development, such as applying national competition principles to water allocation and pricing policies administered by the states. There has also been a renewed interest in Indigenous service delivery models and the application of 'mutual obligation' principles to social provision. This reformist trajectory has been reinforced by the performance audit culture, as outlined below.

PERFORMANCE EVALUATION AND THE 'AUDIT EXPLOSION'

The Australian public sector has developed a strong international reputation for building performance auditing and evaluation into its standard operating systems. This is undertaken for two reasons. The first, traditional, reason is ensuring and certifying the legality and probity of transactions. This 'compliance' approach, often directed at processes to minimise fraud (ANAO 2004) and to ensure due process, has been complemented in recent years by an emphasis on program and organisational 'effectiveness'. The second approach, largely responsible for the 'audit explosion' of recent decades, is aligned with the quality-assurance agenda of management improvement (Power 2003) and the NPM agenda of service delivery improvement. It has a learning orientation rather than a punitive orientation, consistent with building a system of 'meta-regulation' that enhances the 'self-regulatory' capacity of public agencies (Scott 2003).

Performance audit and evaluation is intended to provide rigorous feedback and suggestions for 'better practice' that can assist management's quest for 'continuous improvement' (Barrett 2004). The Australian National Audit Office (ANAO) has played an important role in reviewing and reporting on Commonwealth programs, and on jointly funded national programs. It has reshaped Commonwealth programs by insisting on clearer objectives, better performance information, and measuring outcomes rather than activities. Parliamentary oversight of national performance auditing is undertaken by the Joint Committee on Public Accounts and Audit, which conducts public hearings on many of the ANAO reports. Where performance is unsatisfactory, consequences may be damaging for those most directly account-able – sanctions may include political risk for responsible minis-ters and career risk for the relevant bureaucrats.

Generally, however, parliamentary committees have been more interested in conducting inquiries into policy and program issues, creating forums for social science input into parliamentary think-ing. However, while parliamentary committee reports are valuable in bringing together social research and stakeholder viewpoints, their impact on policy is diffuse. Committees with a majority of government members are wary of making sharp criticisms of government performance, and committees not controlled by the government are labelled as partisan and disregarded. Governments are more likely to pay attention to processes, including commis-sions of inquiry, they have established for specific purposes.

A different but related role has been played by research and advisory bodies established by the Commonwealth since the 1980s. There has been some experimentation with such bodies, and opportunities for social science input. Some bodies have had a limited lifespan, such as the Economic Planning Advisory Council (EPAC) under the Hawke government, which failed to gain a clear ongoing role in its competition with powerful economic departments. The Resource Assessment Commission (RAC) was established in 1989 to provide inter-disciplinary assessment advice on controversial major projects – such as forestry, mining, and coastal zone development. Its work quickly became controversial and it was disbanded in 1993, providing sober lessons on how far an objective approach could be combined with the politics of major projects. The search for evidence-based approaches has also been clear in other aspects of environmental policy, with substantial public investment in scien-tific research findings to identify natural resource and environ-mental problems, and to suggest realistic options for addressing them (Goldie et al. 2005). As with all policy fields, however, there is a challenge in bridging the knowledge/power divide.

An example of a strong and enduring advisory body is the Productivity Commission (superseding the former Industry Commission in 1998) whose core role is to review policy and performance issues in microeconomic reform and suggest ways to reduce the regulatory burden. It is an influential body, with a well-developed methodology of public submissions and hearings, issues papers and draft reports. Its mandate has been broadened to allow for an analysis of wide-ranging issues, such as the socioeconomic implications of an ageing population and the challenges of devising and implementing measures for ecologically sustainable development. One of its most notable tasks has been to work with a federal/state steering committee since 1994–95 to develop and publish outcomes-based performance measures for state and Commonwealth social programs (McGuire 2003), ranging across education, health, justice, housing and community services. The indicators are intended to provide evidence for understanding comparative performance, and thus serve as a spur to improved performance by all jurisdictions (Productivity Commission 2005a).

BUILDING POLICY AND IMPLEMENTATION CAPACITIES

The capacity of governments to engage in robust consideration of policy options will depend on six factors: the availability of digestible social science knowledge; the availability of policy instruments adequate to the task in question; the history of policy fields (coherence, stability and contestation); organisational factors within government agencies (skills, processes and cooperation); linkages with non-government stakeholders (communication, support and involvement); and political leadership and entrepreneurship.

New public management (NPM), as a reformist and normative doctrine favourable to delivery choices, takes seriously the importance of knowledge of the needs and attitudes of clients/customers. Governments have provided more opportunities for non-government players (consultants and think tanks) to become involved in delivering analysis and advice, potentially divergent from that of public agencies. This 'contestability' of advice was celebrated as opening up options and improving the information base for decisions. By extension, external providers also became involved in reviews and evaluations of existing programs and policy settings. To avoid the danger of fragmented pluralism, political steering mechanisms were tightened, including a greater role for advisers inside ministerial offices.

The main alternative to the NPM approach came from a participatory governance perspective on the value of inclusiveness. The likely sources of this approach are twofold: first, the view that citizens affected by issues should be directly engaged in the processes of deliberation about problems, goals and possible solutions; and second, the view that society should tackle complex interconnected problems that have been resistant to standard administrative programs. This second orientation calls for more cooperative and coordinated solutions to complex problems. Where problems are interconnected, and solutions are difficult to determine, stakeholders need to be 'inside the tent' to discuss problems, identify possible ways forward, and consider how to evaluate options. Social science has demonstrated that many problems are linked, and this has policy implications. An example is the increasing resort to 'place management' approaches in social and urban policy, invoking a range of inclusive approaches to inequality and multiple social dysfunction (for example, disadvantaged suburbs regeneration) by pooling funds and expertise, and reconfiguring services in close consultation with communities (Reddel and Woolcock 2004). A recent study of 'network governance' in environmental policy in Australia recommends a new way of approaching complex policy challenges:

> Environmental governance implies the stewardship of issues which are beyond the direct control of any one participant. It implies the reaching of solutions iteratively, by consensus, rather than appealing to an external umpire. It requires networking at the local level, rather

than relying on 'top-down' policy-making. Above all, it requires powerful players to put their energies into building trust, rather than relying on entrenched advantage (Stewart and Jones 2003: 157).

Thus, the important changes to public-sector functions and processes arising from NPM and performance auditing have been complemented recently by 'new governance' approaches embodying the goals of devolved decision-making, community partnerships, and working across boundaries between sectors and levels (Mandell 2001; Kettl 2002; Rhodes 1997; 2003).

POLICY CHALLENGES FOR IMPROVED GOVERNANCE

This section explores three policy governance challenges of recent years from the perspective of how governance has been a strategic focus for achieving improved policy and program outcomes.

JOINED-UP GOVERNMENT SOLUTIONS

The governance challenges arising from multi-level (vertical) coordination in a federation are well known, but overcoming policy fragmentation is very difficult. In terms of vertical coordination between federal, state and local authorities, it is generally expected that 'joined-up government' – the negotiation of a national policy framework, or consistent regulatory arrangements – would provide consistency and coherence. However, in practice there are likely to be many policy areas where tensions, conflicts and lack of cooperation among governments are evident. Complex national programs may require both 'vertical' and 'horizontal' coordination within the governmental sector itself.

As in the United States and Canada (Bardach 1998; Bakvis and Juillet 2004), joined-up government in Australia has mainly been pursued as a challenge within each state and federal jurisdiction, to promote more effective cooperation/coherence between public agencies in related areas (Head 1999; Jackson 2003). This horizontal dimension is concerned with overcoming the rigidity of traditional bureaucratic 'silos' (regulatory and organisational) that tend to dominate each policy arena – economic, social, environmental, defence, security and so on. A related issue is the inconsistency of policy goals and administrative arrangements that can emerge between agencies in the same jurisdiction; for example, agencies encouraging development in locations where other agencies are promoting conservation goals.

The traditional approach to more holistic thinking was to establish an interdepartmental committee (IDC) or taskforce to develop a discussion paper or a possible joint framework for action. This mechanism is still deployed to initiate thinking on a shared problem, but sometimes engenders mutual veto or lowest common-denominator politics. One structural solution to bureaucratic rigidity was the establishment of a reduced number of larger agencies, such as the 'mega-departments' that emerged in 1987 from the Commonwealth's restructuring exercise. Here, related areas from different agencies that service the needs of particular 'clients' are combined into one new 'integrated' agency (for example, community services). Another type of structural solution is to group corporate management and business support functions into a specialised unit that services a range of departments. Central information services (for example, call-centres) that service the general public are also a variant of this approach. These structural approaches are still being pursued in most jurisdictions.

Their common weakness is that structural change, even when supported by efficient database technology, is not sufficient to engender cooperative problem-solving cultures. If the funding for business-as-usual behaviour remains in place, and the core business of agencies is not redefined, the incentives to change towards a more cooperative framework will be very weak. A further type of 'joined-up' approach is to establish new special-purpose agencies with a broad responsibility for special groups; for example, the rise and fall of ATSIC in relation to Indigenous Australians. Indigenous program governance is perhaps the most complex area in contemporary public policy (see Chapter 9), owing to the strong overlays of politics, culture, values and administrative histories. The recent shift towards a model based on strongly coordinated service provision by Commonwealth agencies dealing directly with communities, reflects a widespread frustration with apparent policy failures in the face of seemingly intractable problems.

This and other policy examples are driving the Commonwealth to reassess what can be achieved by better coordination (MAC 2004). However, there is a large difference between, say, coordinating disaster relief operations, and better coordinating interrelating programs and delivery points in social policy:

> ... while case managers should be well placed to coordinate the delivery of services in their local areas, it may well prove to be a considerable challenge to ensure the desirable exchange of experience and ideas between those responsible at the centre for setting the rules and those responsible for carrying them out (Keating and Mitchell 2000: 148).

Social science research suggests that improved coordination among Commonwealth agencies can shift the policy paradigm to a limited degree. Taking a less technocratic and more holistic view of policy problems requires involving stakeholders, who need to be part of redefining the problems and owning the broader solutions. It also requires the demonstration effect of new leadership models and training programs to promote innovation and relationship management.

REGULATING INTEGRITY AND ACCOUNTABILITY

There is a great deal of normative and prescriptive discussion of 'good governance'. Effective democratic forms of governance 'rely on public participation, accountability and transparency' (UNDP 1997: 9). In Australian public policy, following a flirtation with deregulation in the 1980s, there has been increased attention to specifying standards of behaviour required for those who exercise decision-making power in both the public and private sectors.

Corporate governance in the business sector has been in the spotlight because of scandals involving fraud, corruption and reckless disregard of integrity. The response has been tighter standards rather than deregulation. There are also broader influences at work, such as the need for international consistency in business standards and accountability to shareholders, reflected in evolving international standards on accounting and reporting. Good governance debates in the Australian business sector have been not just about fraud and corruption – generally seen as an audit systems issue – but more importantly about 'corporate governance' practices and standards; for example, disclosure requirements, duties of directors, codes of conduct, and corporate regulation under federal and state legislation. The legal and regulatory environment for corporations is complex (Bell 2002), and the burden of meeting diverse standards is keenly felt by industry and professional leaders, who have lobbied for clear and simple standards.

In some respects the public sector has required even higher standards of behaviour of public officials, who are 'entrusted' to exercise their official duties with high regard for probity, integrity and accountability (Preston and Sampford 2002). This expectation is all the more clear in a democratic system with its broad apparatus of complaints and review mechanisms, anti-corruption watchdogs and vigorous public debate. The integrity and probity of politicians and public-sector managers have been scrutinised, with a view to increasing standards of accountability and transparency. Scandals in the public sector, encompassing individuals in all three levels of government, have been the subject of royal commissions, special inquiries, creation of new institutions (police integrity bodies, independent commissions against corruption) and the strengthening of complaints-handling bodies (Brown and Head 2005). Public servants have been subjected to legislated standards, codes of ethics, extensive training and performance contracts. By contrast, the codes and standards in place for elected officials – ministers, MPs and councillors – are less onerous (Hindess 2004). Parliamentary and ministerial codes of conduct are largely controlled by the political executive. Few ministers take responsibility for scandals or fiascos. Political lying and deception are glossed over as largely in the eye of the beholder. Freedom of information is subverted. Politicians are unwilling to tighten campaign finance disclosure requirements. The growth of ministerial advisory staff, linked to asserting political control over the bureaucracy, has left a major accountability gap in the heart of government because they are not subject to external oversight. Social science advice on such topics is often unwelcome.

Despite many qualifications, Australia is generally rated in the top ten nations for its governance standards, among the cleanest and most democratic countries. Public-sector performance is increasingly being evaluated against promised outcomes (effectiveness measures) and published standards (process integrity measures). This has emboldened the federal government to codify aspects of good governance for export, in the form of capacity-building program assistance for developing countries. This accords with concerns by international organisations to combat fraud and corruption in developing nations, the signing of an international Convention to combat bribery of foreign officials in international business dealings (OECD 1999), and a new-found concern to reform 'failing states' in the Asia-Pacific region that could attract organised crime and terrorist groups.

COLLABORATION AND PARTNERSHIP SOLUTIONS

Proponents of 'collaboration' and 'partnerships' claim that inclusive processes increase information, reduce adversarial behaviour, broaden responsibility for identifying and solving difficult problems, and channel disagreements into practical debate about effective and affordable strategies for achieving agreed long-term goals. Critics and sceptics note, however, that much of what is termed collaboration is state-sponsored, and that the discourse of community collaboration and partnerships has become so widespread that it often obscures the power relations, contexts and intended outcomes of joint activities. Governance arrangements that propose 'partnerships' and 'collaboration' may disguise the unequal power relations among the participants, and their different capacities to become involved. Social science research can assist by distinguishing between the analytical and normative usage of 'community partnership' terminology, and then identifying conditions in which various types of collaboration may be useful or appropriate.

In considering the actual relations embedded in shared governance, it is useful to distinguish the relative power of the actors, the extent to which they bring resources to the shared forum, and the extent to which they agree to be bound by the outcomes (Kernaghan 1993). It is important to recognise differences among types of joint activity, ranging from short-term voluntary cooperation around specific tasks, through to the longer term commitments that are necessary to tackle intractable or complex issues. There are important differences between voluntary *cooperative* relationships, more formally *coordinated* joint activities, and long-term integrated *collaborative* activities that involve sharing of power, resources and decision-making. Each type is suitable for addressing certain tasks and challenges, but not for others (Brown and Keast 2003). Trust and confidence in the fairness, integrity and efficacy of a joint process is an important goal for the participants (though this is often overlooked in formal program evaluations that focus on expenditures and business plans). Trust cannot be ignored if a program requires building the capacity of non-government organisations (NGOs) to become effective contributors in democratic governance.

It is common in Australia for government to be a significant player in inter-sectoral 'collaboration', either as a rule-maker, fund-provider, facilitator, key partner with veto powers, or partner with control over implementation. Key examples of participatory governance are structured and sponsored by the governmental sector (Edwards 2003; Head and Ryan 2004). There are costs and benefits of such arrangements. The benefits of state involvement are potentially substantial, through leveraging the resources and legitimacy of the public sector for broadly agreed objectives. Nevertheless, there may be inherent difficulties for participatory governance arising from state sponsorship, in so far as ministers and their public agencies usually prefer quick tangible wins (as against longer term and less certain outcomes), retain ultimate control through funding, impose detailed reporting and compliance obligations on other stakeholders, and neglect to learn from experience on 'why implementation fails'.

Uneven capacity for participation by non-governmental stake-holders is potentially a limitation on the quality of participatory governance. Another limitation is the nature of the structured opportunities for influence provided in the joint forum. Advocates of stronger forms of participation draw attention to the dangers of tokenism and manipulation. It is widely recognised that there is a continuum or 'ladder' of possible participatory forms, ranging from information-sharing, to formal consultation on proposals, through to various types of partnership, delegated power and citizen control (Bishop and Davis 2002).

SOCIAL SCIENCE AND IMPROVING PUBLIC POLICY: RESPONSIVE REGULATION

Social scientists have engaged in innovative research to explain the *effectiveness* of options available to the designers and managers of regulatory systems. Braithwaite and colleagues have developed a range of options configured in the shape of a 'pyramid' (Ayres and Braithwaite 1992; Grabosky 1997). At the base are the self-regulatory options that operate through cooperation, persuasion and the internalisation of standards by industries or corporations. There is a strong preference for such approaches, especially where there are public mechanisms for enforcement of the relevant standards. Where these self-regulatory mechanisms are effective, they will form the preponderance of regulation. They are also relatively economical from a public finance viewpoint, since a fully funded public inspectorate and prosecution model would be prohibitively expensive. On the other hand, complete reliance on voluntary cooperation and internalisation is unrealistic. As non-compliant behaviour emerges, regulatory responses are adapted towards escalation (higher in the pyramid), warnings, public identification of offending firms, and ultimately a variety of economic or criminal sanctions, the nature of which will depend on the context of the industry or sector under consideration (including the harm that requires regulation).

This approach, termed 'responsive regulation', implies there is no single solution, and that regulatory systems need to adjust continuously to the behaviour of the regulated. Effectiveness will also depend on the capacity (powers, information, skills and budget) of the regulator to provide advice and to conduct investigations and prosecutions. A regulator with a real capacity for coercive intervention will be more likely to secure compliance without the need for drastic sanctions. 'Regulatory agencies will be able to speak more softly when they are perceived as carrying big sticks' (Ayres and Braithwaite 1992: 6). But other players can also be drawn in to increase system efficacy; for example, public interest groups can be empowered to participate in monitoring conduct.

The question of encouraging compliance has been raised in research on tax evasion, where data on motivations for non-compliance are helping to test the relevant escalation steps necessary to deal with different categories of recalcitrance. Taxation authorities in Australia and New Zealand have shown increasing interest in utilising the findings of responsive regulation research to improve their collection of revenue, especially from wealthy individuals and corporations that have historically managed to achieve only modest contributions to public revenues (Braithwaite 2003). It is generally found, in most regulatory and policing systems, that compliance is influenced by perceptions of fairness in process as much as by perceptions of good outcomes. Publicity and education are also important.

As more complex regulatory arrangements become routinised and standards internalised, it becomes possible for the State to step back and regulate 'at a distance'. This allows for the emergence of 'meta-regulation', whereby the State oversees the constitution of fair markets, and the setting and enforcement of standards by industry bodies and accredited professionals (Grabosky 1995). Under this scenario, the State devotes energy to information and relationship management systems, though without neglecting its responsibility for public accountability. This meta-regulation role has many analogues; for example, the meta-audit role in which the auditor-general verifies the robustness of audit systems in agencies or corporations, rather than centrally monitoring and responding to the actual behaviours. Or the requirement under public-sector legislation for agencies to develop, implement, review and adjust their codes of ethics, rather than for a central agency to impose and enforce such codes.

Thus, the 'responsive regulation' approach transcends the sterile debate between defenders of traditional prescriptive/coercive regulation and the champions of deregulation. The debate is about engaging the subjects of regulation in more appropriate and effective relationships, with a view to achieving social and economic objectives consistent with the public interest.

An example of responsive regulation is in the field of crime control and prevention – 'community justice', including the application of 'restorative justice' practices. Community justice aims to develop effective prevention and early intervention initiatives, to reduce the likelihood that persons who have not already begun to offend will enter the criminal justice system. The objective is to develop broad preventative and supportive processes in the community rather than react to criminal activities. Social science research on crime prevention strategies combines a normative grounding in principles of social justice and empirical testing of options for effective interventions to reduce the escalating social/human and economic costs of crime (National Crime Prevention Strategy 1999). Much of the focus is on youth and juvenile justice (White 2003), but the broader social and educational strategies are of wider application. The anti-social behaviour of an offender is seen as a community issue, requiring a collective response. The community justice model encourages the self-growth of offenders, and the repairing of damage to the community in which they live and work. However, the State retains ultimate responsibility while allowing some flexibility for local level initiatives. Restorative justice takes up the questions of how offenders can best be persuaded to take personal responsibility for their unlawful activity; how to meet the needs of victims and communities for redress; and how to improve the relationship between offenders, victims and communities (Miers 2001; Strang 2001; Braithwaite 2002). Relevant community members should play an integral role in the decision-making processes.

Community-based restorative justice approaches may have particular value in repairing the harm endemic in unequal or divided societies (Daly 2000). Indigenous communities are widely considered to be crucial in relation to improving social outcomes. Indigenous community justice initiatives are premised on capturing and reinforcing community ideals. These initiatives focus on the community as the legitimate site of intervention and draw on participation and self-determination as guiding principles. Initiatives building on these ideals in the last 20 years include community policing, community conferencing, community courts and circle sentencing (Marchetti and Daly 2004; Harris 2004). Limitations on the effectiveness of these initiatives may include insufficient funding, the uncertain capacity of some communities to perform the desired roles, and the limited range of offences for which these alternative processes may be invoked.

CONCLUSION

This chapter has considered institutional and policy change in recent decades, some recent 'big issues' and their links with governance debates, and suggested how recent insights of social science could assist in opening up policy options and achieving better outcomes. Major themes of the current era include more integrated governance, responsiveness, policy effectiveness and accountability. Closer interaction between the three sectors of government, business and the community is welcomed. Partnership approaches offer promise of progress in complex policy arenas where other approaches have not been successful. In complex and interconnected fields, 'adaptive management' approaches need to be applied to ensure that positive outcomes are attained. Lessons are not yet clear, but will be diverse.

Social research has engaged with many of the key emergent issues, and the implications for policy governance are being considered by many groups of researchers. Searching for practical insights into the factors that facilitate successful new policy governance frameworks is valuable, but it is difficult to distil concepts of 'best practice', given the diversity in the organisational and cultural context of programs. Much social science is undertaken within the public agencies themselves, but their focus is often instrumental and administrative. Building bridges with independent social researchers is not a simple matter. Nevertheless, the incentives for research directions to be policy-relevant have never been stronger. There is strong encouragement for 'evidence-based' social research. Ideas suggested or refined by social research have been influential (Edwards 2004). There is substantial public funding for applied social and economic research, and recent encouragement of networks that link researchers with the main governmental, industry and community users of applied knowledge.

Social science research can build a better understanding of community participation in policy governance arrangements. It is necessary to explore the tension between program *control* (by the fund-providers and designers) and shared accountability for program *performance*. This bears upon the extent of program legitimacy and *support* (by diverse participants). Research may also assist in responding to the concerns expressed by many stakeholders about local and regional capacity: the adequacy of funds and support services, the seeming inability of government to underwrite long-term commitments, and the local availability of management skills to undertake the major responsibilities placed on new local and regional bodies (for planning, consulting, ensuring compliance and reporting).

Within each element of the knowledge/power/practice triangle there remain substantial deficiencies in understanding and awareness of each other's contributions. Bridging the divide will require more joint activities, rather than simply calls for relevance. A 'learning' orientation is essential – for policymakers, program delivery practitioners, stakeholders and researchers. This is more likely to occur if at least some of the learning processes are mutually constructed and experienced.

4

EDUCATION AND
HUMAN CAPITAL
Simon Marginson[1]

EDUCATION IN AUSTRALIA

Education is one of the core Australian activities. Consider its dimensions. There are five sub-sectors: preschool to age five years; primary (elementary) and secondary schooling; vocational education and training (VET), including public technical and further education (TAFE) and private training; higher education, mostly in public universities; and on-the-job training, largely unfunded and uncodified. In 2003 almost six million people were enrolled in formal institutions, including 3.3 million at school, 1.7 million in VET and 0.9 million in higher education. Almost half the population are involved in education, if informal on-the-job training is included. There are 350 000 foreign students (ABS 2005b; DEST 2005; NCVER 2004a; AEI 2005). The 2001 census found that education employed 595 398 Australians, 10.2 per cent more than in 1996 (ABS 2003b: 67). Total national spending on education in 2002–03 was $46.8 billion, $34.4 billion from governments and $12.4 billion from private sources (ABS 2002c), constituting 6 per cent of GDP. Education also creates part of that national product itself: in 2003–04 international education earned $5.6 billion in export revenues, including tuition fees and other spending by students (IDP 2005).

Continuous expansion of the role of education is a worldwide trend that is driven as much by the advance of human aspirations and agency as by economic modernisation. In 1939 only two Australians in every 100 undertook post-school education. The 2001 census found that among 25–34-year-olds, 24 per cent held bachelor degrees or higher and over 50 per cent had tertiary qualifications (ABS 2003b). It is through education, above all, that Australians better themselves, rather than farming or small business. Tertiary education is essential to all kinds of skilled and professional work. Unemployment among degree holders is half that of the general population. The private rate of return to bachelor degrees is between 9 and 15 per cent (Borland 2002). The precise economic advantages fluctuate, but the economic, social and cultural advantages of tertiary education remain robust despite rising private costs.

EDUCATION POLICY

Because education (in this chapter, defined to include training) has become central to individual and family aspirations, to work, to economic capacity, to global competitiveness and national identity, it is an important site of policy. It is a highly politicised sector, in which government is pervasive even in subsidised private institutions and family decision-making; and much policy attention is focused on efficiencies and cost containment. In all sub-sectors of education, funding and provision are shared by a mix of public and private agents, and both federal and state governments are involved. Under the constitution the states carry responsibility for education, except that in 1946 the Chifley Labor government secured a referendum concerning federal provision of social services, which included a clause on 'benefits to students'. The federal government uses its superior taxing powers to intervene selectively. Canberra has never taken complete responsibility for maintaining institutions or securing policy outcomes, even at the peak of nation-building policies in education under the Whitlam Labor government (1972–1975), and its role varies by sub-sector of education.

The federal/state fault-line has become associated with a divergent administrative evolution. On one hand there are federally fostered independent private schools, higher education and private training institutions, now modelled as self-regulating markets. On the other are school and TAFE systems subject to more traditional public administration by the states. (Systemic Catholic schools, educating almost one student in five, federally funded but administered as state/territory systems, are an intermediate form). The result is a fragmented policy environment: institutional educational cultures subtly at variance with each other; government blame-shifting and buck-passing across the constitutional fault-line; and coordinating arrangements that are incomplete, complex and poorly understood even in policy circles. Although all ministers meet in the Ministerial Council for Employment, Education, Training and Youth Affairs (MCEETYA), there is no solid agreement on administering and financing education. Only when federal funding and/or ideological leadership carries all before it, pushing the states towards a residual policy role (as in the early 1970s and late 1980s) is there temporary national coherence.

It is often difficult to identify what drives policy. This is because:

- of federal/state factors
- institutions and government agencies are engaged globally (UK policies and practices are particularly influential)
- the government draws eclectically on social science inside and outside the public service (economics, psychology, sociology and demography all contribute, and statistical methods are indispensable)
- education policy is not autonomous.

Federal economic policy has often been more powerful than education policy in shaping educational practices, especially in the last two decades of neo-liberal ascendancy. The federal departments of Treasury (especially), Finance and Prime Minister and Cabinet have more policy clout than the spending departments. The potent intersection between economic policy and education policy positions economics as king of the social sciences in education. The Nelson reforms in higher education in 2005 were carried through by Treasury. Likewise, state treasuries have the last word on government schools and TAFE. Other portfolios intersect more sporadically with education. Agriculture, Health and Science are interested in research and universities; and when they exist, Departments of Industry are concerned about training. In the late 1980s and early 1990s, Foreign Affairs helped to launch the international student market; and Immigration now shapes the entry of international students by nation, facilitating and retarding the market by turns, and using conditions attached to student visas and skilled migration to build population in regional areas.

THE STATE OF HUMAN CAPITAL

Just as the problems and tasks of health policy can be understood in terms of the wellness of the population, so the problems and tasks of education policy can be understood in terms of the state of human capital. In this chapter 'human capital' is understood not in the technical sense of an economic quantity measured by rates of return on educational qualifications, but as a sociological metaphor, the meaning it often takes in global policy discourse (for example, UNESCO 1968; OECD 2001). Rates of return calculations are informative in themselves; but as one World Bank Taskforce on higher education argued, when governments use rates of return as a proxy for the total social and economic value of education and basic research, they miss many of the benefits (Taskforce on Higher Education and Society 2000: 39). Rates of return analysis are used to comprehend the value of education by measuring the additional earnings created by the educated, against the cost of their education. The equivalent in health policy would be to calculate the wellness of the population by measuring the additional earnings created by the healthy against the costs of their health care. The additional earnings would be ascribed to health care, a tendentious assumption, while other health indicators such as infant mortality would be ignored. The terrain of health policy is best mapped by combining a range of indicators of the wellness of the population and using complex expert judgment to integrate what can be measured with what cannot. Likewise, education policy is best understood by combining available indicators with expert judgements about the state of human capital.

The term 'human capital' is used here to encompass not just the actual earnings of people but their *potential* to create value under one or another set of conditions. 'Value' is not just economic, but also takes social and cultural forms. Human capital as an ongoing social potential is constituted by individual and collective investment in education, formal and informal. Like the wellness of the population, education is a resource for a broad range of possible public and private projects. Its long-term potential is not exhausted by current costs and revenues; and conditions other than education itself affect whether its various ranges of potential are realised. To take one example, if the economy is down, people holding advanced levels of education create less wealth: not because their educated potential is less, but because there is less scope to use such potential.

Possible indicators of the state of human capital include: (1) student achievement as measured by international comparisons; (2) rates of participation in education, or the nature and number of qualifications; and (3) national investment in education from public and private sources as a proportion of GDP. Another factor, requiring complex judgments informed by various indicators, is the *capacity* of educational institutions.

TABLE **4.1** *Selected data on participation rates and spending on education, Australia and other OECD countries, 2001–02*

Country	Percentage of 25–34-year-olds attaining degree-type[a] tertiary study, 2002	Average duration of degree-type tertiary study, 2001	Spending per student over total of degree-type study, 2002	Percentage of 15–19-year-olds not in education, 2002	Spending on educational institutions as a proportion of GDP, by source:		
					public	private	total
	%	Years	US$ PPP[b]	%	%	%	%
United States	31	n.a.	n.a.[c]	18.8	5.1	2.3	7.3
Canada	26	n.a.	n.a.	16.3	4.9	1.3	6.1
Korea	26	4.2	34 756	n.a.	4.8	3.4	8.2
Japan	25	3.8	52 555	n.a.	3.5	1.2	4.6
Netherlands	25	4.9	63 186	19.3	4.5	0.4	4.9
AUSTRALIA	25	2.6	34 954	20.3	4.5	1.4	6.0
Denmark	23	4.4	59 834	11.3	6.8	0.3	7.1
United Kingdom	23	3.8	41 209	24.7	4.7	0.8	5.5
Sweden	22	4.7	69 981	11.6	6.3	0.2	6.5
Finland	21	4.5	49 972	19.6	5.7	0.1	5.8
France	19	5.3	46 103	5.4	5.6	0.4	6.0
New Zealand	18	n.a.	n.a.	n.a.	5.5	n.a.	n.a.
Germany	13	6.5	73 488	9.9	4.3	1.0	5.3
Mexico	5	3.4	14 858	46.6	5.1	0.8	5.9
Average	19	4.7	42 906	18.2	5.0	0.7	5.6

NOTES (a) Enrolment in programs classified by the OECD as 'tertiary type A and advanced research'; (b) PPP = Purchasing Power Parity; (c) n.a. = not available

SOURCE OECD 2004c: 71, 217, 229, 338

SOME INDICATORS

Data from federal agencies and the OECD, summarised in Table 4.1, indicate that:

- Australia's preschooling capacity is poor, covering only 35.9 per cent of 3–4-year-olds in 2002, compared to an OECD country average of 67.8 per cent (UK 81.2 per cent). Australia spent 0.1 per cent of GDP on preschooling – well below the OECD average of 0.4 per cent (OECD 2004c: 231 and 278).

- In school student achievement in reading, maths and science, Australia is in the top group of nations, except for primary school maths (Masters 2005: 8).

- Participation in tertiary education is above the OECD average and strong among older age groups. In 2002,

Australia's participation rate for 30–39-year-olds was 15.2 per cent, behind only the UK (16.2 per cent).

- The educational achievements of most (though not all) migrant groups are superior to those of the native-born; for example, Chinese-born Australians were 0.62 per cent of the population aged 20–24 years in 2001, but 1.34 per cent of higher education students in 2003 (ABS 2004b; DEST 2005).

- Educational resources, especially government funding, are increasing at school but declining at tertiary stage. The length of average degree level study is short. In 2001 the average tertiary student received $34 954 of education over the course compared to $42 906 in the OECD (2004c: 215, 217 and 221).

- Education funding is relatively private-sector dependent. In 2001 public spending at 4.5 per cent of GDP was below the OECD average (5.0 per cent); private spending at 1.4 per cent of GDP was third highest in the OECD after Korea and the United States. From 1995 to 2001, despite a 15 per cent increase in per capita GDP, Australia's total public spending on tertiary education institutions fell by 11 per cent (OECD 2004c: 229–32).

POLICY PROBLEMS AND DILEMMAS

But these quantitative indicators do not tell the whole story. They mask underlying policy problems that have continually retarded the evolution of human capital.

First, there is the tendency towards the bifurcation of human capital between education haves and have-nots. Australia has greater inequalities of school student achievement than in Western Europe, Korea and Japan. Early school drop-out is higher in Australia than in most OECD nations, and it is stubborn: retention to Year 12 of secondary school has been stuck around 75 per cent for a decade (ABS 2005b). No doubt weak preschool coverage is one foundation of later bifurcation, but this is also exacerbated by the policy reliance on private spending. All else being equal, this disadvantages families without the private capacity to pay, and it steepens the hierarchy of supply quality. Much private investment in education in Australia is by families who would participate at lower levels of spending but want to buy special advantages. Though it improves the capacity of certain (already strong) institutions, it is questionable how much such investment contributes to the stock of human capital. Meanwhile, when people from other social groups find that high value educational places are closed to them, they have less incentive to participate in the low-priced lower value high-access institutions.

A second ongoing policy problem is the identification and monitoring of educational outcomes and outputs. During the massive expansion of post-compulsory education from 1960 to 1975, when public spending tripled in ten years (Marginson 1997), following first-wave human capital theorists such as Denison (1962), it was taken for granted that education was economically and socially beneficial and would pay for itself in the longer term by generating growth. Little thought was given to the composition of investment; the mix of benefits; the location and mode of delivery; or efficiency, incentives and behaviours. Keynesian economics supported education psychology in its drive to extend the boundaries of participation across the whole school-age population and maximise the potential talent. For sociologists, whose objective was equal educational outcomes by social group, as in the Karmel (1973) report on schools, the universal expansion of education was the path of least political resistance through the problem of distribution. But when fiscal pressures demanded a less generous and more nuanced approach, government looked to identify educational outputs, so as to maximise the benefits of investment and to target particular outcomes – and neither economics, psychology nor sociology had devised a plausible function relating investment in education to the comprehensive outcomes associated with it.

Psychology is strong on individual cognitive outcomes but weak on social determinations: the only sociology it recognises uses linear analytical methods to model non-linear and contingent social relations. Educational sociology is divided between atomistic quantification, critical policy analysis and cultural theory, none of which can imagine comprehensive outcomes. Economists draw on partial measures of output such as private rates of return. But rates of return analyses assume perfect competition in the markets for education and labour; enhanced earnings are attributed to education alone, not social selection; and calculations of externalities and collective benefits are arbitrary. Larger questions remain unanswered. What are the social and economic conditions and determinants of student achievement? How much does education make a difference? Is education consumption or investment? Is advanced education necessary to economic competitiveness, or do strong economies spend more on education because they can (Wolf 2002)? What are the relations between private benefits and public or social benefits? Are they zero sum, so that the greater the private benefit (and private cost) the lesser the social benefit (and public cost)? Or are they positive sum, requiring distinctive policies? To what extent *should* education be assessed in terms of direct benefits, given its larger contribution to social, economic, cultural and political capacities?

The unresolved ambiguity of outcomes runs through every debate. When mass tertiary education becomes the norm and the engine of complex social practices there is often nostalgia for simplicity and certainty, such as the reassurance of traditional literatures. In Australia, nostalgia often takes the form of demands for vocational utility (or sometimes for traditional literatures), whereby outcomes are measured in terms of employment rates, wage rates and the lifetime earning of graduates; and the work-related attributes they have acquired. The measure of education is how 'practical' it is; how well it prepares, screens and selects students into jobs. The formation of cognitive and cultural attributes, let alone social values, is not seen as significant. Neither human capital theory nor policies of equal opportunity challenge the utilitarian vision. Yet the holes are obvious. Education is never the sole factor that determines economic and social destinations. It does more than prepare people for work, and it does less – learning on the job is more effective than simulated vocational learning in education. Again, the lacuna is a holistic theory linking investment in educational capacity, including direct and indirect effects, to the full range of human and social potential.

POLICY SCIENCE AND NEO-LIBERALISM

SOCIAL SCIENCE AND EDUCATION POLICY

The social sciences have their moments in education policy, when key ideas appear at the right time, or make their time; pushing out (or closing in) the boundaries of education and changing the way it is thought, said and organised. Early 1960s human capital theory was one such moment. Another was the needs-based funding of private schools in the 1970s. A third was the Higher Education Contribution Scheme (HECS) with income contingent repayment, introduced in 1989 (Chapman 1997; 1998). HECS reconciled fiscal savings with expanding access, taxed the private benefits of education and subsidised the formation of human capital for non-vocational purposes, and balanced public and private costs and benefits in transparent fashion. It was designed by the ANU's Bruce Chapman, with involvement also from Bob Gregory, Meredith Edwards and others, and is perhaps *the* outstanding example of how the theoretical and empirical tools of social scientists have contributed to Australian education policy.

The original design was novel and was initially resisted by the Australian Taxation Office, but proved robust, rigorous and flexible enough to survive for almost two decades, albeit in increasingly altered form. HECS has been the major catalyst for income contingent loan developments in New Zealand (1992), the United Kingdom (1997/2005), South Africa (1994), Ethiopia (2002) and Thailand (2005). The World Bank has recommended income contingent loans in Malaysia, Rwanda, Mexico, Colombia, Nepal and Hungary, among others. All because an Australian economist had an idea for solving a policy problem.

There is always potential for cross-fertilisation between academic disciplines and government. But the high points of government/academic collaboration do not translate into a permanent ongoing chemistry. The rhythms and breaks of education policy (like all policy) are other than those of social science; and the relations of power/knowledge are not symmetrical. Social science only rarely drives education policy. The reverse relationship normally prevails. Educational economics, psychology and sociology evolved as specific policy sciences to serve the needs of government. Only learning theory in psychology has constituted major innovations in the parent discipline. The autonomies of all three are problematic: undermined by short-term incentives and imperatives in decision-making, crowded out by fiscal imperatives. Policy is politicised and rarely stays fixed, even for brilliant solutions to complex problems like the early HECS. The needs of the social sciences for long-term horizons and critical spaces are not always understood. Where social science fails to provide ready answers to real (or illusory) policy problems, or to speak back in the values of those with power, it can be shut out, like much of education sociology. Yet when social science tracks its trajectory to the twists and turns of policy, it places its long-term autonomy and coherence at risk.

Educational economics has continually adapted to the shifts in official ideologies, themselves economic in content; and now trails behind it a litter of broken universals, theorisations that were useful in their time but inevitably found wanting as total explanations. Denison's 1962 claim about investment in education has lost its fiscal purchase, though not its appeal to educationists. In *Human Capital* (1964) Becker systematised Alfred Marshall's calculations of the rates of return to individual investment. This work is still mobilised by governments in arguing for the transfer of costs to the direct beneficiaries, despite its limited grasp of educational outputs. Screening theory recognises education's role in social selection and the exchange value of credentials, deepening our understanding of the peculiarities of educational competition and markets (Hirsch 1976; Marginson 2005) – but it is cynical about the potential of education to enhance productivity or other human capacities.

Economists have also built education production functions, in which outputs defined by measures of student achievement are mapped against the costs of inputs. This appeals to policymakers because it is output focused, and it measures both system-level and institutional efficiencies. Moreover, evidence of weak relations between inputs and these selected and narrowly defined outputs (for example, Hanushek 1986) is mobilised to constrain demands for spending. But the method has little credibility with educationists, precisely because most of the outcomes of education are left outside the equation.

NEO-LIBERALISM AND ECONOMIC POLICY

For governments, it is often simpler to put on the vocational blinkers, confine policy attention to measurable direct effects, and use private rates of return as neo-liberal ideology suggests – despite the violent policy reduction that follows. For neo-liberalism offers automatic economic mechanisms and formulas in place of the responsibilities and hazards of public planning. It transfers risk from government to the users of education. Tuition markets, competition and subsidised private sectors naturalise unequal educational outcomes and unequal producer status and quality. It is still widely expected that public policy will deliver a broad framework of opportunity and provide good quality public institutions, but the political and fiscal pressures have been reduced. However, when neo-liberal economic meta-policy is in command, education-specific policies are dumbed down and the potential of the social sciences is constrained.

One outcome is that the education policy work of the 2000s is impoverished, compared with that of the 1960s and 1970s. (The exception is statistical data, including student achievement measures, which are much improved). The Martin report (1964) and the Universities Commission were followed by a first national report on TAFE and the creation of the statutory Tertiary Education Commission and Schools Commission to manage policy and programs. Each developed a distinctive body of autonomous policy knowledge, drawing from different social sciences, and from quantitative and qualitative methods that profoundly affected educational institutions, systems and people. This work is marked by dispassionate intelligence and the accumulation of wisdom. Successive reports built on each other in response to a long-term horizon of objectives, rather than constituting a disconnected series of problems.

Policy inquiry drove deeper, foregrounding obstacles and creating new lines of inquiry and programs to address them. Policy benefited from the freedoms of triennial planning and government willingness to invest in selective policy interventions. Nevertheless, in the 1980s the federal education commissions became more politicised by the education interest and by pressures to rein in spending and reduce the expectations of government. The last was impossible for the commissions. Reforming Labor Minister John Dawkins (1987) saw them as potential sites of resistance and abolished them. Ostensibly, their functions were transferred to the federal department, but the main lines of semi-autonomous policy work were deconstructed. This opened education policy to the play of neo-liberal reform.

Policy papers now eschew genuine inquiry: the only questions they pose are those with pre-given answers. Policy objectives are either piecemeal, or expressed in vacuous generalities, and policy statements tend to be polemical in tone. From time to time, strategic initiatives are taken up but not sustained, being always vulnerable to fiscal pressures: one case in point is Asian languages policy.

The only funding initiatives that readily gain official support are those that strengthen private schooling or kick-start tertiary markets. The fiscal imperative leaves little scope for a social science designed to improve educational outcomes, which would require nuanced public investments designed to generate specific cause/effect relationships. Instead, government simply assumes that once buyer/seller relations are in place, mediated by competition and prices, institutions will improve more or less continuously.

The fuller pedagogical potential of innovations in psychology are eclipsed, in a policy environment in which the political economy of education (reforms in the practices of management and governance; and economic resources, mechanisms and incentives), rather than pedagogies and curriculum, is the medium of modernisation. Instead, educational psychology is configured to serve policy-generated markets in a more subordinate fashion. Learning achievement can be differentiated by institution and school type, and when freed of social context, league tables can be constructed. Yet the same tools of inquiry are never used to interrogate market reform itself. Have the dezoning of government schools, nurturing of private schools, tertiary competition and student fees led to higher student achievement overall? The question is yet to be asked.

CONDITIONS OF NEO-LIBERAL POLICY

There are policy double standards here. It seems that the public funding of private schools (unlike public schools) is positive sum, generating collective as well as private benefits, and producing better educational outcomes. Federal funding of private schools is double that of government schools, which are largely left to the states, though average student–staff ratios in private secondary schools (12.0) are better than in government schools (12.4). The government school share of enrolments has dropped from 78.7 per cent in 1975 to 67.5 per cent in 2004 (ABS 2005b). The absolute social value of government schools and their long-term contribution to human capital are higher than their relative market value. However, the drive for individual social position foregrounds market value. Policy might have stood back from the financing of private investment in educational position, and focused on maximising the quality of the common open access public systems. But instead governments chose to fashion the market and cultivate electoral constituencies within it. This in turn has fed powerfully into popular culture.

Here neo-liberal policy rests on historical conditions of possibility: on one hand, groups with clout (independent schools, Catholic school systems); on the other, participation itself. As the educational frontier moved up the age structure, and employers raised the threshold for work, especially in the 1975, 1982–83 and 1991–92 recessions, the advantages of credentials and the drawbacks of early school-leaving became obvious. Once advanced education becomes a defensive necessity for all, it is no longer necessary for governments to 'buy' participation except for under-represented groups such as the Indigenous. The number of degrees grows, even though national investment falls. But only some places confer premium benefits, creating incentives for private investment. Thus policy strategies shifted from public investment in the human capital of a population prone to under-investment, to policies designed to facilitate self-investment and freedom to pay. But like thrift in earlier times, self-investment financed by debt is a middle-class virtue. Investor panache is premised on a prior level of family education. The ebbing of public financing and weakening of open access public institutions hurts migrant groups, Indigenous students, rural families, welfare dependants and the disabled who depend on public investment and universal solidarity to advance their position.

The status problems of government schools are compounded by a lack of agreement on the school-leaving age. Most educationists see Year 12 as a general preparation for degree courses, VET and the rest of life. Yet Australia specialises early by international standards: Year 12 subject choices are shaped by undergraduate professional courses; and despite vocational programs in schools, some political leaders still favour separating the trades/apprenticeship stream at the end of Year 10. The stratification between high-status academic and low-status vocational streams is another factor reproducing the bifurcation of human capital. Ironically, vocational institutions are major losers. Almost four of every five dollars of VET funding is provided by governments (NCVER 2004b). Low private rates of return restrict full fee markets. But federal–state funding agreement has broken down; and federal spending on VET in terms of costs per student hour has fallen by 16 per cent since 1997 (Campus Review 2004). In the 2004 election, the coalition parties announced that rather than overhaul funding and coordination holistically, they would establish a new sub-system of corporate technical schools/colleges with industry sponsors and non-union labour. As in schooling, creating a public/private 'wedge' is fiscally cheaper than taking responsibility for the whole system, and it fragments the pressures on government. The states continue to carry the main burden in TAFE, which along with preschools is the most under-funded part of education. Meanwhile, on-the-job training receives no policy attention.

THE UNIVERSITIES

Neo-liberal reform has been carried further in higher education. In the Dawkins reforms, which were centrist rather than neo-liberal, a 50 per cent growth in student numbers financed by the non-market HECS was balanced by the promotion of competition, self-managed efficiency and selective commercial markets in vocational postgraduate degrees and international education. Institutions were positioned as self-serving corporations competing for fee-based private revenues and performance-based public research funding. Full indexation of public funding was dropped in 1995. Under the Howard government from 1996, HECS moved closer to a market fee and the advance of domestic student participation slipped. By leading the OECD in reducing public outlays per student, the federal government drove market incentives deep into the minds of university executives. Between 1996 and 2003, public source funding fell from 58 to 44 per cent, with only 25 per cent from federal money for teaching. Funds from students rose from 19 to 34 per cent, with 17 per cent from fees other than HECS (see Table 4.2).

The reforms in 2005 led by Minister Brendan Nelson (2003) include HECS increases of up to 25 per cent and a full-fee undergraduate market supported by income contingent loans, FEE–HELP, again shifting costs to the private side (Marginson 2005). Australian universities are among the least affordable in the world. Over two-thirds of full-time students work during semester, double the proportion of two decades ago. Australian universities are more accessible than rising costs would suggest, primarily because of income contingent repayment (EPI 2005). But for students, the question is not so much access to degrees, as access to high-value degrees. The deeper changes have not been in social access to higher education, but in the production and

TABLE **4.2** *Changes in university revenues by source, 1996 to 2003*

Source of funding	Total funding from this source		Proportion of total funding by source	
	1996 $ million[a]	2003 $ million[a]	1996 %	2003 %
Federal government	4566.3	4919.5	56.7	39.9
State/territory governments	110.4	506.0	1.4	4.1
HECS/PELS from students(b)	932.8	2094.9	11.6	17.0
International student fees(c)	531.1	1700.9	6.6	13.8
Postgraduate student fees	89.9	194.0	1.1	1.6
Undergraduate student fees	0	80.6	0	0.7
Continuing education fees	79.3	93.4	1.0	0.8
All other sources(d)	1741.8	2742.5	21.6	22.2
Total	**8051.6**	**12331.8**	**100.0**	**100.0**

NOTES (a) current prices; (b) PELS = income contingent loans scheme for postgraduate tuition fees; (c) includes international students at all levels of study; (d) includes payments for contract research, donations and bequests, investment income.

SOURCE DEST 2005

culture of the education that is accessed. The market reinforces vocational and instrumental perspectives, blurs policy focus on the longer term and collective benefits of education, and unleashes stratification between universities no longer mediated by policies designed to standardise degree parity and research functions across the national system.

Marketisation has both narrowed and broadened the human capital stock. Between 1996 and 2001, domestic students increased by only 5.7 per cent, though the domestic fee-paying postgraduate load grew by 84.8 per cent and international students by 112.2 per cent. Internationals peaked in 2003 at 210 397, 22.6 per cent of all students, and contributed 13.8 per cent to revenue. The main source nations are China, Hong Kong, Singapore, Malaysia, Indonesia and India (DEST 2005). The majority of international students gain permanent residence, becoming part of national human capital while bringing global sensibilities to it. Australia now provides 10 per cent of the world's international student places. However, the nation is less strong in research, with only two of the top 100 research universities (Marginson 2005), and universities have been slow to recruit international research students, who need scholarships, not fee-based places. Only 4.5 per cent of Australia's international students are research students, much lower than the United States (16.6 per cent), the United Kingdom (10.0 per cent) and parts of Western Europe. Yet such students provide a globally mobile labour force of often exceptional quality.

Meanwhile for most universities, business acumen has become a more important source of competitive advantage than academic capacity; and a growing portion of resources is siphoned into marketing, promotion, fundraising, offshore branches, financial management, quality assurance, status-oriented buildings and facilities at the expense of academic infrastructures. Between 1993 and 2002, average students per staff rose from 14.2 to 20.4 (DEST 2005). This weakens Australia's capacity to produce human capital. The problem will worsen, given that in 2001, 44.5 per cent of university teachers were aged 45 years and over. Universities use marketing and quality assurance to conceal variations in quality. Policy turns a blind eye to the link between national investment and educational capacity. In the longer term, these Nelsonian gestures have diminishing returns, especially in global markets.

CONCLUSION

The infrastructures that generate Australia's human capital are undervalued at school level, perhaps overvalued at university level, and ignored in relation to VET. Human capital is bifurcated between haves and have-nots. All sub-sectors except private schooling suffer from chronic public under-investment. Public goods are under-recognised and undervalued. As in other English-speaking nations, private investment and subsidised market competition are now at the heart of human capital formation. In the universities, though not other sub-sectors, income contingent repayment modifies the regressive effects. But everywhere win/lose markets stratify value, weaken lower status institutions and discourage participation at the margin, subtracting there from the absolute and relative value of human capital, though the relative value of high status participation is enhanced. Apart from the large-scale psychological testing of student achievement, the contribution of autonomous social science to education policy is weaker than in the 1960s and 1970s. Education policy has lost autonomy in the face of neo-liberal economic meta-policy. There is reduced scope for nuanced public investments, for specific interventions and for expert judgments informed by situated cases and accumulated wisdom about the education sector.

Nevertheless, there is scope to develop education by bringing the social sciences to bear on lacunae and obstacles retarding policy. There are three kinds of possible research initiative. The most important is theorisations that extend policy imagination and capacity. Perhaps *the* crucial innovation is a theorisation that could comprehend, monitor and augment the full range of educational costs and benefits; taking into account individual and collective, private and public. This would be inter-disciplinary, combining psychology, sociology and economics; combining quantitative and qualitative techniques with informed synthesis.

Another key move would be to focus research and policy attention on vocational learning in the workplace in order to begin to refashion the division of labour between vocational and general learning. This could help to free institutional education, including VET, to prepare students in the full potentials of human capital. In 2001, three-quarters of the workforce were involved in work-based training (ABS 2002d: 60). We need to know more about what is learned on the job and how it can be systematised, augmented, codified and carried between workplaces. This would help to enhance productivity and address skill needs. In addition, policy research should begin to map a national framework for life-long learning, with funded learning entitlements and portable educational credits.

The second kind of research initiative is investigations that create reflexivities within present policy approaches. For example, what do we know of the efficacy of the mix of market choices and centrally directed pricing variations in meeting both workforce and other needs? What do we know of the larger social consequences on family formation, and the housing sector, of debt-based tertiary education? How does international recruitment of students affect migration policy and vice versa? What are the consequences of the low provision of preschool education? And what about the bifurcation of human capital? Here, the first step is to recognise unequal educational outcomes (Teese and Polesel 2003). Socioeconomic inequalities should be monitored with hard-edged indicators, such as income deciles and parental occupation, instead of ambiguous instruments like residential postcodes. Equity analysis must begin to focus on the distribution of opportunities in the context of producer stratification; for example, rates of return studies targeted to particular qualifications and institutions.

The third kind of research is work that might improve education within the terms of present policies; for example, studies of the information available to parents and students when educational decisions are made, and the potential for new modes of communication to reconstitute the decision-making space. Finally, though the solutions to federal–state problems are beyond the unaided power of social science, it would help if there were a single national agency for the collection of education data.

ENDNOTE

1   The author thanks colleagues for their feedback and ideas, especially Stuart Macintyre.

5

RIGHTS AND RESPONSIBILITIES: WELFARE AND CITIZENSHIP

Peter Travers

One of the most pressing social policy issues in Australia is how to reconcile the expectation that all citizens should enjoy a decent standard of living and the expectation that all should play their part in carrying out the duties of citizenship. For more than 30 years, concern over the extent of poverty and inequality in Australia has been the focus of intense debate, both in academic literature and in the media. This focus has been rivalled in recent years by the seemingly inexorable rise in 'welfare dependency' and the worry that measures designed to counter poverty and inequality have perverse behavioural outcomes.

The claims and counterclaims include:

- payments are too mean

- payments are too generous and undermine the work ethic

- conditions of payments are demeaning and punitive

- the interaction of the welfare system with the tax system results in effective marginal tax rates that are so high as to impede the transition from welfare to work

- the welfare system as a whole is morally pernicious in that it leads to and sustains irresponsible behaviour

- the fiscal burden of this vast system is unsustainable

- the entrenched interests that have been built up over the past century are so powerful as to render the system unreformable.

In the face of these and similar considerations, policymakers might be forgiven for subscribing to one or other of the two reactionary theses that Hirshchman identifies as afflicting the social policy world: the futility thesis (social policy operates at a superficial level – it cannot touch the basic structures which go on inexorably to produce their inevitable outcomes) or the perversity thesis (whatever policymakers do only makes matters worse) (Hirschman 1996).

If policymakers turn to the social sciences seeking a counter to the gloom of the futility and perversity theses, they get mixed messages. The social sciences have a long tradition of highlighting the gap between aspirations and reality. Research findings do not always offer consolation to policymakers. The social sciences do, however, give good reason to reject the reactionary theses that social policy in Australia must inevitably do more harm than good, and the even more insidious claim that social policy intervention is of its very nature doomed to futility.

This chapter begins at the most general level with the claim that the complex of social policies generally known as the welfare state was always doomed to failure. It then moves to the specific issue implicit in the chapter title: the tension between the claims implied by the notion of citizenship, and the demand that citizens behave responsibly. It takes up some more specific contributions of the social sciences in Australia, and briefly asks what might be done in the future.

MAKING A SQUARE MEAL OF A 'STEW OF PARADOX'

In 1949, the British sociologist TH Marshall addressed a question central to the social science debates of his day: Are the equalities implied by 'citizenship' compatible with the inequalities inherent in a capitalist economic system? As he surveyed the Britain of 1949, he saw a more or less intact market economy promoting unequal outcomes, side by side with a welfare state giving access to a degree of income other than market income, and access to a host of services where one's income was irrelevant (Marshall 1949). The problem with the social rights implied by welfare states is that they are based on a quite different principle from the market. They are based on the common status of citizen, a principle of equality, rather than on one's purchasing power, a principle of inequality.

Marshall never does resolve his original question, but keeps insisting that the problem is not due to muddled thinking. There really are opposing principles. But this is not a ground for despair. 'A human society can make a square meal out of a stew of paradox without getting indigestion – at least for a long time' (Marshall 1949: 127). Half a century later, Marshall would probably be surprised to see how both capitalism and welfare states have evolved, and perhaps even more surprised to see the extent to which, despite frequent predictions of their demise, both are entrenched. As welfare states have matured, they have tended to converge at a very high level of aggregate expenditure as a proportion of GDP (Castles 2003). This applies even to Australia, for years regarded as a 'welfare laggard'. Indeed, if we examine net (after-tax) social expenditure, the differences between welfare state leaders and laggards are surprisingly small (Adema 2001). On closer inspection, however, the structure of welfare states, the way in which they are financed, their interaction with the taxation system and with the labour market vary sharply. It is at this level that Marshall's question as to what would come of the 'stew of paradox' is especially relevant.

In one of the best known analyses of comparative welfare state development, Esping-Andersen groups countries according to how they have addressed Marshall's question. Following Marshall, his measuring stick is the degree to which welfare states weaken the

cash nexus by granting entitlements independent of market participation (Esping-Andersen 1990: 35; 1999: 43). Viewed from this
perspective, which he calls the process of 'decommodification', he
identifies three clusters of countries: a liberal English-speaking
group where the cash nexus is at its strongest; conservative
Continental European countries where occupational-based insurance systems give stronger protection against the vagaries of the
market, but always linked to one's occupational status; and social
democratic Scandinavian countries where the split between entitlements and market participation is at its strongest.

More recently, Esping-Andersen has modified his earlier analysis to take account of feminist critiques that he paid insufficient
attention to the very different ways in which welfare states take
account of the aspirations of women, and specifically, how they
assign welfare obligations to the household (Esping-Andersen
1999: 43–6). In the re-formulation of his theory, labour market
and family policies are added to the original social insurance
focus. The original three regime clusters remain, but the dimension of 'de-familialisation' (the degree to which 'family obligations' are removed from the household) has now been added to
'decommodification' (the degree of access to benefits – cash and
services – independently of one's income). Sweden rates highly
both on de-familialisation and decommodification. Conservative
countries such as Germany and Italy also rate highly on decommodification – at least for the main breadwinner, but they are at
the lower end of the scale for de-familialisation. The liberal countries, including Australia, are the least decommodified, but they
rate relatively highly on de-familialisation.

What this adds up to is a quite complex answer to the original
question whether entitlements based on citizenship are compatible
with a capitalist economy. The design of welfare states differs,
above all, according to the degree of responsibility placed on the
market (what can be purchased), the State (what is provided and
under what conditions by it), and what is left to the family.

Market economies themselves are no longer dominated by the manufacturing sector of the mid-twentieth century, but by the post-industrial service-based economies of the twenty-first. Families have changed in quite radical fashion, above all in terms of the aspirations of women. The upshot is that some countries appear to have welfare state institutions that sit more happily than others with market economies. On the basis of economic growth, unemployment rates, levels of inequality, and relatively high fertility rates, and their ability to adapt to changing circumstances, the Nordic countries have been the most successful in juggling the competing claims of markets, social policy and functioning families. On the whole, the liberal regimes also score well, though with poorer performance in terms of social equality. As John Quiggin notes in Chapter 2, the Continental European countries face the gravest challenges, with high unemployment, pension systems that at their worst are both unsustainable and close to unreformable, and fertility rates that are the lowest ever recorded in peacetime.

One can challenge some features of this analysis, such as whether Australia and New Zealand are sufficiently unique as to represent a 'fourth world' of welfare (Castles and Mitchell 1993; Castles 1996), or whether one should collapse the Nordic and liberal worlds into a single 'progressive liberal' axis (Hicks and Kenworthy 2004). There does seem, however, to be a very strong consensus that Australia is among the countries that deal rather well with the paradox involved in combining a strong welfare state and a market economy in the twenty-first century.

THE CITIZEN WITH RIGHTS AND RESPONSIBILITIES

It has been pointed out that much of the history of the welfare state has been one of stability and path dependency, punctuated by three eras of intense reform. Path dependency refers to the tendency of nations to become locked into their institutional incentive structures (North 1990). Despite this bias to inertia, there was a period of upheaval in the late nineteenth century and a second in the 1930s and 1940s. A third epoch of reform is with us today, as all nations face a family revolution with new winners and losers; a service economy with winners and losers; with both processes compounded by homogamy – our common tendency to share life's resources with like partners (Esping-Andersen 2002: 1–6). Though the history of the Australian welfare state gives ample evidence of the power of path dependency, it is not so powerful as to be paralysing. Most of the issues that Australian policymakers are grappling with today are not peculiar to Australia, but are common to other OECD countries.

THE GOOD CITIZEN

The Commonwealth Invalid and Old Age Pension Act of 1908 providing taxpayer-funded pensions based on citizenship has been decisive in shaping Australia's welfare state. As with existing New South Wales legislation, the non-contributory feature was justified on the ground of reciprocity: it gave recognition to the prior contribution of older women and men to building up the wealth of the nation (Travers 1991; Sawer 2003). There were misgivings, however, when it came to allowing all older citizens a similar claim on the nation. In response, moral qualifications were attached to eligibility. Applicants had to establish that they were 'of good character' and that they were 'deserving of a pension'. In practice, the moral provisions were only occasionally applied, mainly to exclude habitual drunkards and husbands who deserted their wives (Jordan 1989).

By the 1930s, the infrequency with which the moral provisions were applied had become a source of concern to the Auditor-General. By the 1970s, the moral provisions were seen as both an anachronism and as an administrative problem owing to their technical inefficiency, with the ever-present risk of inconsistency in their application. The last recorded exclusion was in 1972, and the following year the new Minister for Social Security, Bill Hayden, could write, 'The present approach to social security is that benefits are a right rather than a privilege, and during the current review of our program consideration will be given to deleting from the statute book anachronistic and moralistic provisions' (cited in Jordan 1989: 55). The moral provisions were indeed removed from the Act in 1974.

THE CITIZEN WITH RIGHTS

On the face of it, the rights-based approach referred to by the Minister for Social Security in 1972, together with the removal of discretionary powers in relation to good character, mark a sharp break with previous theory and practice. A pre-modern vestige of a discretionary tradition had now been removed. However, it would be more accurate to say that it represents a limitation of the areas where discretion can be applied, rather than its elimination. No social security system can be free of discretion (Goodin 1988). In the case of the age pension, the areas where discretion could be applied had indeed been restricted to less problematic matters such as residency, age, income and assets. But other payments involve far more subjective decisions such as an applicant's willingness and ability to look for work and accept employment, effective marital status, and physical and mental disability (Jordan 1989). It is these payments that are at the centre of debate in all advanced welfare states today.

THE RESPONSIBLE CITIZEN

A marked change of emphasis took place in Australia in the name of 'activation' following the Social Security Review of the 1980s (Cass 1988) and in the name of 'mutual obligation' following the Welfare Reform process of the 1990s (McClure 2000). This change in emphasis was by no means unique to Australia. On the contrary, it is one strongly advocated by the OECD (1989; 1990), and one which has been taken up more or less vigorously by all OECD member countries. Authors vary in the degree to which they emphasise a shift in values (Schmidt 2000), or a rather more complex interaction of values, existing welfare state institutions, and changing labour market conditions (Plant 2003; Clasen and Clegg 2003; Dingeldey 2004).

It made sense until the recent past to contrast Australia's tax-funded system with the far more common insurance-based European ones. Yet the insurance-based countries now face increasing numbers whose work history is such that they have little prospect of building up sufficient entitlements. To this extent they are joining Australia in their reliance on the tax system. We now see governments of all persuasions being concerned with issues of welfare dependency (which is likely to lead to long-term poverty), moral hazard (acting imprudently, in the expectation that the State will provide) and free-riding (leaving others to pay for one's benefits). These concerns are expressed above all in increasing emphasis on payments being conditional on responsible behaviour.

Welfare reform always combines in various ways a punitive 'workfare' aspect, and an apparently more benign 'enabling' one. In a study of recent welfare state reforms in Denmark, the United Kingdom and Germany, Dingeldey (2004) asks whether their very different welfare state structures and traditions would result in a differing degree of dominance by either the workfare or enabling state orientations. Her first conclusion is that the sharp either/or contrast with which she began is not appropriate. All three countries use a mix of compulsion and enabling strategies. All have individualised services (as distinct from passive payments, where 'one size fits all'); all use compulsion; all have improved employment placement, training, and work experience. Despite convergence at this broad level, there are real differences in the mix of workfare and activating state components. The expected differences resulting from path dependency do exist, but they operate in conjunction with other factors, such as the state of the labour market in each country, and the determination of political actors to bring about a change in direction.

As the path dependency literature would suggest, Denmark is exceptionally generous in its enabling programs; what was not expected was that it is also quite rigorous in the demands it imposes on the unemployed. Despite its long tradition of apprenticeships (an 'enabling' feature), German practice is characterised by rather punitive measures associated with the sheer scale of current unemployment. What this means is that one cannot read off from the supposed ideology of the three countries just how they will implement activation policies.

THE UNITED STATES: THE END OF WELFARE AS WE KNOW IT

US welfare reform is of particular interest to Australia in that it represents by far the most radical of the OECD welfare reforms. The Centre for Independent Studies strongly recommends it as an example from which Australia might learn (Saunders 2004a). For all its weaknesses, the US welfare reform also offers striking evidence against the futility thesis according to which nothing ever changes.

The US debate is centred on reform of the 60-year-old Aid to Families with Dependent Children (AFDC) program. The initiative to 'end welfare as we know it' had come from a pledge of presidential candidate Bill Clinton in 1992. As President, Clinton did not have a free hand, however, and the Bill that he eventually signed in 1995 was shaped by a Republican Congress and contained truly radical features. The Personal Responsibility and Work Opportunity Reconciliation Act (PRWORA) renamed AFDC as Temporary Assistance to Needy Families (TANF). Its key features included transforming the program from a federal entitlement to a block grant to the states, with the states having very considerable discretion in determining not only the level of benefits, but also the details of eligibility and work requirements. The fiscal implications of this are huge, in that an entitlement program is open-ended in terms of costs, whereas a block grant is a fixed amount. An equally important feature is that aid under TANF is, as its name suggests, time-limited. These features in combination achieved the rare feat of a welfare reform that actually saved money.

In terms of his own agenda, Clinton had greater success in achieving enormous expansion of the Earned Income Tax Credit (EITC). The bipartisan support for this 'big government' initiative is undoubtedly due to the fact that benefits are reserved for workers, and hence it is not 'welfare' (DeParle 2004: 109). In subsequent studies of the separate effects of the various components of the reforms, it is EITC rather than TANF itself that is credited with producing the strongest boost to employment among single women (Meyer and Rosenbaum 2001).

A decade after the abolition of AFDC, it is clear that the reform has exceeded all expectations in one of its aims: getting welfare mothers off the welfare rolls. In his highly acclaimed account of the fate of three Wisconsin women under TANF, DeParle paints a graphic picture of what the changes have meant over time at the individual level. He points out that welfare reform for these women did not involve a transition from no-work to work. They had always had three sources of income: work, boyfriends/partners and welfare. Now they receive money from work, boyfriends/partners and EITC. The change lay in the proportion of their income that now came from work. Those in work are indeed marginally better of financially, though one of DeParle's 'success stories' involved a woman who moved from 103 per cent of the poverty line during her last three years on welfare to 114 per cent today. To pass the threshold of being truly better off, she would need to be on about double the poverty line – a goal she has no prospect of achieving (DeParle 2004: 288).

Among the many striking features of US welfare reform is the extent to which the debate has moved on from what is generally understood as 'active labour market policy' (individualised training programs, job-search assistance, work programs) to ending welfare, pure and simple. A second striking feature is the strength of the so-called 'message effect' of the reforms (Brookings Institution 2004). The argument here is that their sheer scale was such that there was a profound change in people's expectations and behaviour, even before the legislation actually came into effect. Two classes of people 'got the message' that welfare was no longer an option. The most obvious group are the former welfare mothers. But when they do work, they discover that they cannot live on the income they can command. Even Lawrence Mead, one of the most vocal advocates of welfare reform, concedes that the former welfare mothers themselves are only marginally better off financially, but argues that they now have greater bargaining power since they are now 'more deserving' (Brookings Institution 2004).

The less obvious, but even more important group in the view of the Brookings Panel, are those who would have gone on welfare in the pre-reform era. With a life on welfare no longer an option, and a single income insufficient to raise children, they may be encouraged to marry, and to marry a working spouse. Robert Rector already sees evidence that the 30-year rise in illegitimacy up to the mid-1990s has come to a halt. Ending welfare was merely a precondition of the more important goal of ending illegitimacy (Rector 2004).

AUSTRALIA: MUTUAL OBLIGATION

We saw how Dingeldey's analysis of welfare reform in Europe made a convincing case that in the face of large rises in the unemployment rate and in the numbers claiming disability and lone-parent pensions, countries as apparently diverse as Britain, Denmark and Germany had all adopted more punitive measures to move people from welfare to work, but they differed in the extent of their 'enabling' measures. Australia, too, has experienced a sharp change from the long period from 1942–74 when unemployment was consistently below 4 per cent, to rates above 10 per cent in 1983 and 1991–94. According to the 2001 census, 18 per cent of children under 15 years lived in a household with no employed parent, with over half (61 per cent) of these living in one-parent families (ABS 2004a). Between 1981 and 2001, the number of persons receiving disability support pensions increased almost threefold (FaCS 2003: Table 7). In response to these developments, Australia followed a path of welfare reform that has much in common with other OECD countries. However, to date, Australia's version of welfare reform under the banner of 'mutual obligation' has more in common with the European countries than with the US welfare reforms.

Australia differs sharply from the United States, both in terms of the level of net (after-tax) minimum wages and also the generosity of social assistance, or 'benefits of last resort'. When measured against relative poverty lines (40 per cent, 50 per cent and 60 per cent of median household income), Australians on full-time minimum wages are the best off of 17 OECD countries, while US households are towards the bottom of the list (OECD 2004b: Figure 2.7). A similar picture emerges when one considers various family groupings with no income other than social assistance (OECD 2004b: Figure 2.4). An even more dramatic contrast arises if one asks what percentage of an average production worker's (APW) salary a beneficiary would have to earn to get to the 60 per cent of the median poverty line. In Australia, a lone parent with two children on benefits alone is just below this poverty line; her US counterpart would have to earn 100 per cent of APW to reach the poverty line. The situation is similar for a couple with two children (OECD 2004b: Figure 2.6).

In view of these differences, it is not surprising that in Australia the focus of debate is how to encourage those on social assistance to enter the workforce. In a significant symbolic move following the 2004 federal election and the return with an increased majority of the conservative Howard government, a large number of programs were transferred from the Department of Family and Community Services (FaCS) to the Department of Employment and Workplace Relations (DEWR). The stated aim was to reduce welfare dependency among working-age Australians and to increase their participation in the workforce (DEWR 2004). These programs cover payments to the unemployed, people with disabilities and lone parents. The reaffirmation of the principle of mutual obligation had been one of the election themes. The unambiguous message is that employment is the ultimate goal, and 'welfare dependency' the evil to be avoided.

THE SOCIAL SCIENCES AND AUSTRALIAN WELFARE REFORM

AUSTRALIA IN A COMPARATIVE SETTING

I have argued that we cannot make sense of welfare reform by looking at Australia in isolation. Comparative studies show Australia, like other countries, grappling with the dilemmas identified by Marshall, but also with the added weight of entrenched institutions, and today's new challenges. We have seen that some versions of the welfare state are faring much better than others. Several of the Continental European countries have entrenched welfare state institutions that are not well suited either to present economic conditions, or to current family structures. Though the liberal English-speaking and the Northern European countries are faring somewhat better, none would claim to have produced a model with which it can rest content.

The most dramatic example of a break with a well-entrenched program, and one that fits well with the notion of the present age being an epoch of intense reform, has surely been the US experience of 'ending welfare as we know it'. In terms of Marshall's paradox, the United States has gone further than any other country in resolving the dilemma in favour of the market – at least in the case of lone parents. Yet even here, 'the market' is not the market of *laissez faire* liberalism, but one where former welfare mothers who have entered the labour market are now the recipients of substantial public largesse in the form of tax credits. Good behaviour is rewarded.

CITIZENSHIP AND THE LABOUR MARKET

The rhetoric of citizenship entitlement even in Marshall's day always implied that most able-bodied citizens, most of the time, would participate in the labour market and pay insurance premiums and taxes (or taxes only in Australia), or share resources with someone who did. The Australian tradition began with the additional recognition that older citizens, especially women, deserved to be rewarded for their non-labour market contributions to the nation (Sawer 2003). Today's more explicit focus on reciprocity in the form of labour market involvement in part reflects the fiscal implications of the very large increase in the proportion of the population for whom any labour market connection is tenuous, and always was tenuous. But it is also based on wider concerns. One is the prospect of a country with a shrinking labour force becoming uncompetitive in global markets; another is the prospect of society becoming polarised between families with strong labour market attachment and those with none.

The labour market indeed offers hope for some, but it is fraught with difficulties. Most of the commentary on the strong focus on the labour market in the US welfare reform is guardedly favourable, but even analysts who are enthusiastically favourable concede that it has not yet produced the expected transformation in people's lives (Brooking Institution 2004). The income of the former welfare mothers is little changed; they have little time to look after their children; their slight prospects of forming a relationship with someone who is earning a reasonable income remain unchanged; and despite generous funding, the casework services that are supposed to assist them are a joke (DeParle 2004: 322–38).

No other country has yet followed the US in making a major welfare category time limited. Yet all face problems with their more attenuated versions. Not only are the more successful activation programs such as Denmark's extremely expensive, but Plant has highlighted a more basic problem. Supply-side measures such as training, education and counselling still leave a substantial group without work. There is little prospect that governments will step in as employers of last resort, and in any case, it requires a strong belief in the inherent value of employment, any employment, to believe that a compulsory make-work program will transform lives (Plant 2003). Finally, individualised activation programs by their very nature involve a high degree of discretion. This is one of the very ills that modern welfare states were designed to avoid. It is at this point that the wheel does indeed appear to have come full circle.

SOCIAL POLICY RESEARCH INSTRUMENTS

If the biggest advance in recent years has been in comparative welfare states studies, this has only been possible because of the existence of vastly better data than previously existed. The Luxemburg Income Study (2004) to which the Social Policy Research Centre has long contributed (Saunders 2002) here takes pride of place. Until recently, little had been available in Australia by way of longitudinal studies that track people's lives over time. This is now being remedied, above all by the Melbourne Institute's Household, Income and Labour Dynamics in Australia (HILDA) survey (Melbourne Institute 2004).

The National Centre for Social and Economic Modelling (NATSEM) has achieved prominence, both at the direct policy-making level through its microsimulation models STINMOD (which is used both by the Federal Treasury and FaCS in policy formulation) and DYNAMOD. The distributional effects of government taxes and benefits based on these models are given wide coverage in the media. They serve to counter one of the most frequent assertions of proponents of the perversity thesis, that government programs involve a transfer from the poor to the middle class (Hirschman 1996). NATSEM has shown repeatedly that the Australian tax-welfare system is highly progressive (Harding, Lloyd and Warren 2004).

The three major social policy research institutions (SPRC, the Melbourne Institute and NATSEM) also feature prominently in the media. This more diffuse contribution to policymaking has the citizen rather than the policymaker as its prime target.

Since the time of the Henderson Poverty Inquiry in the 1970s, one of the more distinctive features of social policy research in Australia has been the prominence given to the measurement of poverty. Although poverty lines have never been accepted officially by government, they are entrenched in popular debate on the successes and failures of the Australian welfare state. This has had both positive and negative consequences. Australia may have no official poverty line, but the existence of much publicised quasi-official poverty lines has been a strong incentive to policy-makers to ensure that most social security payments are at a level that ensures that most recipients are not 'living in poverty'. A negative feature is that the most commonly used versions are calculated in such a way that it is extremely difficult to show progress. This contributes to the impression that 'nothing works', a conclusion as likely to be drawn by the welfare lobby as by its opponents.

The study of poverty and inequality in Australia has been bedevilled by many problems, above all variability in the quality of income data. Data quality has now been very considerably improved by work done by the ABS in conjunction with the Social Policy Research Centre (ABS 2002b). The policy application of the higher quality data has, however, been limited by the polemical nature of most of the public debates. For instance, the Centre for Independent Studies (CIS) recently issued a brief that made trenchant criticisms of a Senate Report on poverty in Australia (Saunders 2004b; Community Affairs Reference Committee 2004). Most of the CIS critique is valid. But it also contains the jibe: 'Put crudely, poverty is about having insufficient money on which to live, while inequality is about having less money than somebody else does. The first is about need, the second is about envy.' Equating concern with inequality with one of the seven deadly sins may be good polemic, but it is not conducive to serious debate.

MISSING RESEARCH DATA

Social science research has shown that Australia's welfare state shares many of the features of welfare states in other advanced market economies. One of its distinctive strengths is its combination of a system that is both generous and targeted towards those who are worst off. In thus avoids the problems of some of the generous but less targeted European countries, and also the harshness of the targeted but less generous US system. The price Australia pays for its combination of generosity and targeting is the existence of very high effective marginal tax rates (EMTRs) over the range of incomes where benefits are being withdrawn while taxes are being applied. On the face of it, this is a major problem. Why would low-income people bother to work more hours if it means they lose well over half their earnings through a combination of taxes paid and benefits lost? Both the common-sense and anecdotal answers are that they would not bother.

Though there is research on the behavioural effects of the introduction of tax credits in the United States (Meyer and Rosenbaum 2001) and in the United Kingdom (Leigh 2004), there is little research available on what are in fact the behavioural consequences of high EMTRs in Australia. The lack of research in Australia is due in part to the absence of a tradition of policy experimentation, very little access to microdata and no sample of tax returns available for analysis (Leigh 2003). Policymakers are well aware of the fiscal cost of remedying high EMTRs by abolishing or lessening targeting, and they are also well aware of the electoral cost involved in cutting benefits. They would be in a better position to face this dilemma if they had better data on whether high EMTRs do have the serious behavioural consequences that are commonly claimed.

CONCLUSION:
WHERE TO FROM HERE?

Social scientists can be of most use to policymakers when it comes to framing or defining the issue at hand. This chapter, for instance, has cast the issue of welfare state reform within a framework according to which clashing principles may not be a sign of bad policy, nor a ground for concluding that 'nothing works'. The chapter began with the paradox of clashing principles noted by Marshall in 1949. In a 1953 lecture, Marshall's contemporary, Isaiah Berlin, enunciated a principle that would see Marshall's paradox as merely an instance of a more general rule. Most policy choices are not between good and evil, but between good things that cannot be pursued to the full at the same time. The biggest risk is that we simplify life by dogmatic insistence on a single principle (Berlin 1969).

Australia's version of the welfare state that appears so muddled when viewed in isolation stands up well in comparison with the alternative models available in other OECD countries. It is, however, faced with a more extreme version of a common problem when it comes to the disincentives people face in the transition from welfare to work. Though it may seem self-evident that this is intolerable, the alternatives may be worse. The most useful offering social scientists could make to the current reform process would be research and reflection on the actual behavioural consequences of the very high tax rates low-income people face as they attempt to juggle the world of welfare and the world of work.

6

SPATIAL DIFFERENCE
AND
PUBLIC POLICY
Ruth Fincher

Space in public policy is generally understood physically, as the territorial or jurisdictional container of populations and infrastructures. In Australia, such thinking is part and parcel of the country's history as a federation, in which the distribution of resources to subnational jurisdictions is a defining activity of the political structure. Governmental resources can be allocated to give more to those areas containing relatively disadvantaged populations, or to places observed to be competitive. The notion of space as a set of areas whose resources are to be compared contrasts with the idea of all things and individuals having an inherent spatiality, and therefore with the idea that all policies should account for their spatial effects.

In this chapter I will focus on policies that use the idea of spatial difference in the conventional sense of spaces as containers. Accepting that almost all policies have spatial consequences, often unacknowledged – that is, they have differential effects on people and environments in different locations – the chapter discusses policies that have expressly spatial intentions, policies named as urban and regional interventions because of their attempts to shape the conditions of cities or regions directly. The chapter does not refer to the indigenous estate, covering about 20 per cent of Australia, barely populated, and whose needs for social and physical infrastructure are only beginning to be understood.

Examples of spatial policies implemented by Australian governments include the following:

- Since 1933, Australia's Commonwealth Grants Commission has made allocations to lower levels of government that raise fewer revenues, seeking to compensate states, and for a time in the 1970s also local governments, for relative disadvantage. This is similar in policy intention to the Canadian government's strategy of annual fiscal equalisation. Internationally, 'the Australian Federation is unusual in its high degree of vertical fiscal imbalance and the comprehensiveness of its arrangements for horizontal fiscal equalisation' (Commonwealth Grants Commission 1995: 257). This system of allocations is longstanding, despite the political reactions it provokes each year.

- The Whitlam Labor government's Department of Urban and Regional Development sought to improve infrastructure in disadvantaged areas of major cities, and to decentralise urban settlement into specified regional centres. State governments resisted this. The programs did not survive the election of a conservative federal government in late 1975. In the 1990s, Labor governments 'oversaw a limited resurgence in Commonwealth policy attention to regions and social policy' with national programs like Building Better Cities, whose objectives were to improve the conditions of places or locations (Reddel 2002: 52). To the spatially aware social scientist, these federal forays into a national redistribution of infrastructure and other resources were bold and imaginative.

- In the early 2000s the Victorian state government produced a strategic plan for Metropolitan Melbourne, the first since the 1980s, entitled *Melbourne 2030*. Wide-ranging in its scope, it has focused initially on the development of 'activity centres' – central nodes at which high-density housing combines spatially with retail activity and public transport options. Of the examples mentioned here, it is the only spatial policy not definable by its interest in disadvantaged or advantaged locations. Such systematic spatial planning for many facets of a large area's activities is rare. In the scope of its spatial thinking, this plan is a success; in its implementation it is generating some adverse comment. Whether the increased investment in public transport infrastructure on which it relies will be committed is unclear.

The next section examines spatial policies intended to alleviate disadvantage in places, while the subsequent section reviews policies designed to enhance the advantage or competitiveness of certain locations. Central to this chapter are: (1) the fact that spatial policies do respond to and envisage two types of locations – the disadvantaged and the advantaged or economically competitive; (2) the question of whether the spatial policies used to ameliorate disadvantage and enhance competitiveness are appropriate and effective; and (3) the usefulness of ideas of spatial difference as an impetus for policy intervention.

POLICIES TO IMPROVE THE DISTRIBUTION OF BENEFITS IN DISADVANTAGED AREAS

Two interpretations of spatial difference have appeared in policies to ameliorate entrenched disadvantage. These are expressed in the ideas of locational disadvantage and social mix.

LOCATIONAL DISADVANTAGE

Maher et al. (1992: 10) describe the notion of locational disadvantage, used in Australian social science since the 1980s as follows:

> While not as fundamental as social and economic position, locational disadvantage is one element of broader social dysfunction ... Location becomes important because there are spatial constraints on the availability and use of a range of resources which are not universally available but are located unevenly in space.

Living in a certain location can exacerbate people's disadvantage. This is not to say that such an understanding began in Australia, or did so recently. Colonial and later state governments in Australia have long balanced the opportunities of city-dwellers directly through provision of transport, sewerage and water lines, and later educational facilities (Gleeson and Low 2000: 30). Since World War 2 the Commonwealth government has partnered the states in public housing provision, but the take-up of the idea of locational disadvantage by the 1990s Labor governments in Australia was tagged anew as an approach to social justice from the understanding that disadvantage is spatially constituted.

Other expressions of this notion were present in the reports of Ronald Henderson's Inquiry into Poverty in Australia. Henderson described poverty in 1970s Australia as concentrated in particular locations and as structured in part by the conditions of those locations (Fincher and Wulff 1998), singling out inner cities, outer metropolitan areas, and certain rural towns and farming areas as sites where disadvantage was being created (Commission of Inquiry into Poverty 1975). This spatial awareness has not been reflected in government policies aimed at reducing poverty since that time. Australian poverty-alleviation policy before the 1970s was aspatial, focusing on assisting the aged poor by providing pensions. The aged are not spatially clustered. More recently, Australian income poverty has been associated with unemployment (King 1998), a matter more identifiable spatially. Australian anti-poverty policy initiatives have not reflected this spatial reality, though social scientific research has registered it strongly in community-centred studies (see Peel 2003).

Other influential accounts of the contribution of place and

location to the quality of life in Australian cities are Peel (1995), analysing planning for the South Australian new town of Elizabeth from the 1950s, and Stretton (1970), provoking nation-wide debates in a commentary on planning for Adelaide and Canberra. In Elizabeth, the attempt to create a town with loca-tional advantage for its population because of local industrial jobs, created later a site of locational disadvantage for working people when the industry around which the town was planned diminished. Extolling the 'equalising' benefits of suburban living, because spatial arrangements 'can distribute very different costs and advantages to different people', Stretton (1970: 2) argued that cities of great size (more than one million people, in the Australian context) disadvantage the poor by precluding them from accessing many centrally located services, while advantaging the rich who can afford to access those services whatever the cost.

Awareness of locational disadvantage and the understanding that spatially targeted infrastructure investments could improve distributional outcomes underpinned two major federal post-war initiatives: the policies of the Department of Urban and Regional Development (DURD) of the 1970s Labor government, and the Building Better Cities program of the early 1990s. In the former, decentralisation of people, houses and employment to regional towns was begun; in the latter, public transport was extended in major metropolitan areas to increase accessibility. Neither initia-tive was sustained long at the national political level, because of the unsettling of power relations within the federal bureaucracy that would have resulted had spatial policymaking come to rival or influence Treasury (Oakley 2004; Orchard 1995: 67).

Most state governments produced master plans for their major cities by the early 1970s, centred on the physical control of subur-ban expansion and less directly on social development (though attempts were made to avoid large imbalances in the spatial distri-bution of facilities and services). Local governments used zoning regulations to restrict the proximity of incompatible land uses

(Gleeson and Low 2000: 32). But by the 1990s, to varying degrees in different states, state-driven master planning, ensuring some evenness in the spatial distribution of facilities attached to metropolitan suburbanisation, was out of favour. Managerialism was replaced by corporate neo-liberalism, this being significant because '[n]eoliberalism abhors planning and seeks to withdraw the state apparatus from intervention in the market' (Gleeson and Low 2000: 172). Locational disadvantage began to be identified in state governments' limited, local, place-making strategies. These are programs undertaken in partnership with local communities and local governments, seeking to involve local people in helping themselves increase community capacity and social capital (Reddel 2002).

Thus spatial policies centred on reducing locational disadvantage have not been evident in Australia since the 1980s, with the withdrawal of federal (and state) governments from major infrastructural and social planning. The creation of new towns around major manufacturing industries or of whole new working-class suburbs, as were established in (then) outer Melbourne after World War 2, would not occur these days. Private-sector developers now create new suburban or inner city infill estates, and their social intentions are not to provide opportunities for the less resourced. Nationally broad spatial planning for regional and urban development, of the kind begun in the mid-1970s, has not been seen since in Australia. Local place-making initiatives are minor indeed in comparison, and within state governments tend to be located outside the planning and infrastructure ministries (in human services or premiers' departments). But the opportunity for physical and social planning of large areas is now appearing in metropolitan strategic planning in cities around Australia, starting with the new *Melbourne 2030*. Whether the social aims of these major metropolitan planning exercises will bear fruit soon is unclear. The physical dimensions of aligning public transport with the establishment of higher density housing are taking priority.

SOCIAL MIX

In contemporary Australia the idea of social mix as a spatial issue appears primarily in discussions in state housing ministries about whether large public housing estates should continue to contain public housing tenants only. Or, should they be places in which housing is owned as well as rented, and public housing clients are mixed with those of the private housing market? Underlying these questions is the policy concern that poor people may have fewer opportunities if they are spatially concentrated in locations with other poor people. Perhaps there may be a number of 'place effects' associated with spatial concentrations of poverty that will be different to those associated with spatial mixtures of income groups.

Australia's public rental housing sector is about 5.3 per cent of all housing in the country, a small percentage compared to that of some European countries. It endured a major reduction in government funding during the 1990s (Arthurson 2001: 812). With physical deterioration of much of this housing, and the persistent poverty and high unemployment levels of residents, strategies to regenerate public housing estates have been adopted by state governments, including physical upgrading of the estates, employment and participation projects for residents, and strategies of social mix aiming for 'a broader socio-economic mix of residents on estates' (Arthurson 2002: 246). Quantitative limits on the concentrations of low-income housing in any one neighbourhood have been set: in Queensland, public housing should not exceed 20 per cent in a locality; in South Australia 25 per cent (Arthurson 2002). The reasoning for the policies is fuzzy. Reduced concentrations of public housing and its tenants are intended to create more 'sustainable' and 'cohesive' communities in both cases. This is a similar rationale to that of the New South Wales Department of Housing (Ruming et al. 2004: 236). But if the idea is that marginalised groups will benefit from having middle-class neighbours as role models with whom they will interact, then the evidence to date is that very limited interaction will occur (Arthurson 2002: 247; Ruming et al. 2004: 246).

This current interest of state housing agencies with amending the nature of public housing provision is not the first time social mix has appeared in Australian urban policy, although its present political context differs from that of earlier decades. Peel (1995: 39ff) noted the conscious attempt to form in Elizabeth a 'model community' of happy and balanced families, drawing on the British new town movement and its critique of uniformly 'one-class' housing estates in favour of communities with 'the full range of the class structure'. This reflected the view of the time that the working classes were not builders of community like the middle classes, and might take up an opportunity to emulate their middle-class neighbours.

Present-day interest in social mix at the neighbourhood scale in Australian states is encouraged by the strategies of the British government. Neighbourhood is the spatial unit of policy focus chosen by the British government's Social Exclusion Unit (Meegan and Mitchell 2001; Tiesdell and Allmendinger 2001). The desirability of the spatial co-location of poor people has long been discussed in the United Kingdom. Current British government thinking, in turn, has been heavily influenced by that of the American social scientists: Wilson (1987), arguing against ghetto-isation, and Putnam (1993), analysing the development of local social networks (Meegan and Mitchell 2001).

Yet recent evaluations of the results of social mix policies on either side of the Atlantic find that at the neighbourhood scale, within cities, policies that concentrate resources within a bounded locality have been unsuccessful as a remedy for poverty. Neighbourhoods of low-income households are 'typically quite heterogeneous. Only the most chronically poor and socially isolated individuals and families lead lives circumscribed distinctly by the poverty and spatial form of their immediate neighbourhoods' (Briggs 2003: 924). Accordingly, it cannot be assumed that a majority of resources to alleviate poverty should be directed, in a spatial social mix strategy, to bounded (container) neighbourhoods, because people do not undertake all their activities locally. People are rarely encased by their neighbourhood. We might recognise that mixing with a range of people is desirable for everyone, and resist the spatial exclusion that can come from locating similar people together spatially (for example, in gated communities of the wealthy). Nevertheless, in the evaluation of policies seeking to develop social mix within bounded neighbourhoods as a way of reducing disadvantage, the finding has been that focusing policy resources on the neighbourhood as the root and source of poverty is a limited policy strategy. So is focusing resources on helping households move out of those neighbourhoods. Multiple strategies to expand 'place-opportunity links' are recommended, rather than engineering social mix within a defined, presumed-to-be-bounded, small locality.

In some European cities concerns to promote social mix have to do with the place of immigrants in society, as well as the politics of class or income groupings. Evidence from the Netherlands provides an example. They have a well-resourced policy of mixing residents in disadvantaged neighbourhoods (where many immigrants live), so as to integrate immigrants into Dutch society (Uitermark 2003), combined with national urban strategy, to which the revitalisation of marginal neighbourhoods is central (as in Britain). Government reports from the early 1990s singled out recent immigrants as the apparent 'bearers' of the lack of 'liveability' of certain parts of major cities (Uitermark 2003: 540). 'The affluent' were encouraged to locate alongside low-income residents, as a means of increasing 'liveability'. But the Dutch findings are that poverty is not reduced by social mix in disadvantaged neighbourhoods, and policymakers' fear of the segregation of marginalised groups is attributed to the uncritical importing of ideas about ghettoes from the United States, following the influential work of Wilson (1987) (Ostendorf, Musterd and De Vos 2001).

Though Australian state governments, in their public housing estate regeneration strategies, seem consistent with overseas policymakers in seeking to engineer social mix of low-income people with those of higher income people, they are less aligned on questions of the spatial deconcentration of immigrants. In Australian cities, where levels of ethnic segregation are not high, the debate over the advantages or disadvantages of clustering by immigrant groups has emphasised the advantages for the settlement process of the spatial co-location of immigrants (Burnley, Murphy and Fagan 1997). That there has been so little concern politically about this question in a country with so many immigrants from diverse sources, is no doubt due to the success of nationally supported services like migrant resource centres, English language training and ethno-specific community groups in settling immigrants in their new destination, under Australia's national policy of multiculturalism. This is a major success story.

There is no evidence that area-based policies to engineer social mixing at a very local scale, in order to improve the social mobility and life chances of marginalised groups, works. A 'light touch' is required in the social planning of local areas and communities, including in public housing estates, with emphasis on opportunities for capacity-building and effective local consultation about changes. At the larger-than-local scale, however, the appearance of a number of metropolitan strategic plans in the early 2000s is evidence that infrastructure planning in the public interest is an area where social scientists and policymakers could combine their energies.

POLICIES TO INCREASE THE COMPETITIVENESS OF CERTAIN URBAN AREAS

In the last two decades, governments have used particular spatial policies to make already-successful cities and regions more competitive. These policies have arisen from ideas about the spatial incidence of the benefits of globalisation, in which certain types of city and region are associated with economic advancement. Two forms of spatial difference are recognised within this body of knowledge – competitive cities and learning regions.

COMPETITIVE CITIES

Seeing the city as a 'key stakeholder' in the processes of globalisation dates from the 1980s (Yeoh 1999: 613), with recognition that 'the combination of spatial dispersal and global integration [of economic activity] has created a new strategic role for major cities' (Sassen 1991: 3). Central is the idea that global cities form a network of economic influence exceeding in some ways, though not replacing, the economic influence of nation states. This thinking is about the actual lumpy geography of globalisation: it is not claiming that global flows of capital are fluid and uninfluenced by spatial differences.

Other analysts have extended the concept of the global city to that of global city-region. Scott et al. (2001) observe a newly inten-sified spatial clustering of services and manufacturing sectors in large city-regions. Because of competition from city-regions else-where, governments frequently find themselves 'engaging actively in institution-building and policymaking in an effort to turn globalisa-tion as far as possible to their benefit' (Scott et al. 2001: 14). When 'competitiveness' is seen to be something that cities and city-regions, rather than firms, should develop, then particular place-based poli-cies of this kind result. As Kim (2001) notes, in Korea after the 1997 economic crisis in East Asia, a common result of such policies was an increase in spatial and socioeconomic polarisation, as less 'prom-ising' city-regions received fewer resources than those seen as more competitive, and more 'balanced' economic and social development was replaced with economic growth.

Not only is competitiveness sought by national policymakers envisaging their large cities and city-regions as effective players in global economic networks, it is sought as well by local policymak-ers pitting their cities against other cities even within a country. But of course:

> Many of the innovations and investments designed to make particu-lar cities more attractive as cultural and consumer centres have quickly been imitated elsewhere, thus rendering any competitive advantage within a system of cities ephemeral (Harvey 1989: 12–13).

Noting these two scales, international and within nations, at which policymakers try to make cities competitive, how do Australian policymakers' efforts compare with those elsewhere? It seems evident that participation in major networks of global cities and city-regions has been pursued in Europe and Asia but not in Australia, probably due to the latter's geographical location, but also because regional initiatives are interpreted in Australia as related only to areas outside major cities. Competing with other cities within the nation for scarce investment is certainly evident among Australian state governments, as it is in the United States; it has been less prominent in Europe until recently, when encouraged under European integration (Cheshire 1999).

Consider these scales of competition for cities in turn. Networks of global cities or city-regions, more loosely defined than those analysed by Sassen (1991), have long existed in Europe. Friedmann (2001: 127) sees them as 'the basis of European integration'. Major European cities have, in addition, been forming alliances recently. An important one of these, developing since the 1980s, is EUROCITIES, a group based on a charter lauding Europe's traditions of urban citizenship and seeking to share knowledge about urban governance (Friedmann 2001: 127). For example, Rotterdam sought competitiveness by attachment to an important network of European cities, using strategic projects like the Rotterdam High Speed Train (HST).

> The intended effect of the HST stop transcends the level of the city. It is associated with the strengthening of the position of Rotterdam as part of the European urban network. Instead of being one of 600 stations in Europe, Rotterdam will be one of only 20 HST stops. Above all, Rotterdam will be the point of arrival in the Netherlands and gateway to the Randstad. Furthermore, it will be the one and only stop in the centre of a city in the Netherlands. (Wigmans 2001: 210).

Despite the inter-city cooperation these examples signal, European integration is 'differentially benefiting "core" or central regions of

Europe compared to peripheral ones' (Cheshire 1999: 850). If city governments in core areas develop competitive policies, setting themselves against other cities and regions, they are likely to be more successful; entrepreneurial policies coming from governments in peripheral areas are not likely to change their circumstances much (Cheshire 1999: 861). The Structural Funds policy of the EU requires matched funding for its projects, setting up a competitive relationship between city-regions in bidding for funds against others, in ways counter to the networks emerging on other levels.

In Australia, by contrast, national governments have not sought explicitly to link major cities into globally powerful economic networks as a means of making them competitive spaces. (Though Sydney is presented often as the 'gateway' to Australia.) In the debate about whether cities and regions can be 'competitive', or whether only firms have that possibility, national governments in Australia have preferred the latter policy pathway. Since the 1970s when the Whitlam government tried to develop new growth centres around medium-sized regional cities to provide some balance in an Australian urban hierarchy dominated by the main-land state capitals, there has been little sympathy in national governments for regional development through policies to expand medium-sized urban centres (Self 2005). Comparisons of European regional development priorities with those of Australia show also that in Europe policies are directed at both rural and urban regions, while Australia's much weaker regional policies have been aimed, since the early 1970s, only at non-urban areas (Gleeson 2003: 234). Even if there were a political will for regional urban programs, the geographical context of Australia's cities is very different from that of Europe. The earlier example of Rotterdam's linking into the European rail network make this clear. While some Australian state governments' efforts to link cities within their states by new, fast, rail lines may indeed aid regional towns, there is no possibility of linking Australian cities to those of numerous other nearby and large countries, as there is in Europe.

The Council of Capital City Lord Mayors, and the Property Council of Australia, have called upon the federal government to develop a Capital Cities Strategy (Spiller 2000), emphasising the benefits of such a strategy for the country's rural regions and its global economic position. Their paper draws upon international policy thinking about competitive cities, provides case studies from around the world of the benefits of governments investing in cities (for example, in subsidising physical infrastructure), and requests a 'new partnership between the capital cities and the Commonwealth' in which it is acknowledged that Australia's capital cities 'drive' the country's economic performance (Spiller 2000: 75). There is no evidence to date that the Australian federal government has shifted its position on these matters.

At the sub-national scale, Australian city and state governments have engaged in entrepreneurial attempts to enhance their own prospects as investment destinations, in the ways described by Harvey (1989). Competition between state capital cities to obtain major sports events is an ongoing feature of national life; for example, ten years ago the Grand Prix car race was 'attracted' from Adelaide to Melbourne. The manner in which the Victorian state government of the 1990s 'place-marketed' Melbourne within the Asia-Pacific region was 'one of the most ambitious place promotion … campaigns ever witnessed in Australia' (Engels 2000: 489).

In a country as large as Australia, it would take great commitment federally to establish substantial networks of globally oriented cities, cooperating for mutual economic benefit. There has been no interest in this in Australia. The shadows of the Whitlam government's attempts to encourage regional and urban economic development, even though not in a time when 'competition' was the focus of spatial development discourse, are long. The only aspect of a 'competitive cities' orientation presently in evidence in Australia has been one of pitting cities against others. Social scientists have a solid critique of this practice, but that cannot halt the engagement of individual cities' powerbrokers in it.

LEARNING REGIONS

Some economic geographers see regions as places facilitating the
growth of innovation and increased competitive advantage in
particular social and institutional conditions, though little empirical support for these theoretical proposals has been offered
(MacKinnon et al. 2002). Derived from the observation of 'new
industrial districts' are the hypotheses that successful clusterings
of interrelated businesses and firms in local areas are underpinned
by cultural ties and institutional support (Raco 1999). A famous
example is the growth of industries in Silicon Valley, California, a
region experiencing five post-war 'major technology waves' with
a variety of institutional forms facilitating the resulting growth
(Henton 2002). Different institutional characteristics appear in
the 'new industrial district' of Baden-Württemberg in Germany
(Raco 1999: 960).

It is clear that the conditions for economic success in local
industrial regions of innovation and mutual learning vary between
regions. A one-size-fits-all model of how to achieve such success
will never be effective (Lovering 1999; Gleeson 2003). This
observed spatial specificity need not prevent governments and
policymakers from trying to create the conditions for innovative
learning regions in their localities. But analysts caution that
seeking a successful region rather than focusing on more balanced
growth overall, and focusing on conditions internal to the region
rather than to its wider context, will fail (Raco 1999: 963).

Do Australian governments' policies reflect this thinking about
regions of mutual learning and innovation, and are they seeking to
facilitate regional clusters of firms in encouraging institutional
conditions? Gibson-Graham (1994: 149), analysing the emergence
of the Australian Labor government's White Paper *Working
Nation* in the early 1990s, saw there new thinking, of the 'new
industrial districts' kind, about regions:

> ... as places of potentiality and plenty. This discourse reflects the
> influence within federal policy circles of a post-Fordist model of

industrial development in which growth is linked to techniques of
flexible specialisation and the important role of regional industrial
ensembles/assemblages/districts. ... The emphasis is upon changing
or instilling a new business culture within local areas. This
program of development starts with what is there and builds from
this, rejecting both the cargo cult mentality of waiting for the right
business to relocate and the strategy of out-competing the regional
neighbours with bigger and better incentives to attract the coveted
sunrise industry. Now regions are the homes of 'stakeholders' who
have it in their power to make their regions into 'pockets of excel-
lence' or 'entrepreneurial hotspots' – in short industrial growth
centres' (Gibson-Graham 1994: 149).

A decade later, pointed strategic thinking based on fostering such
competitive districts appears absent from the government's policies about Australian regions. Regional policies remain solely
about non-metropolitan areas (Commonwealth of Australia
2001). Certainly, the ideas of partnership, stakeholders and potential in regions that Gibson-Graham (1994) saw in earlier federal
policies are there in contemporary policy thinking, but there is
little federal drive of a targeted kind apparent. Rather, there is the
sentiment that members of a community are responsible for
advancing their area's and population's economic prospects. The
considerable resources given by the European Union for regional
assistance are not in prospect here.

Consider one State, Victoria, to examine its government's policy
thinking. In major strategic statements there is interest expressed in
industrial innovation and networking for economic and social
improvement, but it is not spatially envisaged. The particular
support the Victorian government gives manufacturing, long important to its economy, recognises the global context of that sector,
although innovation and industrial/economic development are not
known as spatially specific in the regional-networking terms
advanced in the literature on spatial difference, with the exception
perhaps of the food processing industry (Victorian Government
2004: 21).

On the other hand, regional (spatial) thinking about the metropolis of Melbourne in relation to other parts of Victoria is not driven with economic projects and competitiveness, innovation or learning in mind. The recent metropolitan planning strategy *Melbourne 2030* (Victorian Government 2002) provides an example. A 30-year plan to manage the growth of Melbourne sustainably, it 'emphasises the city's interdependence with regional Victoria, to provide maximum benefit to the whole State' (2002: 12). Accordingly, it proposes a 'networked cities model' for linking the cities and towns of the State with improved transport facilities. The networking between towns and cities envisaged is primarily about encouraging people to move out of the metropolis and into the regions, assuming that a spread of housing outside Melbourne will spread the State's economic prosperity to those places.

In sum, though a few social scientists in Australia propose regional development strategies like networked learning regions, there is little evidence that their voices are heard in policies at the federal level. At the state level, it seems that innovation and regional development are part of economic policy thinking, but not in the targeted and spatially specific way suggested in the international literature. Of course, as social scientists agree, a one-size-fits-all model should not be suggested; for reasons institutional, political, financial and spatial, we in Australia could not expect to see European-style policies. The use in policy of ideas from other places can be helpful or not, and must be monitored. In addition, some theorists claim there is inadequate empirical evidence that it is possible to create learning regions through policy intervention. There is also the possibility that a too-frenzied focus on policies to enhance regional competitiveness will create greater socioeconomic imbalances within a country, unless that is taken into account in policy settings.

CONCLUSION

The first set of policies and thinking mentioned in this chapter, aimed at ameliorating disadvantage expressed spatially, is about reducing spatial difference. Policies and thinking about improving the competitiveness of cities and regions are about increasing spatial difference, unless attention is paid in policy settings to prevent this. This two-part categorising of spatial policies is not an organisational artefact of this chapter alone. Rather, in the way that spatial difference is understood in public policy as physical differentiation on the basis of bounded areas (where it is thought about at all), spaces are containers of less resourced or more resourced populations or circumstances. The policy response is to allocate resources and strategies accordingly, in whatever fashion the politics of the day demand.

If one were to view spatial difference through the conceptual lens of spatiality, mentioned in the first paragraph of this chapter, the policy response might be different. From this view, every policy initiative would understand the spatial character of its object – every allocation and priority would be made knowing the spatial circumstances of the phenomenon to be changed. Regional clusters of economic activities, or social networks of myriad kinds, overlapping each other's boundaries, would be resourced for the characteristics they have spatially (as well as economically, politically or socially). Then, for example, a situation might not emerge in which telecommunications were permitted to be far better in major cities than in minor cities, for each would have been resourced with their spatial character and needs in mind. A spatial audit of policies would be routine. Such a thoroughly spatial reorientation is most unlikely nationally, however, beyond the allocations of the longstanding Commonwealth Grants Commission, due to philosophies of small government and of communities and regions helping themselves, along with the difficulties of inserting spatial thinking into major bureaucracies like Treasury.

At the state government level a serious interest in spatial difference seems more likely, since it already exists in some areas. Perhaps past resistance by state governments to the Commonwealth's direct interventions in the fate of regions (Reddel 2002) has enhanced this interest. The policy players in any renewed discussion of spatial difference in Australia, then, are likely to be in state governments (even were these governments not all Labor governments, as they are at the time of writing). There it is that attention is paid currently to social mix and locational disadvantage, though principally not in planning ministries, but in aspatially focused ministries of human or community services. It is here that focus is maintained on enhancing competitive economic advantage, or identifying clusters of networked industries, though again in economic ministries whose spatial awareness is limited. For social scientists concerned with spatial difference, useful links could be made with these aspatial departments of state governments. Especially useful could be the participation of spatially interested social scientists in whole-of-government initiatives.

Are the particular spatial policies observed in this chapter the most appropriate, useful and effective forms of spatial intervention? Accepting that 'appropriate' can never be defined outside its political context, the conclusions must be as follows. Policies of redressing locational disadvantage by the distribution of infrastructure are crucial, for the redistributive aspects of evenly spread access to facilities and services are profound. What the infrastructure is, how much, how funded and precisely where it is provided, are matters beyond the scope of this chapter, but they are most important for public policy and they are utterly spatial in character. Policies seeking to achieve social mix, which seems perhaps to be the code for the privatisation of public housing, are based on dubious social assumptions and have been found to be unsuccessful by researchers in Europe and the United States. They are fuzzy in the relationship of their stated aims to their design and outcomes, especially at the local, neighbourhood scale where presently they seem directed.

Turning to policies seeking to establish globally competitive cities and urban networks, and learning regions of economic innovation, the social scientific literature is very cautious about suggesting policy models that might be transferred between countries. A one-size-fits-all model is nowhere suggested by spatially sensitive social scientists, though the elements of success (networks, institutional support, balance of economic, social and environmental policies) are identified in their work. To develop a model for learning regions of innovation in Australia, and to resource it, would be a fascinating research project for social scientists working with governments.

7

WORK, FAMILY AND THE SHY SOCIAL SCIENTIST

Barbara Pocock[1]

If newspaper column space is any indicator of the significance of an issue to public debate, then issues on the general terrain of 'work and family' rank high on the agenda at present in Australia. Many questions around work and family are the subject of regular public discussion. They include the impact of work and its changing shape on the health and wellbeing of women, men and children and households; future labour market supply, population and fertility; the challenges that employers face in attracting, retaining and employing Australians; and the public policy response to these issues.

The reasons for this interest are multiple. Australia exhibits a poorly configured 'work and care regime', where paid work increasingly encroaches upon care, with significant implications for those who work, those who care, and those who rely on the care of others, as well as for the State and employers (McDonald 2001a, 2001b, 2002; Pocock 2003; Campbell and Charlesworth 2004). These issues affect the majority of Australians – including politicians, journalists and researchers – making industrial, work and family issues of significant interest to social scientists at the turn of the twenty-first century – in Australia and beyond.

Unfortunately, the existing body of social science analysis around these issues has not prevented a muddle in relation to policies around work and family in Australia. Why are good policy regimes around work and care so slow to emerge and so encrusted with historical sediment? Several things beyond social science may explain this: the absence of strong political voices in sustained agitation for better policy (especially among mothers, carers and children); the conservative Australian attachment (not confined to the conservative side of politics) to the primacy and almost exclusivity of maternal care; the powerful but confused political discourse around key concepts like 'the family'; and finally, a retreat of the State from care, alongside strong employer resistance to picking it up. However, the slow change in the policy regime also raises questions about the nature and efficacy of the link between social research and policy.

In this chapter, I first review the current challenges that arise in the sphere of work and family policy. Second, I consider the ways in which this debate is assisted (or not) by social science and its key conceptual categories and intellectual organisation. Third, I propose some ways forward for a better interface between social science and work and family policy that could improve Australian outcomes.

Discussion about these issues is often assisted by social science research and by the large and growing body of helpful statistics and data collection around work and households in Australia. However, it is also, on occasion, muddied by unclear thinking about key terms (like 'work', 'choice', 'flexibility' and the 'family'), and is inhibited by a poor connection between social science research and policy. It is also constrained by both the intellectual silos and the lumbering gait of engagement that sometimes characterises publication and social science scholarship. While a flurry of public talk characterises this terrain, policy change is slow, narrow and lags well behind international provision in key areas like the care of children and support for working parents. These lags are not the result of the failure of social science – their causes are deeply institutional, cultural and political. However, they may be better met by more social research that brings a greater array of evidence forward, in timely and comprehensible ways, using a range of mechanisms, so that better policy outcomes can be found.

WORK AND FAMILY: KEY CHALLENGES

Australia has seen a great deal of change in patterns of work and household arrangements in the past 30 years. These changes expose serious policy gaps and failures in relation to the ways in which Australians now work, live and care. These gaps and failures arise because significant change in work and in households has not been accompanied by change in institutions or in dominant cultures to support these new constellations.

Taking work patterns first, the proportion of Australians in the labour market has been gradually increasing over the past few decades. However, the gender profile of workers is significantly shifting. Employees are increasingly likely to be women, and – while care responsibilities change over the life-cycle – their care responsibilities are very different from those of men. Since the 1970s, across Australia and the industrialised world, women have joined men in their labour 'fetish' (as Guy Standing (2002) terms it) in unprecedented numbers. This means that a shrinking number of women are at home to undertake the necessary work of social reproduction. Women in paid work have not, however, been able to give up their other jobs of social and family reproduction, with Australian women still doing around twice the level of unpaid work as men (Bittman and Pixley 1997; Baxter 2002). Their total work is intensified and doubled up, with the effect of exhausting many women, increasing the support-load falling to those who remain at home, and the thinning of the social fabric around the household.

On a cultural level, changes in work participation also have important effects. At the turn of the twenty-first century, young women are much more attached to a work identity than their mothers. And that attachment increasingly collides with their later identification as mothers and carers (Pocock 2003; Probert 2002; Reed et al. 2003), creating an acute squeeze between home and work. For many women of all ages, this squeeze results in feelings of guilt and inadequacy as they try to square how they must mother (and work) with how they think they *should* (or others think they should). Cultural beliefs about the appropriateness of female and maternal care remain strong in Australia, as do notions of 'proper motherhood' (ever available and boundlessly caring), as well as 'proper workers' (mostly full-time, available for overtime, placing work centrally in their lives) (Pocock 2003).

Positive evaluations of work as an enjoyable activity beyond mere monetary reward confirm the centrality of work to Australians' sense of themselves. For many women and men, work is a positive source of enjoyment, social connection and contribution. In the 2001 HILDA survey, over half of respondents said they would enjoy having a job even if they didn't need to work for the money (Pocock 2005a). While such positive evaluations of work are higher among white-collar and professional workers, more than half of cleaners, labourers, and elementary clerical, sales and service workers agreed with the statement that they would enjoy having a job even if they didn't need the money. There is every sign that paid work will increase in its significance to future Australians, partly driven by its positive returns, and partly by a spending cycle fuelled by the high level of indebtedness in Australian households. This means that a collision between home and work is unlikely to abate.

Within the population of Australian workers, the nature of work has changed significantly. Not only are workers more likely to be female, white-collar and working in the service sector, their jobs are increasingly part-time or precarious. Most recent jobs growth has been part-time. This suits many working carers (and their employers). Part-time work is a work/family vehicle of choice within the Australian context, with 44 per cent of all women working part-time, compared to the OECD average of 26 per cent. However, Australian women who work part-time pay a high price in terms of job security and other entitlements. Two-thirds of these jobs are casual with little job security and weak entitlements.

A growing proportion of all Australian employment is in jobs without paid sick or holiday entitlements (most of these employees are self-identified casual employees). At a moment when sick leave and holidays are vital to a much larger proportion of workers who need them to care for their children, access to these entitlements is in decline. Forty-two per cent of the change in full-time and part-time employment in Australia between 1992 and 2003 occurred in jobs without paid sick leave and holidays; that is, casual jobs. This has been much remarked on in the literature, and its implications debated (Campbell and Burgess 2001; Wooden and Warren 2003). Casual density (that is, the proportion of employees without paid leave entitlements as a proportion of all employees) grew from 21.5 per cent to 25.5 per cent of employees between 1992 and 2003 (ABS 2005c). Many are young people in jobs that will perhaps be short term and underpin their studies. But, a growing proportion are not – they are in long-term casual work, and a growing proportion are men and non-students. This has important implications for families, who need stability of earnings, and predictability of hours, along with some control over working time.

The rise in casual employment shifts the risks of daily, weekly, monthly and annual fluctuations in production to the employee – especially women – who shoulder the risk in their pay packet and loss of time sovereignty, liberating their employer from these burdens. The growth in limited term contract and some forms of self-employment similarly shift these income and temporal risks to workers (Watson et al. 2003: 66). This new level of riskiness is accompanied by a low level of union protection (now less than a quarter of all employees).

These changes in participation are accompanied in many

workplaces by more intensive work (Watson et al. 2003; Allen et al. 2005) and by longer working hours (OECD 2004a). The OECD has recently commented on the growth in working hours in Australia, with over one in five now working on average 50 hours a week, making Australia one of the few OECD countries to show a rising trend (OECD 2004a). While some workers who do long hours enjoy their jobs, the pleasure is not always shared by their partners, who often become de facto sole parents (Pocock et al. 2001), or by their children (Pocock and Clarke 2004). Not all workers doing long hours enjoy them, and many such hours are unpaid in Australia. Common family time is also hard to find for some dual income families.

A further element in the transformation of Australian workers is the shape of the household in which they live. Over the past 30 years Australia has seen the decline of the 'male-worker/female-carer' household type, and a rise in dual earner and single mother/earner households. Two-thirds of households where children are present are now dual income households. These trends are likely to continue. Dual earner and single-parent households are time-poor, care-rich and consumption dependent (that is, they replace domestic labour with purchased services like childcare, elder care, prepared food, clothing, cleaning, gardening and other services).

The increasing allocation of household time to paid work (through dual-earner households and women's increasing labour market participation, and growth in the hours of work of full-time workers) has contributed to both *a squeeze on time* (at the individual and household level) and *a struggle for control of time* (Watson et al. 2003; Pocock 2003). More and more households feel this.

This shift in household forms and the very significant reduction in the proportion of women at home providing unpaid care, drives spending on commodified care, and a 'work/spend' cycle (Schor 1998). It also fuels demand for workplace flexibility to assist the growing proportion of working carers who populate the paid workplace – now up to 40 per cent of all employees on any day of the week in Australia (Pocock 2003). They are looking for a new level of 'give' in their workplaces, as households try to combine care with paid work. Unfortunately, when they look to institutions for support, they find all too little change.

Australia's work care regime sits near the bottom end of the OECD league in terms of its support for working carers. A recent study suggested that among 20 countries, Australia's childcare, leave and tax/benefit provisions were ranked seventeenth after countries including the Nordic group, France, Germany, Great Britain, the United States, Ireland, Canada and Japan (Jaumotte 2004). Only New Zealand, Turkey and Mexico were worse. A brief analysis of just two issues is instructive: childcare and parental leave.

In 2002, the parents of 130 000 children who sought childcare could not find it, and issues of cost, quality and accessibility remove real choice from many parents in relation to the labour market. This has caused the federal government to offer a 30 per cent rebate for the costs of childcare. This response addresses the important question of cost, but neglects other important issues like supply and quality. Australia's system of care for preschool children is ragged and patchy. Care is increasingly offered by a small number of 'for profit' companies whose focus is on shareholder value. Given what we know about the importance of early life experience to long-term life chances (McCain and Fraser Mustard 2002; Coffey 2003), it is unfortunate that policy and practice in this area lags so seriously behind behaviour and need.

The other major area of deficiency concerns leave entitlements. With over a quarter of working Australians not eligible for paid sick and holiday leave, access to even basic, long-established rights is in decline. But Australia begins well behind the pack in terms of other forms of leave. It shares the dubious honour of being the only OECD country alongside the United States that does not provide a national system of paid maternity leave. Most Australian women lack an entitlement to paid maternity leave. Around a third have some paid leave because of a local industrial agreement or the generosity of their bosses. Most of these are in the public sector or on higher incomes (Human Rights and Equal Opportunity Commission 2002). Much of the existing leave is for only a few weeks, while the International Labour Organisation recommends 14 weeks paid leave. Even unpaid leave is unavailable to a growing number of women who do not have 12 months tenure with their employer prior to childbirth.

The issues of childcare and paid leave illustrate the institutional lags that characterise Australia's response to changes in labour force participation, its gender composition and family formation. By comparison, with many other industrialised nations, these lags are startling (Pfau-Effinger 2004). The costs are high for women, men and children. With a tighter labour market in view, along with a higher dependency ratio as the Australian population ages, the costs for labour supply and employers are also high. In 2005, 174 000 women nominated lack of childcare as their main barrier to working (ABS 2005d). Such basic structural inadequacies create a strong argument for a policy response and relevant social research.

CONCEPTUAL CATEGORIES AND CHALLENGES

Turning to conceptual issues, there are some important challenges; I will consider seven. First, work and family discussion obviously crosses the disciplinary boundaries. It reaches across health sciences, sociology, industrial relations, politics, demography, gender studies and economics. This means multi-disciplinary study and exchange is essential to defining and pursuing problems. Increasingly, this is best done through research teams and networks, and their development in Australia is a welcome advance.

Second, work and family study is often characterised by an uncritical and rather undifferentiated notion of (nuclear, heterosexual) 'family'. This family – a magical black box of goodness – is assumed to be a place of benign care, and a place that mitigates the 'drain' of paid work. In fact, not all families are either benign or stable. This calls for a closer examination of what families do to individuals. 'Family' policy assumes a stable family form that keeps family transitions (or individual transitions within or through families) out of view. Such transitions are often hazardous, risky, or financially costly, and they are understudied.

Further, this idealised 'family' entity is assumed to sit amid a sustaining and stable community of extended family, friends and social relationships. This community is the essential support for the paid work participation of many. However, the precise nature and diversity of such communities is rarely studied, and is highly variable by ethnicity, class, region, urban/rural location and among Indigenous/non-Indigenous Australians. At present, in policy terms, the ideal family is being asked to do more care, without close critical examination of the diversity of family types, or their capacity to provide such care. In many cases, the de-commodification of care of family members with health problems means more work for women, though the gendered effect of such policies is also often under-studied. The family is loaded up with care, without enough examination of how this locks in socioeconomic status, or how it affects the many who do not live in a benign or stable family.

A further effect of the prominence of family in these debates is the disappearance of women, and women's policy, into the family and family policy. As Anne Summers has pointed out, the identity of women is increasingly lost within the notion of 'family', as if dealing with women here, means they do not need to be dealt with beyond the family (for example, in relation to civic power and voice, gender inequality, discrimination, violence and so on) (Summers 2004).

A third conceptual problem exists around the divide between the public and private spheres, and the failure to recognise the private sphere of unpaid care and work. This limitation afflicts some social sciences (especially neo-classical economics) more than others (like gender studies and sociology). Neo-classical economics continues in the main to ignore the ways in which unpaid labour and reproduction underpin the public world of work and production. Consider for example its analysis of labour supply. Conventional neo-classical economic theory uncouples labour supply from the messy social and physical business of reproduction and care. It assumes that labour supply arises from the choice between 'hours of work' and 'hours of leisure', with men and women maximising their utility by allocating them in optimal ways. This binary 'choice' between two exclusive activities does not take into account the work of care or reproduction, much less understand how care is distinct from leisure, how it is often involuntary, how it intersects with paid work and leisure, and how it is shaped by institutional and cultural norms that constrain 'choice'. These are 'given'. This theoretical weakness in the 'queen' of social sciences, economics, has important practical consequences. One is that public policy in Australia, often led by economists, has been inattentive to important aspects of the labour market, production and reproduction.

The notion of 'choice' is a fourth general conceptual difficulty in the field of work and family policy. Social scientists have argued over the true extent of choice, arguing over the true extent of agency or voluntary untrammelled choice, in the face of structures, contexts, and social expectations that shape such choices. Liberal politicians give great primacy to the notion of choice and draw comfort from social science that gives weight to it as a determinant of wellbeing. They are happy to see a focus on private choice as relieving them of policy intervention. However, a careful social science in the area of work and family must investigate the true boundaries of choice, considering how institutional supports and cultural constraints determine it.

Fifth, discussion about work and family is often uncritical of the increasing role of markets in shaping work and family outcomes – whether labour markets, the commodification of services and care, or the ways in which markets construct social life. The market is often taken as a given, not 'made strange' to social life and reproduction. A greater role for the market in family life is evident through an entrenched work/spend cycle, competitive consumption and the commodification of many forms of care (like food preparation, domestic services, sex, and care of the aged and young). The boundaries of commodification are shifting around the family and intimate relations more broadly, with changing contributions by the State and households. These changes drive higher levels of private indebtedness, which in turn have important effects on household and individual welfare.

Sixth, the idea of 'work and family *conflict*' sits centrally in most discussions about work and family in Australia, with the State seen as mitigating the harsh inevitabilities of 'draining' work, while employers are moved by 'the business case' to implement work and family policies on a firm-by-firm basis. This framework poses work and family in perpetual conflict when in fact a sustainable labour market increasingly relies, at the macro level, on the reproduction of workers. Further, this framing of the role of employers, acting at the enterprise level, means widening inequality between those in (and those outside) large workplaces, the public sector or where a senior manager champions work/life balance (Pocock 2005b). Meanwhile, the State, led at the federal level by a government hostile to increased rights or support for workers, refuses to mitigate the effects of work and family collision. Does social science research have a role in better probing these frames and their implications, and thus contributing to greater progressive policy momentum?

Finally, Australian social scientists are generally diligent in placing their work in its international context, so that it stands atop the best international work that has gone before. However, it is also important to recognise that a practical, new, Australian work and family policy will be shaped by a historical and institutional sediment, and will thus be peculiarly Australian. This requires a confident Australian social science, and the avoidance of an overly Euro- or US-centric comparative frame.

TOWARDS A BETTER INTERFACE
BETWEEN SOCIAL SCIENCE AND POLICY

A number of social science researchers, working from a range of disciplinary bases, have over many years influenced public policy in this sphere, through publication, public events and commentary. Despite this work, policy remains poorly coordinated, partial, compartmentalised and often driven more by the electoral cycle than good social research. For example, in the 2004 federal election, work and family issues figured prominently in public discussion, but in policy terms were poorly served by hastily developed proposals from both the major parties. These focused narrowly on private household finances, rather than on structural and workplace questions.

A considerable amount of social research has focused upon the issues of work and family in recent years. The Australian Institute of Family Studies has played an important role in generating research, holding conferences, fostering the research of others and promulgating discussion, as do new research networks that cross disciplinary boundaries: see, for example, the Australian Research Alliance for Children & Youth (www.aracy.org.au). Study of these issues is greatly assisted by the statistical collections of the Australian Bureau of Statistics (ABS), now supplemented by longitudinal surveys that bring rich new sources of quantitative data to the discussion and have generated a number of new lines of study (see Negotiating the Life Course study at ANU (lifecourse.anu. edu.au), and, more recently and significantly, the Household, Income and Labour Dynamics in Australia (HILDA) survey (www.melbourneinstitute.com/hilda). These are of great importance to the field of study and a boon to work and family researchers. There are also some important gaps with the deferral of both the Australian Workplace Industrial Relations Survey (last conducted in 1995) and the National Time Use Survey (last conducted in 1997). These important surveys have provided vital data for social scientists and policymakers in the past.

There are some international stand-out successes in bringing multi-disciplinary social science to bear on work and family issues. Professor Fraser Mustard, from the Canadian Institute for Advanced Research, provides one exceptional example. He and his colleagues have brought a variety of health and social research to public debate, and changed public policy both in Canada and beyond, through studies about development of children (McCain and Fraser Mustard 2002). This articulation of research and policy provides an effective example of social research put to work to make change. Professor Mustard's instruments have been varied: the generation of major new robust studies, their wide publication in academic literature and beyond, along with accessible Web publication and an energetic championing of research findings to many governments, the corporate sector, community organisations, and individuals in many walks of life. A local example is provided by the Australian Research Alliance for Children & Youth led by Professor Fiona Stanley.

These examples illustrate the benefits of multi-disciplinary research, research teams, active promulgation, and energetic researchers who are willing to take discussion of social science well beyond the university and across the political spectrum, including through the use of private sources of funds.

Most of the research in the field of work and family, and throughout the social sciences, is undertaken by individual researchers. At the level of the individual, there is an undeniable tension between doing good social research, and shepherding it into public discussion. Time is a major constraint for most researchers, especially those who combine teaching and research.

For some social scientists, *doing* research is their primary goal. They are very focused, and carefully marshal their time to maximise it for research, often on a narrow terrain where they are expert. They frequently publish – mostly in academic journals – and often become professors. Their ideas can be influential despite their determination not to be diverted by public forums or media requests. These researchers take the JD Salinger approach to publication: they pack their academic article a sandwich, put in on the bus, and send it out into the world to find its own readership and effect. Unfortunately, not all articles are the social science equivalent of *The Catcher in the Rye*, and many sink without trace (especially given the distorting incentives that the current academic practice of 'publication-counting' creates in favour of multiple publication, rather than reward for public, policy or scholarly effect).

At the other end of the spectrum, some social scientists are keen to see their research linked to public discussion and policy, and actively respond to, and create it.

There are powerful tensions between these two approaches: between *doing* research and *talking about it*. The processes of promulgation almost always drain efforts that could go into the generation of new research (though they do have their own pleasures and can usefully stimulate new insights and new lines of research). What is more, promulgation can be bruising. It is more comfortable behind the desk than in front of the camera or in the witness box. However, there are good arguments for finding some kind of middle road between the monk-like path of isolated scholarship and 'celebrity-researcher' status.

Academic texts and journals have narrow readerships, and are increasingly lost in a world where accessible Web-based publication is a significant means of public communication. If a key ethical test for social research is that it *matters* (to whom and why, being highly arguable and subjective questions of course), then social research deserves public discussion; indeed, an ethical obligation exists for it, given the large Australian public investment in social research.

What are the mechanisms available to link social science research with public policy? In my experience in the fields of industrial relations, work and family a range of influential actors exist, along with a set of mechanisms that can affect them (see Table 7.1).

TABLE **7.1** *Technologies of influence: Transmission mechanisms for research*

Actors who shape policy	Instruments that affect them
Public policymakers (bureaucrats, advisers)	Publications (academic journal, newspaper, opinion pieces, Web-based, other) Direct communication Personal relationships Pressure generated by public interest and response
'The public'	Publications (academic journal, newspaper, opinion pieces, Web-based, other) Communication via other media
Politicians	Publication (academic journal, newspaper, opinion pieces, Web-based, other) Direct communication Personal relationships Pressure generated by public interest and response Submissions to public inquiries (for example, Senate)
Law-making	Publication (academic journal, newspaper, opinion pieces, Web-based, other) Evidence in legal proceedings Expert witness testimony
Other scholars, researchers (including 'think tanks')	Publication (academic journal, newspaper, opinion pieces, Web-based, other) Conferences Direct communication Deployment of 'the international expert'
Media	Publication (academic journal, newspaper, opinion pieces, Web-based, other) Flow-ons from initial media contributions Direct communication Personal relationship Research assistance to journalists

Clearly, publication (in all its forms) potentially reaches all the actors who shape policy, so focusing on it is a wise first step. However, in my view, Australian social science academics over-rely on publication in academic journals. Alone, it is a weak instrument to affect policy. This is especially the case when unaccompanied by any complementary publication (for example, press release, media feature, opinion piece or Web-based). These complementary forms of publication are seriously under-utilised by many social scientists. It goes without saying that, however results are published, clear writing is a first requirement for a closer connection between policy and research. Unfortunately, some social scientists continue to conflate impenetrable, inaccessible writing with good research and intellectual depth. There is no excuse for this in social science.

Beyond publication, social science researchers in Australia under-utilise a range of other means of communication with significant actors, especially personal and direct communication of their work to the media, politicians or policymakers. In 2001–02, I spent just over a year working for a federal political leader, advising on industrial, work and family issues. I was very struck by three things in relation to the connection between public policy, law-making and research. First, how little research was being done on some key social issues in Australia. For example, unfair dismissal rights in small businesses have been frequently discussed in federal parliament over the past five years, and the issue is relevant to many thousands of businesses and workers. However, there is very little good research to underpin many of the claims that recur in this debate – most notoriously in relation to the number of jobs that will be created if small businesses do not have to use fair dismissal procedures. This debate has proceeded without much reference to evidence, not least because few social scientists have been collecting it in Australia.

Second, social scientists too rarely directly approach politicians (or journalists or policymakers). It can also be said that many politicians rarely make such approaches. Fortunately, federal politicians in Australia are well served by a very competent parliamentary library and research service (which vigorously scans and critically summarises social science literature). However, in my brief experience in Canberra, there appeared be a weak personal connection between politicians and researchers, especially researchers beyond Canberra. Politicians rarely seek out researchers directly (there are exceptions), and researchers rarely approach politicians. Indeed, there appears to be some nervousness on both sides.

Third, where such meetings do occur, communication is sometimes hampered by researchers' lack of ability to summarise

research and communicate it succinctly, emphasising policy implications (it is also hampered by the short-term horizon and the
distractability of law-makers). In my observation, parliamentary
life, policymaking and media influence are very often built around
personal relationships. People approach those they know and seek
them out again. Newspaper editors commission opinion pieces
from those they know – or those who approach them. Journalists
in particular approach those they know, and the circle of social
policy 'media talent' they pursue is small. The gateway into this
circle is fairly wide but often requires a personal approach.
Policymaking and public discourse is in part a social process.
Researchers who eschew it may be undermining some of their
policy-focused work and leaving the field to a small circle that
'work' such relationships.

In my experience, many scholars are hesitant about taking their
research into new forms (short summaries, opinion pieces, personal
briefings, Senate submissions, witness appearances and so on).
Some of this reluctance reflects a shortage of time. But, some of it
arises from a shy reluctance to take risks by pursuing more public
discussion beyond traditional academic forums, especially through
personal discussion with actors in the media, political life and
public agencies. This reluctance is also about comfort and habit.
There are good arguments for a greater academic-led social science
engagement with a wider variety of actors using a broader range of
public policy instruments. This engagement will not always be
productive, and it has its hazards. However, better public policy,
greater use of a wider array of evidence, and perhaps even some
personal pleasure for researchers, may well be its fruit.

CONCLUSION

There is much that social science is contributing to the understanding of work and family in Australian life. But the dissonance
between institutions, cultures and the practical realities of
working and caring life in Australia are a strong argument for a

better effort. Some good data sources and multi-disciplinary platforms exist to underpin this effort. However, more are needed, along with social scientists who are willing to pursue the many pressing questions that exist in relation to appropriate institutional, work, labour market and household forms of the future – forms that ease the combination of work and family, and the many transitions made within and between them. Given the urgent nature of these challenges, and their impact on the welfare of so many women, men and children, there are good arguments for more engaged social research in this field, one that better connects good research with public effect.

ENDNOTE

1   I would like to thank Marian Sawer and Meredith Edwards, along with the book's editors, for their helpful comments on an earlier draft.

8

Gender Policies: Hers to His

Chilla Bulbeck[1]

A REVOLUTION IN GENDER RESEARCH

In the summer of 1969–70, women returning from the United States met in Sydney and announced the inaugural meeting of the Women's Liberation Group (Curthoys 1992: 430). This was the start of 'second wave' feminism, an explosion that spread through the Australian community and into universities, parliaments and bureaucracies. Conceptions of gender issues have since changed beyond recognition, so that post-feminism now means young women who have known nothing but a discourse of gender equality, as well as a men's backlash attempting to turn the clock back to pre-feminist days. This chapter outlines the impact of feminist theory in policy practice, changes wrought via alliances between social science researchers, femocrats and feminist politicians. The chapter then discusses the contemporary backlash climate, before exploring the possibilities for restoring issues of gender-related disadvantage and advantage to the policy agenda.

SOCIAL SCIENTISTS ON THE GENDER ORDER: 'WHAT'S THE PROBLEM?'

Ann Curthoys (1998: 179) describes 'official feminism' as 'a uniquely Australian configuration' legitimating 'the perspectives of political science, history, sociology, economics and law' in applying a 'gender lens' to public policy (Hancock 1999: 4). As well as feminist intellectuals, femocrats (or *Sisters in Suits,* Sawer 1990) also worked with an activist women's movement, securing funding and a stable future for many women's movement initiatives, such as refuges, rape crisis centres, women's health centres, working women's centres, legal aid and women's legal services (Sawer 1999: 38). The Women's Electoral Lobby (WEL) monitored the policies and activities of the political parties, recommending that women use their vote to advance women's issues and policies, contributing to a 'gender gap' in voting on issues where women's and men's votes diverged. Such activities prompted bipartisan policies; for example, affordable childcare and domestic violence prevention.

In 1958, the then Social Science Research Council of Australia commissioned pioneering research by Norman MacKenzie, published as *Women in Australia* (1962). In 1983, even though almost all the Fellows of The Academy of Social Sciences in Australia were male, 'The Academy took an interest in the social position of women before it became fashionable to do so' when it held its annual symposium on 'Women and the Social Sciences: New Modes of Thought'. 'By 1983 the impact of feminist arguments, questions and challenges had been felt in most areas of academic life, especially in the disciplines of the social sciences' (Goodnow and Pateman 1985: vi). By the end of the 1990s, the research areas gender/medical/family, at more than one-fifth of members, constituted the largest research concentration of The Australian Sociological Association (reported in Western 1998: 226).

Before the 1970s, most Australians, including social scientists, treated gender as equivalent to sex: a natural difference. Where it was of sociological interest, sex was seen as an empirical variable in data analysis, sex differences being presumed to rest on a series of dichotomies, such as emotional–rational, private–public and dependent–independent. Table 8.1 below identifies three overlapping 'phases' in feminist research and policy. These phases track the revolutionary impact of social science research on public policy and Australians' understandings of their social and private worlds. Feminist researchers named new objects of analysis, such as 'gender', 'embodiment', 'sexualities' and 'patriarchy'. They developed new policy concerns such as 'sexual harassment', 'domestic violence survivor' and 'rape in marriage'. These concerns identified new ways of understanding issues. For example, the concept of the 'carer citizen' captures the complex set of impediments to women's public participation in work and politics, based on women's presumed responsibility for childcare and housework. The invisibility of women's unpaid work meant it was not recognised in a tax/transfer/family law regime that favoured the head of household and disadvantaged the dependent spouse (see Cass 1985). Table 8.1 could contain many more columns, on legislation to improve women's rights, media representations of women, women's political representation and voting patterns, and battles to shift the understanding of gay and lesbian sexualities from a mental illness to a political identity, for instance. Pocock's chapter in this volume outlines some of the changes summarised in relation to work and the carer citizen. The focus here will be on embodiment issues and, to a lesser extent, education (for background, see Marginson in this volume).

In the first phase, feminist social researchers asserted the need to study 'women', hidden from analysis by the presumed universal category of men. Major policy developments were framed around overcoming 'women's disadvantage', rather than focusing attention on 'men's advantage' (Connell 1995: 82; Eveline 1994), since policies directed at removing advantages were akin to electoral suicide. Unfortunately, the focus on women's disadvantage implied that women needed 'special measures' because of their weakness or inferiority, whether programs were framed in terms of women's difference (for example, embodiment issues) or the goal of equality with men (for example, education). Carol Bacchi (1999) explores some of the negative effects of framing women's difference as disadvantage, also expressed in 'individualising' the problem: 'the denial of power relations that keep oppressed groups oppressed'. For example, affirmative action has been redefined as special measures for a less deserving group, rather than as compensation for structures that privilege male workers. Domestic violence is understood as chivalrous intervention by a State that protects women as weak victims who require one man to save them from another. Abortion is offered to those 'too poor, too young, too physically or mentally incompetent' for motherhood. Only in the 'carer citizens' strand of research, was women's difference translated into women's positive contribution, women's equivalence with men. Time use surveys charted the enormous contribution made to national wellbeing by women's unpaid labour dedicated to childcare, housework and community work. This contribution, represented in satellite national accounts, underwrote women's claims to independent social security support and a fair share of family property at the time of divorce.

In the first phase, sex was seen as the biological bedrock on which socially constructed gender was built (see Edwards 1989). In the second phase, the notion of the 'gender order' combines agency and structure, embodiment and life story to produce a complex picture of numerous masculinities and femininities in hierarchical and conflictual relations with each other. The gender order is produced through 'gender projects': 'a social pattern [that] requires us to see it as a product of history, and also as a *producer* of history' (Connell 1995: 81; Connell 2000: 28). The notion that 'women' was not a homogenous category and that gender was a social construct informed policy developments in this second phase. For example, the 1986 National Action Plan focused on girls who benefited least from schooling, addressing disadvantages produced by location (geography), class and ethnicity (Boulden 2004). In the mid-1990s, Professional Development Projects, including those for 'Developing Gender Inclusive Curriculum', were federally funded. These projects were administered by the Association of Women Educators working with state education department equity officers and academics as advisers and evaluators.

Similarly, domestic violence policies were developed to respond to the different needs of women from different cultural backgrounds. According to all the indicators, violence is more prevalent in Indigenous than non-Indigenous communities, due to the accumulations of dispossession from land and culture, and ongoing third world health and economic conditions, in a climate where police were often seen as the enemy rather than as friends of the community. Renaming the problem 'family violence', researchers such as Judy Atkinson (1990) sought to promote holistic community-wide interventions responsive to the enormous difficulties experienced as much by perpetrators as victims, offering, for instance, alcohol and drug rehabilitation programs, and better mental health delivery services (see Robertson 1999). Women from non–English-speaking-backgrounds also lobbied for culturally appropriate domestic violence shelters whose workers were sensitive to the difficulties of leaving a violent home when, due to isolation, cultural and language barriers, wider society might seem just as dangerous. Immigrant women relying on Australian-born husbands for their residency rights were particularly vulnerable. One policy intervention was to extend independent citizenship rights to immigrant women suffering domestic violence, while the past violent records of abusers were revealed to women applying to migrate to join such men.

Just as feminist scholars developed more complex understandings of the relationships between gender and other factors of disadvantage, academics researching boys' disadvantage also uncovered which boys were losing (working class and Aboriginal, for example), and why, in terms of hegemonic masculinity. For example, poorly performing boys often persist with 'masculine' subjects, like mathematics, rather than changing to 'feminised' subjects that would threaten their masculine identity. In many school boy subcultures, studiousness was disparaged as feminine, requiring academically successful boys to develop complicated strategies to disguise their academic commitment. Boys express their masculinity in aggression, particularly targeting girls and gays, behaviour that can only be redressed with anti-bullying policies, anger management courses and deconstructions of gender in the curriculum (for example, see Gilbert and Gilbert 1998; Kenway et al. 1997).

Bacchi (1999) argues that an exception to the women's disadvantage model is the women's health movement. The movement both challenged the framing paradigms of the medical establishment and claimed better access to its services. Table 8.1 indicates some of these joint strategies, reframing women's bodily experiences as normal rather than aberrant, and seeking women's control over their bodies through alternative service delivery. Adopting the orientation of the women's health movement, in the early 1990s a men's health movement developed. The movement responded to the facts that men's health is worse than women's, at least as measured by indicators such as longevity. However, rather than seeking funding for programs such as prostate cancer prevention, academic research explained men's health in terms of aggressive masculinity, which commends risk-taking behaviour, in terms of industrial and traffic accidents, and also in terms of refusal to visit the doctor, which is tantamount to admitting 'weakness' (Connell 2000: 177). Men's health initiatives worked with men to reconstruct those aspects of masculinity that were detrimental to men's health.

Recognised internationally for its success in limiting the AIDS epidemic is the liaison between social scientists as public intellectuals, gay advocacy groups and the former Labor government to promote AIDS-awareness in the gay community. The government was reintroducing Medicare, against the wishes of the medical profession, and was prepared to challenge the medical profession's 'ownership' of the disease. Encouraged by the development of the public health Ottawa Charter of 1986, promoting a community-based response to health care, the Minister of Health, Neal Blewett, and Bill Bowtell, in the minister's office, were sympathetic to a non-medical approach. The gay community had become politicised and was readily mobilised around the issue. Social researchers established that the spread of AIDS was linked to risk-taking behaviours by gay and bisexual men. Instead of policing the social actors involved, the policy treated a group of stigmatised men as the experts who would develop and implement programs to spread safe sex strategies. Working with public intellectuals like Denis Altman and advocacy organisations such as NACAIDS, instead of driving the AIDS-affected underground with a punitive approach, education, peer-group support, non-discriminatory access to treatment, and voluntary testing with counselling support produced a containment of AIDS in Australia that was the envy of many nations (Drielsma 1997).

Although research on gender has become more sophisticated, gender patterns in some areas remained intransigent. Boys' aggression at school barely abated. Men continued to resist sharing housework and childcare. The third frame in Table 8.1 explains these resistances in terms of the continued marking of some activities or occupations as either 'male' or 'female'. In 'doing gender', males eschew housework and affirm aggression; females eschew engineering and blue-collar trades and affirm attractiveness. This new scenario is complicated by a discourse in which women assert their equality, even when evidence proves otherwise. This discourse was labelled by Bittman and Pixley (1997: 145–171) as 'pseudo-mutuality' in relation to claims concerning shared housework. 'Date rape' entered the feminist research lexicon as increasing numbers of young women described their experiences of sexual coercion, but refused to call it 'rape' (for example, see Chung 2002). Young feminists in particular disputed what they saw as the 'victim' feminism of the 'collectivist' women's liberation movement. As a result, research findings are emerging which suggest that inequality is something 'other' women suffer, women marked as different due to a marginalised ethnicity or class. Anita Harris (2004) charts media and political celebration of the 'can-do' girls as model future workers, consumers and citizens. The 'can-do' girls are role models for the 'at-risk' girls, girls defined by 'juvenile delinquency, nihilism, and anti-social attitudes'; and, most particularly, the pathology of young motherhood (Harris 2004: 10–19, 25, 28, 67 and 73). Nobody wants to be seen as an 'at-risk' girl, a victim who can't get her own life together. In the contemporary climate, while theoretical research on gender has become more complex, the opportunities for gender-inflected policies have retreated dramatically.

DISCURSIVE SHIFTS: NEO-LIBERALISM AND MEN'S DISADVANTAGE

Given that social scientists contributed to such a dramatic impact on the lives of Australian men and women, it is little wonder that a defensive backlash movement was provoked (see Marsh this volume), almost from the inception of women's liberation. However, it is only since 1996 and the election of the Howard government that groups such as the right-wing men's movement and Family First have received extensive political support. Women's machinery in government has been particularly targeted, with drastic budget cuts to the Human Rights and Equal Opportunities Commission (HREOC) and the Office of the Status of Women (OSW) removed from the Department of the Prime Minister and Cabinet in October 2004 and incorporated into the Department of Family and Community Affairs as the Office for Women. Other agencies that monitored women's status, such as the Australian

Bureau of Statistics' Women's Statistics Unit, were closed down (Sawer 1999: 43 and 45). As the relocation of the Office for Women indicates, women as individuals and workers have been displaced for the notion of women as family members. The role of the Affirmative Action Agency was redefined from equity for women in employment to support for business (Summers 2003: 130–1). Three units which supported women's workforce roles were abolished: the Women's Bureau (abolished 1997), the Equal Pay Unit (abolished 1998) and the Work and Family Unit (abolished 2003). Feminist community organisations, alternative sources of policy production and lobbying, have been silenced by defunding.

The catalyst for such changes was the shift away from a welfare-oriented State towards neo-liberalism and economic rationalism. It was no longer acknowledged that society is marked by patterned structures of inequality on the basis of class, ethnicity and so on. Instead, individuals are charged with responsibility for their own life outcomes, producing, among other things, pseudomutuality. One response of femocrats was 'ideological bilingualism', as it was called in New Zealand, 'speaking one language (managerialism and economic rationalism) while thinking another' (Sawer 1993: 17). For example, besides claiming the justice outcomes of preventing domestic violence, femocrats calculated its costs, and to the community and employers as well as to victims. There have been at least seven such studies in Australia since 1988 (Access Economics 2004: 11), with the most recent study suggesting that domestic violence cost Australia $8.1 billion in 2002–03, ranking among the top five risks to women's health (women constituted 87 per cent of the some 400 000 victims in 2002–03). As Access Economics (2004: 6) points out, costs borne by employers in the first instance are passed on to consumers, while the costs of support services provided by the government are paid for in taxes. As noted above, domestic violence policy can be framed in terms of 'good' men's chivalrous protection of 'weak' women from 'bad' men. Unfortunately, such men now have the ear of government, and claim that women are just as capable of violence as men and so do not need any government protection.[2] Within the powerful counterframes of the neo-liberal anti-elitist discourse, the women's machinery and policies developed over the last 30 years constitute unfair positive discrimination, disadvantaging men and advantaging women.

Men's groups campaign for policies to correct men's disadvantage, discerned particularly in the areas of education and work. For example, in 2002, there was a House of Representatives enquiry called *Boys: Getting it Right,* while a 2004 tender to review the gender equity framework was won by the Centre for Boys, Family and Life (Boulden 2004). In 2004 both the Prime Minister and the Leader of the Opposition proclaimed the need for more male teachers to provide positive male role models in an over-feminised and hence alienating educational environment. Neither leader recommended the strategy most likely to succeed: increased salaries for teachers. In the same year, the Sex Discrimination Commissioner, Pru Goward, asserted that the 'crisis in masculinity' was an issue for unemployed working class men, who, like their more fortunate brothers, needed to 'sit at the head of the family table' (interview on Radio National's Life Matters, Thursday 22 April).[3] These discussions reveal that gender equity is still on the political agenda, providing a potential toehold for feminist social researchers to contribute to policy formation.

GENDER EQUALITY: WHY BOTHER?

Social scientists optimistically believe that evidenced-based research will speak for itself, yet evidence that runs counter to the present climate is buried or ignored. For instance, the newly elected Howard government refused to release HREOC's report detailing widespread discrimination against pregnant women at work. More recently, the Access Economics report on the costs of domestic violence was released only after a successful Freedom of Information request, the report possibly suppressed because of its finding that the overwhelming majority of perpetrators are men and victims are women (Sawer 2005). The government has failed to replicate foreshadowed studies, such as the ABS Women's Safety Survey, last undertaken in 1996, and the National Time Use Survey, due in 2002. Given debates concerning the effects of lengthening and unpredictable working weeks on marriages and children, a time use survey would provide significant data, for families as much as women. Papers commissioned from academics, for example as part of the celebration of 20 years of the Sex Discrimination Act, are published on HREOC's web site, but there is little bureaucratic or political will to implement their recommendations. Among the recommendations are calls for a parliamentary review of the effectiveness of the Commonwealth sex discrimination and equal opportunity legislation (Marian Sawer), a right for parents of young children to request flexible work and be given a serious response by their employers (Beth Gaze), and Superannuation Guarantee contributions for women on maternity leave and for carers (Diana Olsberg) (HREOC 2004).

When Anne Summers (2003) bemoans *The End of Equality,* she treats gender equality as a self-evident goal: as indeed it was for 20-odd years in Australian public policy. However, the profound discursive shift created by neo-liberal individualism and populist anti-elitism have reversed previous understandings of the world, so that outcomes are the result of individual effort or laziness and government intervention is positive preferment. The capacity to formulate gender equity policies in this environment is limited, although several possibilities are explored in this section.

AUSTRALIA'S INTERNATIONAL STANDING

Australia has obligations under United Nations Conventions, the main convention in relation to gender being the Convention on the Elimination of Discrimination Against Women (CEDAW). Failure to meet these obligations brings criticism and loss of standing in the international community, particularly European Union members, so that Australia risks marginalisation as a backward nation in its equity policies. Failure to meet CEDAW obligations sits uneasily with the government's commitment to promote democracy and 'governance' among Pacific neighbours, including the participation of women in democratic structures.

GENDER EQUITY LINKED TO EFFICIENCY OR COST-SAVINGS ARGUMENTS

Equity is still an issue in many policy arenas, because it is aligned with efficiency; for example, practical reconciliation in relation to Indigenous policies (see Altman and Rowse in this volume). Social researchers should call for an analysis of alternative mechanisms for overcoming our present skills shortage. The costs and benefits of training 'at-risk' young men and women who have been failed by the present education system, programs for girls to enter 'non-traditional' trades that are responsive to the gender aspects of these choices, identification of appropriately skilled people not working in these areas (as was done several years ago in relation to nurses), and the costs in additional infrastructure of making up the deficit from overseas could be evaluated and compared. Claims concerning increased national productivity, with which feminists promoted the affirmative action legislation, are all the more necessary in the present economic rationalist climate.

'AT-RISK' MALES AND FEMALES

Instead of devising policies that address 'women' or 'men', a focus on 'at-risk' males and females may achieve greater headway in the present climate. Masculinities research has suggested programs by which men can enact masculinities more safely, for both themselves and the women in their lives. The present moment also calls for ensuring that a gender lens is included in policies that attempt to 'strengthen' or 'build' families or communities. In this way, gender issues can be mainstreamed, as is the current orthodoxy in the European Union. Even-handed policies should be advocated: scholarships for male primary school teachers or childcare workers matched by those for trainee female CEOs or mining engineers.

IT IS WHAT WOMEN AND MEN WANT

As Sawer (2002: 259) points out, citing the Australian Election Study, in 2001, 45 per cent of the female electorate felt that more needs to be done to promote equal pay and equal opportunity for women, increasing to 58 per cent of female supporters of the Democrats and Greens.[4] In almost all response categories, over half the respondents agreed that 'guaranteeing equality between men and women in all aspects of life' is 'very important', rising to 60 per cent of men and over 70 per cent of women supporters of Labor, Democrats and Greens. Young women, whatever their class background, imagine futures which rely on the achievements of femocrats and feminist research. They plan to combine mother-hood with work/career (for example, Summers 2003: 22), whether they are young mothers planning education for the future or young corporate women who are, however, 'very unclear about how they might combine having children with their careers' (Probert and Macdonald 1999: 138–9 and 150). The government can support young women's desires by providing childcare, permanent part-time employment, paid maternity leave, ongoing contributions to their superannuation scheme while a full-time carer and so on. Such policies are more likely to reverse the declining fertility rates and secure the votes of young people than withdrawing women's access to abortion (see Travers in this volume on the effectiveness of different welfare state responses to the falling birth rate).

While Summers (2003) bemoans the contemporary government position in which 'women' are disappeared into 'families', perhaps contemporary policy activists and researchers must adapt this rhetoric in another version of ideological bilingualism, working again on the family front, as they did prior to the resurgence of feminism in the 1960s (see Lake 1999). There is some hope for this approach in the evidence of Coalition government activism in supporting women as carer citizens (see Table 8.1). The Prime Minister's fore-word to the 'Australia says no' campaign, devised by the Office for Women, identifies this possible approach. The Prime Minister notes that the 'government believes violence against women is unacceptable' while also, contradictorily, claiming that it is not the role of the government to tell people how to lead their lives. However, the campaign is justified because 'The Australian Government believes that families are the backbone of a strong and healthy community, and loving supportive relationships are at the heart of happy, well-functioning families' (in Office for Women 2004). Parents are called on to assist their children in detecting and dealing with unacceptable relationship violence. While the unacceptability of violence – and against 'women' – is confirmed, unfortunately no women's services were allowed to tender for the counselling service (Sawer 2005), making it unlikely that callers will speak with someone educated in the complicated subjectivities by which young women assert their agency in ongoing situations of gender subordination (which is why many young women refuse to recognise date rape or abuse in their relationships – see analysis by Phillips 2000). While the present government would also like policies to cost nothing and reinforce the role of women as economically dependent married wives and mothers, perhaps these ideals can be stretched towards feminist positions in limited ways. It is true that neither major party promised maternity leave at the 2004 federal election (that is, a payment based on a woman's status as a paid worker), but it is also true that both promised some kind of payment to mothers. Policies that work from the present government's family ideal could stretch the definition of 'family' to enfold the majority, rather than minority, of Australian families. Men and women might be offered universal family-friendly policies, policies for parents such as non-transferable parental leave or a presumptive right to part-time work for any parent of small children. A pro-active government sensitive to financial constraints might be persuaded to introduce a Family-Friendly (or Diversity) Workplace Guarantee Levy, working in the same way as the Keating government's Training Guarantee Levy. Employers would either pay the levy as a tax or, in consultation with their workers, deploy the monies to make their workplaces more family-friendly, boosting staff morale and productivity, and enhancing their public relations profile as 'good corporate citizens'.

CONCLUSION: WORKING AT OTHER LEVELS

Feminist researchers will continue to work with offices for women at the state government level, with the unions (presently mounting cases for both paid maternity leave and to increase the basic wage), community groups, and perhaps they should redouble their efforts to work with the corporate sector. Pay inquiries in NSW (1998), Queensland (2001) and Western Australia (2004) have drawn on social science research findings to reiterate 'the extent to which gender inequality is often historically embedded in the way work is valued' (Todd and Eveline 2004). These precedents provide a support base for other cases seeking to expand the principles of pay equity (Whitehouse 2004).

Possibly, the time is ripe to call on the federal government to form an 'office of gender equity', staffed with men and women trained in gender issues. With the dissolution of femocrat-staffed offices in the federal bureaucracy, social researchers must seek other transmission belts or 'bridging networks' (see Head, Chapter 2) to formulate socially useful research and publicise research findings. A range of these are detailed by Pocock in this volume, to which could be added alternative media such as Web-based organisations and publications; alternative advocacy organisations framed in terms of self-help, but which do not always understand gender to be a core aspect of their members' identity; innovative research proposals such as gender impact assessments, and randomised social science experiments (Leigh 2003); and publicising gender debates and research issues through public forums such as deliberative forums (which might bring men's groups and feminists together in an attempt to produce an agreed platform concerning domestic violence or women's reproductive autonomy). An optimistic scenario is mutual information exchange to produce novel policies for some of the still intractable gender discriminations in Australian life.

TABLE 8.1 *Gender-oriented research: objects of analysis & examples of policy change*

Focus in gender relations	Health and violence (women's embodiment) Women's difference
Before 1970 and gender-based research	• rape was women's fault • police and courts treated domestic violence as a 'private' matter • the law recognised almost no sex-based harms against women • women had little control of their interactions with doctors • women's different is 'nature' or 'choice'
1970s–1980s: research focus is 'women'	• rape laws amended to reflect unequal power relations in sexual encounters • domestic violence a public policy issue; for example, refuges, violence protection orders • new legal remedies, such as sexual harassment, rape in marriage • women's health centres educate and empower women re their bodies • alternative health delivery; for example, home births, breastfeeding
1980s–1990s: research focus is 'gender', women are diverse	• instead of 'domestic violence' Aboriginal women experience 'family violence', requiring community solutions • shelters to meet specific needs of women of non–English-speaking background
1990s +: research focus is 'femininities' and 'masculinities'	• eating disorders, cosmetic surgery as expression of desired femininities • masculinity as reason for men's poor health outcomes • AIDS prevention research and policy • critique medical model of menstruation, pregnancy and menopause as disabilities
After 1996: research focus on 'men' in backlash rhetoric	• women extended 'protection' by chivalrous males; for example, Partnerships Against Domestic Violence program • women trafficked into Australian sex industry protected if self-define as 'victims' who assist investigations • women just as violent as men

OTHER SOURCES See Goodnow and Pateman (eds) (1985) for feminist social science contributions to theory and policy development in the areas of work and carer citizens (for example, Cass and Edwards) and embodiment (for example, Scutt, Goodnow and Eisenstein); see Bulbeck (2003) on contributions in these fields; see also Boulden (2004) for education.

Education Women's disadvantage	Work Women's disadvantage	Citizenship and welfare Women's contribution
• girls and boys trained for their naturally determined different futures • boys outperformed girls educationally	• all men paid 'family wage'; women paid two-thirds of male wage • married women forced to resign from workforce	• women dependent on male breadwinners • women performed unpaid nurturing functions, not seen as work • intra-household resource allocations presumed equitable/equal
• policy activists and teachers amend the gendered curriculum, as a result of studies such as 'Girls, Schools and Society' (1975)	• equal pay • equal basic wage • bipartisan support for affordable childcare, so women can participate in workforce, starting with Childcare Act 1972	• social security regime recognises contribution of carer citizen: benefits from 'wallet' (for example, tax deductions) to 'purse' (for example, payments to primary care-givers) (under Fraser) • women's unpaid household contributions accounted for at divorce, including share of superannuation (under Howard)
• education policies focus on girls suffering multiple disadvantage • school curricula explores construction of gender	• due to failure of equal pay cases, move to comparative worth cases • superannuation not tailored to women's broken work careers	• pension categories responsive to needs of different women; for example, for older women no longer responsible for dependent children
• protest masculinity expressed against girls and homosexual students • studiousness defined as feminine and abjured	• gender segregation of workforce due to sexualisation of occupations • sexual harassment against women in non-traditional occupations	• despite claimed commitment to sharing housework, men refuse to share equally, partly because it is marked as feminine
• boys' disadvantage at school explained as due to feminisation of teaching profession	• due to structural changes in economy, claimed that males more disadvantaged than females	• mothers to be supported by male breadwinner • men contest child support for women beyond patriarchal control of ex-husband (see Winchester 1999)

ENDNOTES

1   My thanks for the valuable feedback provided by various readers, particularly Meredith Edwards, James Walter and Marian Sawer. I have especially benefited from Marian Sawer's ideas concerning content and scope, as well as her careful editorial suggestions.

2   For example, see 'Australian News Commentary', http://www.australian-news.com.au/feminist_propaganda.htm for a diatribe against the Access Economics report on domestic violence.

3   The evidence that females are doing better than males is less clear than backlash commentators claim. For example, in 1999–2000, the average weekly income of males aged 15–24 was $355 compared with $336 for females. In 1999, over 3 per cent of young men aged 20–24 were long-term unemployed compared with about 1.5 per cent of young women, but 3 per cent of young women aged 15–19 by contrast with less than 2 per cent of men aged 15–19 were long-term unemployed. Ninety-four per cent of young men with children are in the labour force compared with 38 per cent of young mothers, motherhood also disbarring young women from educational participation (Australian Bureau of Statistics 2005a; Probert and Macdonald 1999: 135 and 147). Men still dominate apprenticeship courses, while, due in part to gender segregation in fields of study, graduate women's starting salaries are about 95 per cent of graduate men's (Williams 2000: 13).

4   According to the 2001 Australian Election study, more respondents claim that equal opportunities for women have not gone far enough (38 per cent) than believe they have gone too far (11 per cent), although half the respondents believed that the present situation was 'about right' (Australian Social Science Data Archive 2001).

9

INDIGENOUS AFFAIRS

Jon Altman and Tim Rowse

Should the goals of Indigenous affairs policy be to achieve equality of socioeconomic status or to facilitate choice and self-determination? The former tends to imply integration and urban migration, while the latter may require adherence to different life worlds and resistance to transformation. In Australia, different social science disciplines have framed this 'problem' at the very heart of Indigenous affairs policy in different ways and correspondingly have put forward different policy proposals. For instance, whereas anthropology dwells on cultural difference and presumes that difference to be a social good, economics dwells on socioeconomic inequality and presumes that difference to be the legacy of historic exclusion, racism and neglect. One history of the policy-relevant social sciences can be told as a playing out of the competition between these two discourses of difference.

ANTHROPOLOGICAL ADVICE ABOUT REMOTE AUSTRALIAN FRONTIERS

Colonial Australian governments took advice from settlers whose long association with Aborigines and systematic inquiries qualified them as 'experts'. AW Howitt (1830–1908), a magistrate in Victoria who published many ethnological papers, was convinced that Aborigines, while very interesting as a specimen of primitive humanity, were a dying race. Serving on the Royal Commission on Aborigines in Victoria (1877), Howitt co-authored its recommendation that all remaining Aborigines in that colony should reside at self-supporting institutions managed by missionaries. The location of the missions would not need to take into account the customary associations between people and land. No Aborigines were invited to give evidence to the Royal Commission, but four were interviewed by it when they turned up to a hearing (Barwick 1998: 155). In short, in this first engagement of an 'expert' with public policy, there was 'a dissociation between the Aboriginals as an object of scientific interest and as a challenge to social policy' (Stanner 1972: 433).

The policy era known as 'protection' (lasting from c.1880 to c.1940) was based on two widely held ideas. First, that as members of an inferior civilisation, Aborigines quickly lost their social cohesion upon contact with non-Aborigines and became prey to unscrupulous colonists. And second, that they were entitled to protection from these predators and to the improving influences of some kind of education and of steady employment. Where there were jobs, the role of the State was to supervise their employment; for those not employed institutions were necessary – some combination of the Christian mission, the child-focused institution, and the reserve where contact with colonists could be minimised. Finally, in all policymaking, Whites knew what was good for Blacks. Advocates of 'protection' came to distinguish between 'full-bloods' (who were thought to be dying out) and 'half-castes', 'quadroons' and 'octoroons' (who were thought to be proliferating). As the Aboriginal population became more hybrid, the policy implications of hybridity remained controversial, though it became common to remove children of mixed descent from their natural 'Aboriginal' parents in the hope that their 'white side' would flourish.

The following 'experts' in Aboriginal ways were among those who devised and ran these regimes of 'protection'.

A Meston (1851–1924) was a parliamentarian and a journalist whose study of Aborigines helped to persuade the Queensland government to pass the 1897 Aborigines Protection and Restriction of the Sale of Opium Act. The Act regulated employment, marriage and the relocation of Aborigines to residential institutions. Meston recommended the systematic management of the Aboriginal population, including setting aside land as 'reserves'. WE Roth (1861–1933) served as a protector in the Queensland system and contributed to the Act's extensive amendment in 1901. From 1904 to 1906, while chief protector, he reviewed Western Australia's Aboriginal policies. He advocated setting aside large reserves for Aborigines. WB Spencer (1860–1929) was a biologist at Melbourne University whose research, from 1894, came to include the Aborigines of the Northern Territory. Shortly after the Commonwealth took over the Northern Territory in 1911, Spencer became chief protector of Aborigines for a year and wrote a report advocating a mixture of institutions for Aborigines whose way of life had been undermined by contact with non-Aborigines, and reserves for those people, remote from towns and cities, who had not yet been 'spoiled'. Adelaide-based H Basedow (1881–1933), anthropologist, medical practitioner, geologist, and for a short time also the Northern Territory's chief protector, was another advocate of the large, remote reserve as a device for delaying the degradation of Aboriginal society.

The influence of such experts is evident in the fact that between 1918 and 1920, the Commonwealth, South Australian and Western Australian governments declared three contiguous reserves in central Australia. A leading concern for anthropologists between the wars was to advocate additions to these remote reserves and to ensure their inviolability. Publicly and privately, Adelaide University's Board for Anthropological Research advocated the extension of the Central Australian reserves. When an inquiry into a police killing of an Aboriginal man in 1935 recommended that the Commonwealth recruit an anthropologist as a patrol officer, TGH Strehlow got this job and became yet another advocate of the remote reserve. At the same time, when the people of Arnhem Land killed a policeman and some visiting Japanese fishermen, the Commonwealth asked for advice about how best to respond from anthropologist D Thomson. Thomson's 1937 report insisted that the Arnhem Land Reserve (declared in 1931) remain inviolate. O Pink, though not as credible to authorities as her more masculine and less eccentric colleagues, was another notable anthropologist advocate of the reserve in the 1930s.

Up to World War 2, the most important policy impact of anthropologists' advice to Australian governments was to secure remote reserves, mostly in northern and central Australia, as 'sanctuaries' for Aboriginal people not yet disturbed or dispossessed. Although these experts did not dispute that Aboriginal customs were doomed, they were unsure how long such a decline would take. Reserves were of indefinite duration partly because these advocates were unable to articulate a theory of social change. When Australian governments began to acknowledge 'land rights' (in various legislation from 1966 to 1991), it was relatively simple, politically, to grant Aborigines title to these extensive reserves. That about 20 per cent of Australia's land mass is now under some form of Aboriginal title is a consequence, in part, of anthropologists' advice being accepted from the 1890s to the 1950s.

THE SOCIAL SCIENCE OF 'ASSIMILATION'

First, the reserves had to withstand the challenge of 'assimilation', an idea whose popularity was increased by war. The labour shortage of World War 2 was met, in the north and centre, by the Army recruiting Aborigines (mostly to non-combatant roles). Observing the native labour camps, some anthropologists, including the

University of Sydney's Professor AP Elkin, noticed how quickly and enthusiastically Aborigines had changed from hunter-gatherer to useful citizen. Added to observations that, before the war's outbreak, Aborigines had not stayed within their reserves, this perception of Aborigines' rapid learning contributed to a reconsideration of reserves. Were they not a dereliction of the responsibility to uplift and to assimilate? In 1946–47, when the Australian public debated whether or not the reserves of central Australia should be included in a new rocket-testing range, Elkin, a member of the Chifley government's Rocket Range Committee, argued that all devices for keeping Aborigines apart would eventually have to be dismantled. Under the new policy of 'assimilation' there was no long-term future for reserves, and in some southern regions (notably in Victoria and New South Wales) authorities had already begun to extinguish reserves and to disperse their enclave communities into the wider Australian population.

Assimilation policies brought their own problems and controversies; for example, in 1959, when Elkin criticised the coerciveness of the Commonwealth's programs in the Northern Territory (Rowse 1998). Addressing a widespread sense of policy malaise, in May 1964, the Social Science Research Council of Australia appointed CD Rowley to be Director of a multi-author project on 'Aborigines in Australian Society' that produced 14 books between 1970 and 1980. Here are some examples of their recommendations.

Schapper, in Western Australia, recommended: that there be no specialist Department of Native Welfare, so that all Departments would have to learn to service Aborigines; and a schedule should be set for the closure of missions, reserves and hostels. A Social Planning Council with elected Aboriginal membership should be established in the Office of the Western Australian Premier. Governments should set targets for integration: 'the children of all Aborigines first married in 1971 and later will be reared *by their parents* as independent persons fully integrated in the mainstream of Australian society' (Schapper 1970: 144). Policy progress would depend on White political will and Aboriginal involvement in 'decision making from the grass roots to the top' (Schapper 1970: 144).

Broom and Jones asserted that, rather than dying out, the Aboriginal population 'will at least double in size within twenty years, and treble within thirty'. They saw urgency in these figures: while 'the cost of advancement is now high', 'it is less than it will be at any time in the next few decades' (Broom and Jones 1973: 72). Noting the absurdity of Australia importing labour when it had Aboriginal labour in excess, they urged governments to divert resources from helping migrants to helping Aborigines. Indigenous Australians should choose their degree of integration, but they emphasised how difficult were such choices to make. On education, they called for 'literacy programs and adult education, for pre-primary schooling, for special vernacular schools, for concentration on the late primary years where a drop in motivation and performance often occurs, for an emphasis on integrated schooling, or the identification and fostering of highly talented tertiary school prospects' (Broom and Jones 1973: 22).

Rowley's authors welcomed Aborigines' 'urbanisation'. Gale's study of the urbanisation of South Australian Aborigines was suffused with a positive view of its cultural effects. In the rural regions, Aborigines were subject to discrimination by non-Aborigines and they were sunk in their own squalor. Rural life was their past, city life their future. Movement to the city gave them social mobility, and, she reported, they liked it (Gale 1972: 1, 5, 12 and 27). Writing in the context of the minerals boom of the late 1960s, Rowley argued that new towns, or old towns with a new economic rationale, could be and should be where Aboriginal people, hitherto isolated on missions and settlements, would now acquire the skills to become part of Australian society. White Australians had tended to 'frustrate' Aboriginal urbanisation, he complained. 'A prime purpose' of reformed policy 'must be to open up the way for Aboriginal re-location, resulting from Aboriginal choice' (Rowley 1970: 29).

Rowley's authors indicated that social scientists lacked data on Indigenous Australians. The 1966 Census was the first to release data on Aborigines in terms similar to those for other Australians, thus making possible systematic comparison of Aboriginal well-being with the well-being of the Australian population as a whole. Finding the Census inadequate, Broom and Jones remarked of Aboriginal affairs administration that 'The management of a rubbish tip is more carefully monitored' (Broom and Jones 1973: 75). For Stanner, 'the very absence of more precise information is itself the best evidence of past indifference' (Stanner 1970: vi–ix).

The Rowley Project initiated the engagement of social sciences other than anthropology with the issues of Indigenous public policy. Indeed, none of the authors recruited to the Project was an anthropologist (though anthropology had been part of the training of the public servant Jeremy Long). Rowley was convinced that what anthropologists knew had little to do with understanding Aborigines' contemporary behaviour.

> If from their origins there are indeed some cultural predispositions, as well there may be, it is not necessary to postulate these as the *cause* of Aboriginal actions and attitudes; these may be adequately accounted for by historical and economic factors and by social factors arising from the relationship of the group with government and with non-Aboriginal society (Rowley 1970: 173).

The agronomist Schapper argued that 'studies for social and economic planning are properly within the scope of the professional economist, regardless of the ethnic heritage of the people involved. However, where plans are to embrace persons in another culture or sub-culture such as Aborigines, special care is required to ensure that proposals are in accord with findings and assessments of the social sciences' (Schapper 1970: xi). According to anthropologist Ruth Fink, anthropologists and administrators responsible for 'assimilation' had developed:

mutual antipathy, since they feel their interests to lie at cross-purposes. The practical administrator usually thinks that the anthropologist is interested only in tribal matters and suspects him of having naïve views about how administrations should be run. The anthropologist, on the other hand, is inclined to fear that his colleagues will label him with the epithet 'social engineer' if he concerns himself with social problems rather than 'pure' research' (Fink 1965: 419).

This obituary for a policy-relevant anthropology was premature. In the late 1960s, Aborigines' defence of their reserve lands against mining put 'land rights' on the policy agenda, and when governments responded to their actions with 'land rights' legislation, they drew on anthropology. Anthropologists now play an important part in the legal processes by which Aborigines' land claims (including native title) are validated.

Anthropology also has potential comparative advantage in enhancing understanding of the thousands of Indigenous organisations that we know as 'the Indigenous Sector' that might maintain its policy relevance. Of importance here, for example, is the notion of 'cultural match' between Western and customary forms in the effective governance of such organisations. Certainly, we can see the hand of anthropology in the origins of the Indigenous Sector. The most important policy product of the Rowley Project was the *Aboriginal Councils and Associations Act 1976*. Rowley argued in 1970 that if Aborigines were to become politically and legally effective, they must do so as corporations, not only as individuals. 'A program involving social change must deal with the social group,' he wrote (Rowley 1970: 417). This influential advice gave policy-relevant expression to Elkin's longstanding cautions against individualistic versions of 'assimilation'. In 1944: 'Group – or community – life is of fundamental importance to persons of Aboriginal descent.' In 1951: 'The Aborigines must move up in groups'. In 1959: 'group life' and 'continuity with the past' are 'essential for a people's well-being' (quoted in Rowse 1998: 125,

128 and 129). Now that the Indigenous Sector exists as the vehicle of so much service delivery and as the unit of ownership of land and other assets, anthropology is one of several disciplines illuminating the emergent political culture of Aboriginal Australians (Martin and Finlayson 1996; Rowse 2001; Schwab 1998).

THE RISE OF SOCIOECONOMIC EQUALITY AS A POLICY GOAL

The 1966 Census was the first complete enumeration of what was then understood to be the Indigenous population, yielding data with which to compare the education and occupations of 'Aborigines' and 'all Australians' (Broom and Jones 1973). However, the 1971 Census introduced a new definition of 'Indigenous' by asking people whether they identify as Aboriginal, or Torres Strait Islander, or neither. Used until 1991 (in 1996 a category of mixed Aboriginal–Torres Strait Islander was added), the 1971 definition became the basis of long-term comparison of the socioeconomic status of the Indigenous population of Australia with the total population of Australia. Social indicators from the five-yearly census have informed policy development and evaluation.

A study sponsored by the federal Department of Aboriginal Affairs (DAA) used 1971 Census data to measure Indigenous inequality (Altman and Nieuwenhuysen 1979: 1–21). Focusing on the enumerated Aboriginal population (excluding Torres Strait Islanders) of just over 100 000 identifiers (less than 1 per cent of the national population), Altman and Nieuwenhuysen showed that Aborigines were very young and that they were much more likely than non-Aborigines to be living in remote, rural and small urban areas. Their education status was low: 25 per cent of Aboriginal adults had never attended school compared to less than 1 per cent for the general population. Labour market participation rates were low, unemployment rates high, and Aboriginal people held relatively low-paying unskilled jobs. Income estimates did not exist in 1971, but with high dependency ratios and with low rates of employment, Aborigines' incomes must have been low by Australian standards.

Home ownership was low, and private dwellings were overcrowded and lacked basic facilities; 18 per cent of Aboriginal people lived in improvised dwellings compared to 0.4 per cent for the general population. Infant mortality rates were far higher and life expectancy far lower for Aboriginal people. This study had little impact on policy, but it demonstrated to social scientists what was analytically possible when using official statistics from large data sets. The analysis confirmed policy practitioners' impression that Indigenous circumstances were regionally diverse.

The DAA sponsored further research in 1978–82, published as *The Aboriginal Economy in Town and Country* (Fisk 1985). Mixing 1981 Census data and case study material, Fisk underlined the high dependence of Aborigines on the many public-sector subventions. Such portraits of deep-rooted economic dependency stimulated the recently elected Hawke government to appoint the Committee of Review of Aboriginal Employment and Training Programs chaired by the late Mick Miller. Miller's committee included a social scientist (HC Coombs) and an Indigenous educationalist (MA Bin-Sallik), as well as government officers. Informed by Fisk's 1981 census analysis, a review secretariat with diverse field-based and Canberra-based policy and program delivery experience, numerous submissions, field visits, community consultation and specially commissioned studies by social scientists, the Miller Report was long and rigorous. The 164 recommendations went to a Commonwealth government that was concerned with social justice (see Hawke and Howe 1990). The result was the Aboriginal Employment Development Policy (AEDP), announced in 1987. The AEDP added little to the range of programs established by the Whitlam (1972–75) and Fraser (1975–83) governments. However, it dedicated much more money to these programs, over five years. The AEDP aspired to 'equity', defined as 'statistical equality' between Indigenous and other Australians by the year 2000 in employment, education and income (Altman and Sanders 1991). The Hawke government sought 'a shift from the welfare dependency of the past towards measures to enhance Aboriginal economic independence' (Commonwealth of Australia 1987: iii).

The Miller Report's last recommendation was for a Commonwealth Bureau of Aboriginal Economic Research (modelled on the Bureau of Labour Market Research) (Miller 1985: 423). The AEDP did not include such a Bureau, but the government helped to establish the Centre for Aboriginal Economic Policy Research (CAEPR) at the ANU in 1990. With help from the Academy of the Social Sciences in Australia (ASSA), CAEPR convened a workshop to discuss how to use Census data to review the AEDP's progress (Altman 1991). The workshop demonstrated that the AEDP had underestimated its task. Indigenous population growth meant that employment equality by 2001 would require a threefold growth in Indigenous jobs. Notwithstanding Miller's realism, the AEDP had not taken into account the high proportion of the Indigenous population living in rural and remote regions, the historical legacy of neglect, the youthful age structure of the population, and cultural difference. Sanders (1991) predicted that the government's pursuit of statistical equality in employment and income status between Aborigines and other Australians by the year 2000 was 'destined to fail'. Data from the 2001 Census confirm his prediction. (See final column in Table 9.3.)

TABLE **9.1** *Socioeconomic outcomes for Indigenous Australians, 1971–2001*

VARIABLE	1971	1981	1991	2001
Unemployment rate (% labour force)	9.0	24.6	30.8	20.0
Employment to population ratio (% adults)	42.0	35.7	37.1	41.7
Labour force participation rate (% adults)	46.1	47.3	53.5	52.1
Full-time employment (% adults)	32.9	19.5	21.9	21.6
Private-sector employment (% adults)	29.7	17.2	20.5	22.9
Median income in $2001 – Individual	n.a.	187.5	211.0	212.6
Median income in $2001 – Household	n.a.	676.5	653.1	787.1
Home owner or purchasing (% population)	26.1	19.7	19.1	26.8
Household size	4.6	4.1	4.0	3.4
Never attended school (% adults)	22.7	10.7	5.1	3.2
15–24-year-olds attending educational institution (% of non-secondary students)	n.a.	6.8	16.0	25.9
Post-school qualification (% adults)	3.2	5.0	9.5	18.2
Population aged over 55 years (%)	7.3	6.4	6.2	6.7

NOTE 'n.a'. means that the data were not available in that year.
SOURCE Altman, Biddle and Hunter (2004)

TABLE **9.2** *Socioeconomic outcomes for non-Indigenous Australians, 1971–2001*

VARIABLE	1971	1981	1991	2001
Unemployment rate (% labour force)	1.6	5.8	11.4	7.2
Employment to population ratio (% adults)	57.8	58.2	56.3	58.9
Labour force participation rate (% adults)	58.8	61.8	63.6	63.4
Full-time employment (% adults)	48.7	44.3	38.9	38.1
Private-sector employment (% adults)	45.6	41.0	40.6	48.0
Median income in $2001 – Individual	n.a.	341.0	342.0	379.7
Median income in $2001 – Household	n.a.	937.7	853.6	1009.8
Home owner or purchasing (% population)	70.5	73.4	70.2	72.9
Household size	3.4	3.1	2.9	2.6
Never attended school (% adults)	0.6	0.7	1.0	1.0
15–24-year-olds attending educational institution (% of non-secondary students)	n.a.	17.9	46.2	59.9
Post-school qualification (% adults)	23.7	27.7	32.3	41.6
Population aged over 55 years (%)	17.1	18.6	19.6	22.0

NOTE 'n.a'. means that the data were not available in that year.
SOURCE Altman, Biddle and Hunter (2004)

TABLE **9.3** *Ratio of Indigenous to non-Indigenous outcomes, 1971–2001*

VARIABLE	1971	1981	1991	2001
Unemployment rate (% labour force)	5.44	4.22	2.70	2.79
Employment to population ratio (% adults)	0.73	0.61	0.66	0.71
Labour force participation rate (% adults)	0.78	0.77	0.84	0.82
Full-time employment (% adults)	0.68	0.44	0.56	0.57
Private-sector employment (% adults)	0.65	0.42	0.50	0.48
Median income in $2001 – Individual	n.a.	0.55	0.62	0.56
Median income in $2001 – Household	n.a.	0.72	0.77	0.78
Home owner or purchasing (% population)	0.37	0.27	0.27	0.37
Household size	1.33	1.32	1.38	1.31
Never attended school (% adults)	39.32	14.42	5.21	3.14
15–24-year-olds attending educational institution (% of non-secondary students)	n.a.	0.38	0.35	0.43
Post-school qualification (% adults)	0.13	0.18	0.30	0.44
Population aged over 55 years (%)	0.43	0.34	0.31	0.31

NOTE 'n.a.' means that the data were not available in that year.
SOURCE Altman, Biddle and Hunter (2004)

In the 1980s and 1990s, governments strove to give social scientists the data that the Rowley authors had lacked. In addition to the five-yearly census, the ABS conducted the National Aboriginal and Torres Strait Islander Survey in 1994; the National Aboriginal and Torres Strait Islander Social Survey in 2002; and the Community

Housing and Infrastructure Needs Survey for approximately 1300 discrete communities in 1992, 1999 and 2001. The ABS improved sampling within the National Health Survey framework; and state and territory governments standardised their registration of Indigenous births and deaths. Here are five examples of research that made illuminating use of these new data.

1   In 1993, J Taylor made a comparative assessment of socioeconomic change between 1986 and 1991 censuses (Taylor 1993a; 1993b). He confirmed that the AEDP had underestimated its challenge.

2   In 1997 and 1998, two studies sponsored by ATSIC (Taylor and Altman 1997; Taylor and Hunter 1998) projected the growth of the Indigenous working age population, stimulating further government labour market interventions in the Indigenous Employment Program launched in 1999.

3   Two ABS monographs by labour economists AE Daly (1995) and B Hunter (2004) argued that governments must adapt main-stream policy instruments if they wished to overcome Indigenous economic disadvantage.

4   In the 1990s, by measuring the unmet needs of Indigenous Australians, social scientists began to estimate the amounts that governments should be spending on services. In 1994, R Jones used 1991 Census data to estimate the housing backlog for Indigenous Australians; he then estimated the cost of addressing it (Jones 1994). A team led by health economist J Deeble demonstrated significant under-expenditure on Indigenous health services (Deeble et al. 1998). M Neutze led a team that measured the extent of under-funding in programs directed at employment, education, housing and health (Neutze, Sanders and Jones 1999).

5   In late 1999, the Howard government asked the Commonwealth Grants Commission (CGC) whether the distribution of Commonwealth Indigenous-specific program expenditures reflected the different needs among Indigenous Australians. The CGC accepted advice from social scientists that it could not

address this issue without also considering many other factors such as Indigenous/non-Indigenous differentials and the role of the state and territories governments in service delivery to Indigenous people (CGC 2001).

Research now contradicts the popular view that governments spend too much on Indigenous Australians; if we consider their measured needs, and apply the principle of equality of outcome, we know that governments spend far too little. In highlighting practices of inter-governmental cost-shifting, this finding may have helped to persuade COAG (Council of Australian Governments) to commit to a 'whole-of-government' approach (Shergold 2004). To monitor expenditure levels on disadvantaged and relatively politically powerless Indigenous minorities across nine governments is a huge challenge to Australian fiscal federalism.

In recent years, the Commonwealth government has claimed to prefer 'practical reconciliation' to 'symbolic' policies. Defining 'practical reconciliation' in terms that social science can measure, such as closing the gaps between Indigenous and non-Indigenous indices of health, education, housing and employment, the Howard government, perhaps learning from the mistakes of the Hawke government, has not specified the period in which these goals are to be achieved. This is more than cautious; it is timid. Perhaps such timidity is an effect of the policy pessimism that is inspired by, for example, the persistence of a 25-year gap between Indigenous and non-Indigenous median ages of death (Ring and Brown 2002). Alarming as that gap may be, the available Census data show that there have been some successes.

Tables 9.1, 9.2 and 9.3 bring together carefully matched information from the 1971, 1981, 1991 and 2001 censuses. The tables show changes in Indigenous absolute and relative wellbeing across 13 social indicators. According to some of the labour market, income and housing indicators, Indigenous wellbeing has improved since 1971. The most striking improvements have been in Indigenous access to formal education. Policies promoting

Indigenous education have been effective (though there is further to go). However, we should note what these figures do and do not reveal. They do reveal a distinction between absolute and relative improvements in Indigenous wellbeing. Take education, for example. Because the non-Indigenous population has also been increasing its commitment to formal education, the *relative* position of Indigenous Australians has not improved as much as it might have. What is not revealed in these tables is regional difference. It is much easier to assemble national aggregate data to deliver a national 'report card' than to show the disparities among Indigenous Australians. Furthermore, census data are limited in their ability to reflect changes in Indigenous household and family composition over time, in part because of mixed households and in part because of changed identification.

Notwithstanding such reservations, Tables 9.1, 9.2 and 9.3 show that in the 1990s, Indigenous wellbeing did not improve as much as one would hope during a period of vigorous economic growth and with a policy-setting that aimed to close the gaps between Indigenous and non-Indigenous socioeconomic status (see Altman and Hunter 2003; Hunter 2004; Productivity Commission 2003; ABS 2003a, 2004a; Jonas 2004).

The Commonwealth's criteria of policy success are now so clear that any research by social scientists on this subject cannot avoid being implicated in political controversy. The relationship between social scientists and government has thus become more uncomfortable. Meanwhile, social scientists are collaborating with policy-makers in many Commonwealth, state and territory agencies, and with regional Indigenous organisations. And social scientists outside the academy are writing discussion papers sponsored and published by 'think tanks' such as the Centre for Independent Studies and the Menzies Research Centre. Although most such papers have not been peer reviewed before publication, they receive as much attention (perhaps more) in the press and Parliament as the refereed social sciences research from the academy.

THE SOCIAL SCIENCE OF 'OUTCOMES'

Although we uphold the relevance of social science to Indigenous public policy, we do not think that it can answer the big political questions about the success and the failure of policies. For example, in 1968, J Barnes (then an anthropologist at the ANU) asked whether we could measure the 'outcome' of 'assimilation' policy. The 'individuals who have successfully made the transition from one community to the other have ... endeavoured to conceal their part-Aboriginal ancestry. They do not appear as 'former Aboriginals' in any official statistics ...' (Barnes 1968: 44). In the 1990s, was the 'failure' of the AEDP also its success? Two goals were stated for that policy: choice and equality. Indigenous Australians would have a choice about the nature and degree of their involvement in the nation's economic activities; and as a result of their involvement, the 'social indicators' of Indigenous and non-Indigenous wellbeing would show convergence in the patterns of employment, education, income, and economic independence from the State. If these Indigenous 'outcomes' were not equal by 2000, but were nonetheless the result, in part, of Indigenous choices, then are we to conclude that the AEDP policy succeeded (Aborigines made choices) or failed (because inequalities remained) (Rowse 2002a: 2–19 and 24–8)?

Now we have statistics seeking to measure 'practical reconciliation'. In April 2002, the Council of Australian Governments (COAG) commissioned the Steering Committee for the Review of Commonwealth/State Service Provision to develop indicators of Indigenous disadvantage on which there could be regular published reports. The Steering Committee Report set out an elaborate framework of statistical comparison. Its choice of variables was based partly on a causal model of disadvantage, highlighting the domestic settings of child-rearing, and the interactions between family and school. Ostensibly, in the Steering Committee's framework we see social science defining Indigenous realities in more detail than ever before. However, the Steering Committee reported that while those whom it consulted emphasised 'the need for adequate government services', so too did they underline 'the need for families to ensure that their children were properly fed and lived in a nurturing environment. Parental responsibility, respect for elders and community leadership were all seen as major factors' (Productivity Commission 2003: 2.12). Yet 'parental responsibility, respect for elders, and community leadership' are not measured variables in the Productivity Commission's statistical framework. The Steering Committee did not propose a causal model that would weight governments', parents' and communities' discharge of their responsibilities as factors affecting measured equality. It is one thing to measure quantitative relationships among variables, and quite another to depict relationships among agents such as individuals, domestic groups, formal Indigenous organisations, formal government organisations and private companies. Governments and commentators (including Indigenous commentators) continue to account for Indigenous circumstances in terms that include (implicit or explicit) conceptions of human agency. For example, the language of 'mutual obligation', favoured by the Howard government, invites us to consider policy failure as a result of someone not meeting their 'obligations'. A social science that is coy about human agency, or that fails to theorise it, will be shoved aside in political debate by political language that is saturated with contentious implications of agency and responsibility. A social science that imagines social processes as relationships among variables is an amoral, technicist fantasy, perhaps a necessary aid to political reasoning, but not to be confused with political reasoning.

CONCLUSION

We began this chapter by highlighting a tension between the social science disciplines of economics and anthropology in their respective approaches to Indigenous public policy. The former emphasises the need for socioeconomic equality, the latter sees potential incompatibility between such a policy goal and Indigenous cultural differences and choice. The competition between these two influential disciplines may also be a conversation – with benefits to Indigenous policymaking.

From 2005 new administrative arrangements in Indigenous affairs include the abolition of ATSIC as a national and regional Indigenous representative organisation. The Howard government is seeking to develop bilateral agreements with the states to ensure a 'joined up' approach that would eliminate inter-governmental cost shifting and neglect. At the same time, the government is proposing that Indigenous-specific programs, and possibly other services, be delivered to discrete Indigenous communities via 'shared responsibility' agreements. This in turn suggests that Indigenous policy may be applied differently in different regions. The need to disaggregate 'outcomes' by region will pose new challenges for social scientists, both in informing policymaking and in evaluation at regional and sub-regional levels. Fortunately, the proposed Indigenous households survey program will allow a more thorough statistical analysis of outcomes at the sub-national level than has been previously possible.

While the current policy rhetoric of shared responsibility agreements on a community-by-community basis will resonate with anthropology's focus on the particular characteristics of each community, we believe that anthropology is also positioned to be a critic of some deeper assumptions of current policy. The Howard government favours 'practical reconciliation' – a goal defined in terms of socioeconomic similarity. This approach ignores a point made by anthropology: that to change peoples' forms of economic activity is to transform them culturally. Some anthropological studies of regional economic activity argue that certain economic adaptations by Indigenous Australians embody complex trade-offs between peoples' desires for cultural continuity and for material prosperity (Altman 2004). It is all too easy for those inspired by 'practical reconciliation' to dismiss these adaptations as mere failures in economic development; to do so is to ignore the cultural needs that these adaptations meet. Anthropology may be more in sympathy with another aspect of current policy: the emphasis on community governance. Anthropologists' focus on the 'local' enables it to help to 'broker' community-based agreements with governments that reflect local aspirations. That is, anthropology may assist in formulating those aspirations in terms that program officers can recognise as consistent with their program's aims (for an example see Rowse 2002b: 346–52).

The challenge facing disciplines, such as economics, that use census and other ABS secondary data is to explore the possible operational meanings of 'equality' in some extremely remote, difficult and structurally constrained circumstances. Generalised models of socioeconomic equality must be realistically informed by cultural, historical and regional particularities. Both quantitative and qualitative social research will have to be considered if policy is to honour the two ideals of 'equality' and 'plurality'.

10

LIBERTY, SECURITY
AND
THE STATE

Jenny Hocking[1]

> History, and not only ancient history, shows that in countries
> where democratic institutions have been unconstitutionally super-
> seded, it has been done not seldom by those holding the executive
> power (Dixon 1951).

In March 2005 a remarkable piece of legislation was presented to
the British Parliament by Prime Minister Tony Blair's Labour
government. The Prevention of Terrorism Bill would suspend
habeus corpus, that defining feature of the rule of law that there
can be no deprivation of liberty without trial, and sought to hand
a government minister the power to place British citizens under
indefinite house arrest. The Bill was to replace the existing detention without trial provisions in the *Anti-Terrorism, Crime and
Security Act 2001* in response to a decision by the Law Lords in
December 2004, which declared detention without trial illegal and
in which Lord Hoffman suggested that 'The real threat to the life
of the nation ... comes not from terrorism but from laws such as
these' (Bunyan 2005).

The intention of the Prevention of Terrorism Bill was therefore, and unashamedly, to circumvent the ruling of the Lords in

this respect. In place of the outright prison detention contained in the *Anti-Terrorism, Crime and Security Act 2001*, the Prevention of Terrorism Bill proposed the use of 'control orders' (including 'tagging' and indefinite 'house arrest') to be based on intelligence assessments drawn up by MI5 and authorised by the Home Secretary. Those held would have been charged with no offence and could not know the evidence against them. Although the Bill had been strongly criticised from several quarters, it also had widespread popular support and received a largely quiescent, timorous, parliamentary consideration, even from those who professed principled opposition.

Politically, opposition to the Bill appeared clear and unassailable. The Liberal Democrat leader Charles Kennedy publicly expressed his party's concerns, 'We are not about to surrender fundamental principles', and attended neither the debate nor the first vote in the House of Commons. The Shadow Attorney-General, the Conservative Party's Dominic Grieve, was equally appalled: the Bill was, 'unpleasant, repellent and disgusting'. Yet Grieve and his party then voted for it in the House. And lawyers, despite the concerns expressed by a former senior member that, 'the defendant is not to be told the nature of the case against him, or the facts that are going to be urged against him, or the basis of the decision', nodded sagely as they noted the requirement that the judiciary would rubber stamp precisely that.[2] There could scarcely have been a more powerful statement of the capitulation of judicial independence to executive decree in the name of countering terrorism.

The UK Prevention of Terrorism Bill is just the latest in a long line of security measures which, like those of many other countries, have progressively whittled away fundamental legal protections primarily through an immense expansion of executive power. For the experience of the Prevention of Terrorism Bill, as dramatic in substance as it has been in process, is unusual in neither respect. Many Western nations, including Australia, have passed similar legislation in the three years after September 11, each further cementing the interests of national security, diminishing legal and political rights, and enhancing executive power and each enjoying an unusually truncated process of Parliamentary scrutiny with minimal public debate. In this respect the 'war on terror' has combined international adventurism with domestic subjection, fundamentally recasting both the relationships and structures of governance and the conceptions of citizen that both underpin and define democracy.

SECURITY, DEMOCRACY AND THE STATE

In the 'war on terror', a war without an object and without hope therefore of conclusion, the legal and political landscape has changed dramatically, nationally and internationally. The elevation of the interests of national security above individual rights and legal processes has been its most remarkable transformation. The unprecedented diminution of legal rights has been matched by the equally unprecedented expansion in executive power and a corresponding reduction in the efficacy of parliamentary oversight and judicial review. Yet, the emergence of this as a recognised public policy field has been, at best, slow. Indeed, the first incarnation of counter-terrorism as a significant policy field came with what I have termed the 'first wave' of counter-terrorism developments in the mid-1970s – a dramatic restructuring of the policing function to accommodate a militarised special force capacity, a renewed peace-time function for the military through the SAS and an involvement in the training of police special squads, an expansion of domestic intelligence collection around perceived terrorists rather than the Cold-war notion of subversives, and a detailed strategy for media control in the event of a terrorist incident (Hocking 1993). The few works to have examined these early Australian developments were predominantly legal and concentrated on specific aspects – ASIO, policing and the use of the military during peacetime (Lee et al. 1995; Raeburn 1978; Blackshield 1978; Beddie and Moss 1982). Historical analyses of security services and policing, and criminological appraisals of the use of force in peacetime, have similarly concentrated on specific elements of national security developments (Cain 1983; McCulloch 2000) and there has been little providing a comprehensive sense of this as a rapidly growing policy field.

The events of 11 September 2001 and the subsequent 'war on terror' have catapulted counter-terrorism into the limelight as the policy field of the moment, a fact not lost on the Australian Attorney-General, Philip Ruddock. He has noted that 'counter terrorism issues have moved to the centre stage of public and political debate'.[3] The globalised, networked construction of a new legal framework that allows for the imposition of executive detention without trial, the compromising of the right to independent legal representation and constraints on public communication on security matters have marked this as the most significant contemporary public policy field. Its implications spread beyond the immediate effects on national criminal justice systems to challenge the very nature of the democratic state itself.

Lepsius has similarly noted in the German instance that the issues relating to civil rights and security in the criminal justice response to terrorism had already been debated during the first wave of counter-terrorism of the 1970s. But Lepsius also recognises the critical distinctions between the two periods, in the nature both of terrorism and of counter-terrorism, proposing two novel aspects to the nature of terrorism and the nature of the State's response to it in the contemporary, second wave. Whereas previously,

> ... [i]t was possible to individualize terrorism; this was deemed no longer possible after September 11 ... Terrorism has become de-personalized and deregionalized. The new threat is global and can no longer be limited to a few perpetrators. Only on the basis of this fundamental perception can one comprehend why this was declared to be a qualitatively new level of threat and why certain legislative measures were taken. The evaluation of the relationship between civil liberties and security has to be seen in this context (Lepsius 2004: 438–9).

Most importantly, the nature of the changes is such that Lepsius asks, 'Do these measures merely represent a quantitative increase in the number of fundamental rights violations, or does this development herald a qualitative change in the relationship of freedom and security? In other words: Does the new perception of terrorism mirror a principle change in the adjustment of freedom and security?' (Lepsius 2004: 454). We might also ask, does this matter?

In March 2002 the Howard government put forward seven major legislative initiatives to 'allow terrorist organizations to be stopped and potential terrorist activity to be stopped before that activity has actually taken place' (Alderson 2002). This aspect of pre-emption is not only central to the security initiatives, but is the basis for many of the concerns about them. Two 'omnibus' pieces of legislation, each of which in turn amended several other Acts, formed the core of this legislative package. First, the *Security Legislation Amendment Act 2002 (No. 2)*, described by the Democrats Senator Greig as 'an ambit claim for arbitrary executive power at the expense of civil rights and fundamental principles of law'.[4] The Act defined a 'terrorist act' for the first time in Australian (Commonwealth) law, created new categories of 'terrorism offences', introduced means for executive proscription of 'terrorist organisations' (originally proposed merely by ministerial fiat, subsequently amended to those listed by the UN as 'terrorist organisations'), and created derivative organisational crimes in relation to membership and other specified connections with such declared 'terrorist organisations' (see Hocking 2004a).

Second, in June 2003, the *Australian Security Intelligence Organization Legislation Amendment (Terrorism) Act 2003* (known as the *ASIO Act 2003*) allowed ASIO for the first time to operate within the policing sphere, to function in part as a police force, able to detain for up to seven days and to interrogate for up to 24 hours within that period, Australians not even suspected of involvement in a terrorist offence, but who 'may have information relating to a terrorism offence'. These provisions caused an outcry during parliamentary and committee investigation, since it was originally proposed that such detention be incommunicado, without access to lawyers and applicable to children as young as 10 years old (Hocking 2004b). With some amendments, ASIO's detention regime now applies to children from 16 years of age and then only if suspected of involvement in an offence; however, detention and interrogation can still be conducted without appropriate access to independent legal advice and, in some cases, incommunicado. Little wonder that the Parliamentary Joint Committee that examined the Bill described it as 'one of the most controversial pieces of legislation considered by parliament in recent times' and one which would 'undermine key legal rights and erode the civil liberties that make Australia a leading democracy'.[5]

Yet despite the impact of these Acts on fundamental aspects of democracy, an impact heightened by the passage of a further 17 security-related Acts since, there has been minimal public debate and scant media consideration. What little scrutiny there has been has come largely from within the law. Sustained analysis of these developments at the level both of public policy effects and broader transformation of the democratic state has been absent. When the government reluctantly put the original security package to review by Parliamentary committee, the call for submissions, procedurally minimised at two weeks, was advertised on the weekend of 23–24 March for final submissions by 5 April. This coincided precisely with the Easter holiday period (including school and university holidays) and the Jewish Festival of Passover – with six working days available for preparation and presentation of submissions on one of the most complex and significant legislative packages ever to come before the Australian parliament. In total it asked for comment on five separate pieces of legislation totalling more than 120 pages.

Nevertheless, the Committee received a remarkable 431 submissions from individuals, organisations and affected bodies such as ASIO and the Australian Federal Police. Submissions from legal bodies, civil liberties organisations, individual lawyers and academic lawyers predominated in the policy debate as they have in the literature. While the dominance of legal analyses has been well grounded in concerns for the protection of legal process and disputed constitutionality, its effect has been to highlight the minutiae of each legislative encroachment, further fuelling the lack of public understanding of and interest in the broader picture. Much of the analysis of these critical developments focused on the legislative adventures enacted in the aftermath of September 11, with an emphasis on ameliorating the worst excesses of these counter-terrorist developments by minimising their impact on legal and political rights and processes. This focus also helped generate what is now an unchallenged view, that there must be a (new) balance cast between the needs of national security and individual rights.

The view that a notional balance can be found between the needs of national security and individual rights has become one of the strongest rhetorical devices for garnering support for the impositions and derogations of the new security regime. It presupposes a particular conception of democracy and a particular conception of citizen, one in which rights do not inhere in every individual as immutable and fundamental *human* rights, but rather are deemed by the State and can be redeemed by it in times of crisis. The security of the State determines the security of its citizens and not the other way around. It is a view put more prosaically by Charles Clarke, the UK Home Secretary and the man responsible for deciding individual cases of home detention without trial. 'I'm all in favour of human rights, but I'm even more in favour of our national security being protected' (Clarke, in Bunyan 2005: 28, fn. 62). In this argued 'balance' between security and liberty, with the security of the individual seen as met by the security of the State, can be seen a reinscription of the absolutist State, a unification of State and citizens through crisis.

The view that protection of the institutions and form of the State is its most fundamental (sovereign) function was not sustainable with the rise of the parliamentary system in contemporary democratic states. The primary legitimacy of the legislature as the expression of a popular (representative) will has ensured that the executive functions no longer as an unfettered holder of discretionary power but as an agent of the legislature (Lustgarten 2004: 4). Yet a return to the earlier conception of the relationship between State and executive is reflected in the gradual shift towards executive dominance, at the expense of both parliamentary oversight and judicial review, of the field of national security during the twentieth century. Lustgarten argues that 'The great irony is that the coming of democracy has brought with it the quiescence of Parliament in the highest matters of state ... Issues of defence and foreign relations, which in the mid-twentieth century were subsumed under the general rubric "national security", are the areas about which Parliament receives the least information, and which it debates with diminished frequency and competence' (Lustgarten 2004: 6). This ceding of matters of national security to the executive expanded in the post-Cold war period with the collapsing of matters of 'terrorism' into the 'national security' rubric and what Lustgarten terms 'a habit of deference to executive power'. In the period since September 11, this 'habit of deference' has intensified around the demands of counter-terrorism. Yet, as Uhr notes, 'Parliament is least effective in contributing to national security when it retreats from active involvement in the processes of civil government, convinced by an assertive political executive that the security of the civil realm is best left in the hands of those responsible for the military realm' (Uhr 2004).

Politically this view reflects the argument that it is for the executive and not the judiciary to determine the requirements of national security. The extent to which 'the doctrine of security' can serve as the basis for an executive rather than a judicial determination in relation to matters deemed by the executive to be 'relevant to security', particularly the relevance of this doctrine in peace-time and the need for an argued link to 'national security' to be real and not illusory, has generated significant legal debate. This was the issue at the heart of the landmark High Court judgement in the *Communist Party Dissolution* case of 1951 in which the High Court interrupted the 'habit of deference' to executive power by ruling the Act unconstitutional since it usurped the principle of judicial review in its assumption of powers it did not have during peacetime (Hocking 2001: 48). The significance of this as a legal rupture in the relationship between the executive and the judiciary has been largely unmatched by any parallel debates within the social sciences.

In the contemporary security debate, the dominant rhetoric of 'balance' places differing types of rights against each other along a mythical scale. Yet the metaphor, seductive in its simplicity, is nonsense. For individual rights, positive rights, cannot be matched against a collective negative right of the State to protection, the latter being only understood in its breach and being termed a 'right' although better understood as an 'interest'. In what sense can it be argued that an individual's personal liberty, right to a trial or right to free association, can be set against the right of the State itself (and hence of all its citizens) to security? The artifice of 'balance' merely ensures the acceptance of the diminution of individual rights and protections in the face of an invocation of 'national security'. Attorney-General Philip Ruddock reiterates this view: 'the unavoidable fact is that any tightening of security arrangements does involve some diminution of rights' (quoted in Hocking 2004a: 335). As Lepsius describes it, 'security now achieved a more equal, if not even a higher constitutional justification' (Lepsius 2004: 436).

The focus on balance is, I have argued elsewhere, 'a flawed equation ... National security and individual liberties, far from being in competition with one another in a simplistic zero-sum game, are in fact mutually reinforcing. Rather than seeing national security and democracy as being in perpetual friction (as if each exists somehow independently yet in tension with the other), political and civil rights and a robust democratic process are the key elements in the maintenance of national security itself' (Hocking 2004a: 336). Above all, the construction of 'balance' presupposes a particular type of democracy that is itself transformative. It is a return to notions of the unity of the executive and the State, and the primacy of that interest above the rights and freedoms of its citizens. This is outside the realm of the separation of powers that is still maintained in all other spheres.

It is disconcerting that there has been no appropriate and substantive justification for the introduction of such significant measures. With the earliest measures the government's stated intention was simple – to combat a 'new level of threat' posed by terrorism in the post-September 11 environment. The shock of those events was such that little more needed to be said. Subsequent developments were similarly accompanied by assertion rather than by reasoned analysis and identification of recognisable failings in the existing counter-terrorism framework. Attorney-General Philip Ruddock, speaking of the Anti-Terrorism Bill in 2004 suggested that 'In the current environment, complacency is not an option ... It is now appropriate to improve the capability of Australia's law enforcement agencies to properly investigate these new terrorism offences'.[6] As Ruddock's remarks make clear, the current counter-terrorism response rests on a universalised notion of threat rather than any specific threat. In this way, the justification for extreme measures is shifted away from the present and into the fear of an unknown future. In this intellectual fortress in which anything is possible and therefore we must guard against everything, arguments for an expanded security sector are no longer based in present-day realities but in the threat of the unknown, and debate on these terms becomes difficult, if not impossible. Nevertheless, in discussing this raft of security measures, Attorney-General Ruddock has made clear the government's determination that, while enhancing security, these developments would not adversely affect democratic rights; 'the community should be protected from the threat of terrorism without unfairly or unnecessarily encroaching on the individual rights and liberties that are fundamental to our democratic system'.[7]

In a reversal of accepted change management practice, these legislative changes preceded any substantial review of either current security arrangements or changing threat levels, and without the consequent identification of areas of strength or areas requiring action. It was not until March 2004 that the federal government commissioned a White Paper on Terrorism to be undertaken by Les Luck, 'Counter-Terrorism Ambassador' with the Department of Foreign Affairs and Trade.[8] The White Paper was commissioned after the government had already spent nearly $2 billion over five years to enhance security arrangements and after Australia's counter-terrorism plans had been reconfigured and its legislative package cemented.[9] However, there is now a means through which further detailed debate and consideration can take place, particularly in relation to the operation of the ASIO Act. Following the substantial Senate amendment of the original ASIO Bill, a three-year sunset clause is in place, to be preceded by a process of review of the Act's provisions and enforcement. The Joint Committee on ASIO, AIS and DSD will also review the operation, effectiveness and implications of these amendments to ASIO's powers in early 2006.

Several aspects essential to informed policy development ought now to be addressed in order to facilitate this process of review: what has the Australian experience of terrorism been? What is the level of terrorist threat in Australia? What are Australia's existing powers and structures to counter terrorism and are they adequate to meet this level of threat? Such a fully informed debate, involving practitioners, policymakers and policy experts, would take the form of a security audit in which threat levels, performance indicators and appropriate measures are canvassed outside the political arena, yet involved with it. A particular focus should be the extent to which these measures have met the aim of enhancing security without impinging upon fundamental democratic rights and processes. These policy questions mirror the legal concerns regarding the introduction of exceptional measures, or the derogation from established criminal justice procedures, that such measures be proportional, appropriate and proximate as measures adopted only in times of crisis. Yet the overwhelming emphasis on legal considerations of the contemporary counter-terrorism framework – its impact on the rule of law, legal rights and process – has failed to fully identify the critical impact on democratic practice. The space for the social sciences to enter this debate lies in just this consideration. These legal requirements of proportionality, appropriateness and proximity need to be considered politically as much as legally, to be reviewed and analysed not only for their impact on established legal structures, but also for their transformation of the democratic state itself.

Two elements of the contemporary reinvigoration of executive power through counter-terrorism have already had a significant impact on democratic governance and provide a starting point for political rather than legal assessment. The first is the contraction of civil and legal rights, in particular freedoms of political association and participation, and the consequent compromising of aspects of the rule of law discussed above. A second, less widely remarked upon, element impacting on the capacity of an informed citizenry to fully participate in democratic practice is that of political communication.

THE CRIMINALISATION OF INFORMATION EXCHANGE

John Keane's optimistic view of 'communicative abundance' proposes a 'galaxy of communications' that 'has the effect of marginalizing representative government' through its vigorous '*symbolic* representation' (Keane 2002). However, despite the plethora of media outlets and forms that excite Keane in their democratising potential, constraints on aspects of information exchange in the realm of national security in general and counter-terrorism in particular, have channelled this apparent abundance into a homogeneous, secretive, authorised information flow. There are several aspects to the contraction of information exchange that have emerged over recent years around matters of national security, fuelled primarily by counter-terrorism: establishment of secret court hearings in matters of national security, denial of public disclosure of material for reasons of national security, criminalisation of the publication of information about ASIO, and the extension of the *Proceeds of Crimes Act* to encompass commercial public disclosure by those held in Guantanamo Bay.

Recent legislative developments contained in the coalition government's second major security package have diminished the institutions for public debate and criminalised aspects of information exchange.[10] Further amendments to the newly revamped ASIO Act were presented in late 2003. These have (among other things) imposed stringent secrecy provisions in relation to public disclosure of ASIO's detention regime. It is now illegal to disclose any information about ASIO's existing detention warrants while the warrant is in effect, including even the name or fact of an individual being detained. Such disclosure carries a penalty of five years of imprisonment. Further crimes relating to the disclosure of 'operational information' relating to ASIO's activities were also introduced and these are particularly broad since 'operational information' is defined as 'information that [ASIO] has or had'. Such disclosures carry a penalty of five years imprisonment if reported or otherwise disclosed within two years of the warranting period. It is now unclear whether reporting on any aspect of this controversial aspect of ASIO's activities would be to risk imprisonment. Attempts by the Greens to introduce a 'public interest' clause to protect journalists from prosecution in cases where national security information was not threatened by the publication of material were unsuccessful.

The ambitious, omnibus legislation of the *Anti-Terrorism Act 2004* has seen a further entrenching of these developments just months after the passage of the earlier security legislation. Through its amendment of the *Proceeds of Crime Act 2002*, the *Anti-Terrorism Act* allows for confiscation orders in relation to any profits gained from the commercial publication by those accused of foreign indictable offences, including those held but never charged and those held, charged and acquitted in such matters. The Act is quite specific that acquittal does not imply immunity from such orders: 'an acquittal does not affect the court's power to make a "literary proceeds" order' (Hocking 2004a: 333). Individuals are liable to confiscation orders even if the illegal conduct they had allegedly undertaken in a foreign country was not illegal in Australia at that time. The Act also recognises for the first time in Australian law the military tribunals operating in relation to inmates held in Guantanamo Bay, with explicit reference to 'the Military Order of 13 November 2001 made by the President of the United States of America and entitled "Detention, Treatment and Trial of Certain Non-Citizens in the War against Terrorism"'.

When the Bill was presented to parliament, it was widely noted that these provisions would ensure that, '[n]either David Hicks nor Mamdouh Habib, nor indeed any other Australians who are, in the future, held in Guantanamo Bay by American authorities, would be able to publish commercially any details of their detention, or their treatment, whether they are eventually charged, convicted, acquitted or even released without charge' (Hocking 2004a: 333–4). Given that details of torture, mistreatment and even death in other American-run facilities have emerged precisely because of such commercial publication, these provisions directly impact both on Habib's freedom of speech and on the public's ability to know and fully debate the nature of the conditions and treatment of detainees at Guantanamo Bay.

Following the release without charge of Mamdouh Habib by American authorities after two years of detention and his return to Australia, the government threatened to institute a confiscation order should Habib seek to profit from the publication of any details of his detention at Guantanamo Bay. The constitutional position of this Act in relation to Guantanamo Bay is by no means clear, on several grounds. Joo-Cheong Tham suggests that the impact of these provisions on freedom of speech may infringe the implied freedom of political communication, one of the few implied rights to have been recognised by the High Court. In that case, Justice Brennan remarked, 'Once it is recognised that a representative democracy is constitutionally prescribed, the freedom of discussion which is essential to sustain it is as firmly entrenched in the Constitution as the system of government which the Constitution expressly ordains' (cited in Barak 2002: 41). The power to punish without necessitating proper conviction also breaches the separation of powers: whether a constitutional issue flows from this is as yet untested, although clearly in the Communist Party Dissolution case it did. The justices in that case pointed to the absence of any such assumed power in peace-time. So the ascription of 'war' to the 'war on terror' could well be determinant if the 'war' is indeed accepted as real, and not illusory in the way that Menzies' 'Cold-war' allusions were. Furthermore, as Tham notes; 'If the government seeks to confiscate income that Habib earned through publicising conditions at Guantanamo Bay, a key factor for the court will be the public interest in making these conditions known'.[11]

These political and legal innovations have drastically affected the capacity for citizens to engage in the full and open political communication essential to democratic participation. As Ian Marsh notes (see Chapter 12), 'In a nutshell, an informed and engaged public realises the promise of liberal democracy and fulfils its ideal of citizenship'.

THE CODIFICATION OF TORTURE

Recent arguments for the legitimation of torture further underscore a paradigm shift within the democratic state. Alan Dershowitz has argued that the practice of torture should be codified as a structured, accountable tool in the 'war on terror'. Despite the absolute prohibition on the use of torture under the

International Covenant on Civil and Political Rights (ICCPR), Dershowitz suggests that 'torture warrants' could be used 'in order to wage the most effective battle against terrorism within the rule of law'.[12] Torture is one of the specified rights from which, the ICCPR indicates, derogation can never be permitted (Charlesworth 2003: 63).

The United States already circumvents the apparent prohibition on torture in two ways. First by torturing with impunity regardless, as has occurred in Abu Ghraib prison in Iraq and in 'the jurisdictional void' (McNally 2004: 79) of Guantanamo Bay. By mid-2004 at least 25 prisoners had died in US military custody in Iraq and Afghanistan, some of them directly at the hands of American personnel.[13] Mamdouh Habib has alleged Australian knowledge of, if not complicity in, the use of torture. Second, and more disconcertingly, the practice of torture is being realised through the process of rendition, where a captive subject under the command of the United States is 'rendered' up to another country that condones and practises torture, in order for that torture to take place.[14] In early 2005, the Pentagon 'rendered' three detainees from Guantanamo Bay to Afghanistan, Maldives and Pakistan. Out of sight, out of mind.[15]

These are examples of the morality of a regime that believes it can absolve its own illegality and impoverished humanity simply by a change of location. They are also an indication of the inevitability of further degradation and dehumanisation once such acts are accepted as an official norm. The broader consequence of a society in which torture is not only accepted, but formal policy, is the incitement to violence and indignity. Behaviour that is officially sanctioned becomes behaviour that is socially sanctioned and acted upon. The events in Abu Ghraib highlight this predictable decay in moral fabric:

> ... as torture moved down the chain of command, it further degenerated from a twisted and illegal means of interrogation into a sadistic sport for ordinary soldiers to apply to ordinary prisoners.

This deterioration is predictable. It has happened under every total-
itarian regime, from Stalin to Hitler to Torquemada. When torture
is official policy, ordinary soldiers and police let their frustrations
and imaginations run wild. This is why civilized nations ban
torture categorically.[16]

The use of torture is incompatible with the core rights and principles of a democracy: the rule of law, the separation of powers, and
civil and political rights. Even to entertain its possibility is to
admit the final transformation of the democratic state. The United
Nations Commission on Human Rights report on the state of
human rights after September 11 reaffirmed the absolute prohibition against the use of torture in any circumstances, and noted
those measures that contribute to its practice as being:

> The wide scope of arrest and detention powers granted to the
> police; overlapping of jurisdiction of various police and security
> agencies; secret detention; lack of or inadequate legal infrastructure
> to deal with allegations of torture; the existence of extensive pre-
> trial detention powers; the use of administrative or preventive
> detention for prolonged periods or time; ... and the denial of access
> to lawyers, family and medical personnel (UNHCR 2002).

CONCLUSION

Despite unprecedented developments in domestic security matters,
for Attorney-General Philip Ruddock, the government's anti-
terrorism policy is not a 'finished canvas'.[17] But can the fight
against the infinite and indefinable 'terror' ever be complete? With
each legislative amendment the need apparently arises for more
and the 'balance' between national security and individual rights
can then be simply recast again. The developments outlined here
have altered the relationships between the arms of government
that have structured Australian democracy for over 100 years. The
shifting priorities of the criminal justice system, an expanded
executive power, the diminution of legal protections and rights

and the marginalisation of judicial review have all enabled the interests of security to prevail. In doing so they have eroded the essential features of a democratic state leaving a formal democracy with a diminished substantive core. Agamben describes this as a State in which, 'security imposes itself as the basic principle of state activity ... Because they require constant reference to a state of exception, measures of security work towards a growing depoliticisation of society. In the long run, they are incompatible with democracy' (Agamben 2002: 2).

This transformation reflects the movement away from an understanding of democracy defined by a universalising core of rights, justice and the rule of law, as well as its institutional political (parliamentary) form, towards an understanding of democracy defined by the interests and preservation of national security and the State itself. We are witnessing the evolution of a new type of State, the post-democratic State, in which the primacy of security has overtaken substantive democratic features of rights and justice, reducing democracy to electoral formality on the one hand and mere acclamation on the other.

The review of the operations of the security legislation in 2006 provides the best opportunity for an extensive engagement by all parties involved in policy deliberation and analysis. The interaction between scholars, practitioners and policymakers can only be of benefit, not only to the development of appropriate security policy but also to the achievement of the government's avowed aims in this complex field. Attorney-General Ruddock has acknowledged that, 'Australians do not want our security agencies to have harsh, excessive or draconian powers. And they do not want security measures which will erode the very rights, liberties and freedoms that we are trying to protect ... we are equally determined to respect and preserve the individual rights and freedoms that define our society and way of life'.[18] Ensuing that these security measures meet the government's intention of enhancing security, while at the same time preserving democratic rights and freedoms, necessitates overcoming both the 'habit of deference to executive power' and the passivity of parliament in security matters. But it also necessitates a reinvigoration of public policy debate in this field, demanding the comprehensive engagement of scholars, analysts, policymakers and practitioners with the policy process. The current security environment does not encourage such debate, nor would its conclusions willingly be accepted. Yet rarely has it been so important that this debate take place.

ENDNOTES

1 I would like to acknowledge the exceptional research assistance of Sara Cousins in the preparation of this chapter and the comments and guidance of James Walter and the project committee.

2 David Charter, 'Law chief's fears over terror Bill', *The Times,* 5 March, 2005: 8.

3 The Hon. Philip Ruddock 'Opening Address', 12th Annual Conference, Australian Institute of Professional Intelligence Officers, 22 October 2003.

4 Senate Legal & Constitutional Legislation Committee. Parliament of Australia, *Inquiry into the Security Legislation Amendment (Terrorism) Bill 2002 (No. 2) and Related Bills (2002):* 82.

5 Parliamentary Joint Committee on ASIO, ASIS, DSD. Parliament of Australia. Advisory Report on ASIO Amendment (Terrorism) Bill 2002, Foreword.

6 The Hon. Philip Ruddock, Second Reading Speech, Anti-Terrorism Bill 2004, House of Representatives, 31 March 2004.

7 The Hon. Philip Ruddock, Second Reading Speech, Anti-Terrorism Bill 2004, House of Representatives, 31 March 2004.

8 Patrick Walters and Sophie Morris, 'Downer orders analysis on terror,' *The Australian,* 30 March 2004: 2.

9 The Hon. Philip Ruddock, 'Opening Address', 12th Annual Conference, Australian Institute of Professional Intelligence Officers, 22 October 2003.

10 The government's second major security legislation, the *Anti-Terrorism Act 2004,* amended the *Proceeds of Crime Act 2002,* the *Crimes Act 1914* and the *Crimes (Foreign Incursions and Recruitment) Act 1978.*

11 Joo-Cheong Tham, 'The Government Should Not Hinder Mr Habib From Speaking', web diary http://webdiary.smh.com.au/archives//000675.html accessed 10 February 2005.

12 Alan M. Dershowitz, 'Stop Winking at Torture and Codify It', *Los Angeles Times,* 13 June 2004.

13 Marian Wilkinson, 'Pentagon Reveals Deaths in Custody', *The Age,* 6 May 2004: 8.

14 Douglas Jehl, 'US Action Bars Right of Some Captured in Iraq', *The New York Times,* 26 October 2004.

15 Suzanne Goldenberg, 'Guantanamo Prisoners Win Transfer Reprieve', *The Guardian,* 14 March 2005: 15.

16 Robert Kuttner, 'The Torturers Among Us: Legalese Can't Protect the Bush Administration from Its Crimes', *The American Prospect Online*, 14 June 2004, http://www.prospect.org/

17 Ruddock, P. on ABC Lateline 2 March 2004, http://www.abc.net.au/lateline/content/2004s1057475.htm

18 The Hon. Philip Ruddock, Opening Address 12th Annual Conference Australian, Institute of Professional Intelligence Officers Canberra, 22 October, 2003, http://www.ag.gov.au/agd/WWW/MinisterRuddockHome .nsf/Page/Speeches_2003_Speeches_22_October_2003_-_Speech_-_Australian_Institute_of_ Professional_Intelligence_Officers

11

THE
QUALITY
OF LIFE

Richard Eckersley

The central purpose of a nation should be to improve the quality of life of its people. It follows that the primary function of public policy should be to improve quality of life; it is an important means to that end. This is not necessarily the assumption on which other chapters are based, nor is it the basis of social science scholarship more generally. Nevertheless, in this chapter I will set out the arguments in favour of this broad approach to the aim and purpose of this book, examine the role and contributions of the social sciences at this level, and consider the implications for public policy.

Put another way, I am not primarily concerned with specific public policy issues, but with the social and political framework within which public policy decisions are made. This perspective is intended to complement, not contradict, the tighter policy focus of other chapters. We need both approaches: the practical achievements of policy reform, but also to ensure this reform reflects and reinforces a more profound re-evaluation of the principles and beliefs that underpin policy thinking and development.

I begin by describing the central importance accorded to economic growth in public policy, and its rationale. I challenge this emphasis on several grounds: the relationship between wealth and wellbeing, at both a national and individual level; patterns and trends in health; public perceptions of quality of life; the evidence provided by other indicators, including alternatives to gross domestic product (GDP); and the effects on wellbeing of the cultural trends in materialism, individualism and consumerism. I then outline the need for a transition from material progress to sustainable development as 'the defining idea' of how we improve quality of life, before, finally, discussing the policy implications of this conceptual shift.

I define quality of life as the degree to which people enjoy the conditions of life – social, economic, cultural and environmental – that are conducive to total wellbeing: physical, mental, social and spiritual. Quality of life is both subjective and objective, as much a matter of how we feel about our lives as about the material conditions in which we live.

GOING FOR GROWTH

Australian governments give overriding priority in public policy to economics, believing economic growth to be the basis for improving the wellbeing of the Australian people. This position is shared by the major political parties: a 'policy constant' that is largely beyond scrutiny or debate. Prime Minister John Howard made much of his government's economic record during the 2004 federal election campaign, claiming repeatedly that a strong, growing economy was critical to Australia's future.

In a major speech, 'Getting the big things right', Howard (2004) said: 'Maintaining a strong, dynamic and growing economy is the ... overriding responsibility of government' (along with, now, national security and defence). At a World Economic Forum dinner six years earlier, Howard (1998) stated unequivocally: 'The overriding aim of our agenda is to deliver Australia an annual (economic) growth rate of over 4 per cent on average during the decade to 2010'. This aim is reflected in the government's overall policy objective for Treasury: 'strong, sustainable, economic growth and the improved wellbeing of the Australian people' (Henry 2004). Indeed, Treasury's mission statement is 'to improve the wellbeing of the Australian people'.

The primacy of growth is at the heart of the concept of material progress, which regards economic growth as paramount because it creates the wealth necessary not only to increase personal freedoms and opportunities, but also to meet community needs and national goals, including addressing social problems. In public policy terms, economic growth means more revenue, bigger budget surpluses, and more money to spend on more or bigger programs, including on health, education and the environment. As Howard (2004) argues:

> If we can sustain our overall growth rates ... we will be a $1 trillion economy in around seven years time [compared to more than ten years at previous rates] ... By 2015, the difference in national income would be about $135 billion a year in today's dollars. That's a difference of an extra $12 billion a year for health and more than $8 billion for education at current spending patterns ...

In other words, as Howard has often stressed, the government's economic objectives are not ends in themselves but the means for satisfying human needs. 'Economic reform is about making people feel more secure, happier, more able to care for their families' (Grattan 2000). Just how well do the means serve these ends?

GROWTH AND WELLBEING

There are, on the face of it, good grounds for the equation of more with better. *The Spectator* magazine recently claimed that 'we live in the happiest, healthiest and most peaceful era in human history' (Hanlon 2004). And if now was good, it argued, the future would be even better. The belief that we live in the best of all times has been most famously and controversially articulated in recent years by Lomborg (2001) in *The Skeptical Environmentalist: Measuring the Real State of the World.*

Lomborg (2001: 351–2) concludes that mankind's lot has improved vastly in every significant measurable field and that it is likely to continue to do so:

> ... children born today – in both the industrialised world and developing countries – will live longer and be healthier, they will get more food, a better education, a higher standard of living, more leisure time and far more possibilities – without the global environment being destroyed. And that is a beautiful world.

Like many others, he credits this achievement to material prosperity resulting from economic growth.

Historically, economic growth has been associated with many indicators of improved quality of life. Today, many more people are living much richer, longer lives than ever before (Maddison 2001). In the year 1000, there were about 270 million people in the world who, on average, could expect to live about 24 years and earn about US$400 a year (in today's dollars). Today there are over 6 billion people on earth who, on average, can expect to live about 67 years and earn almost US$6000 year. All parts of the world have shared in the gains. In the developed world in the past 200 years, per capita GDP has risen about twenty-fold, and life expectancy has more than doubled. In the rest of the world, per capita GDP has increased more than five-fold and life expectancy has also more than doubled.

However, a closer examination of the evidence shows that the picture is rather more complex than these simple correlations indicate, even when we just look at the associations at a broad, international and historical scale. Quality of life is not the same as standard of living, and how well we live is not just a matter of how long we live, especially in rich nations such as Australia. Other issues that we need to take into account in explaining these trends include the role of other factors such as the growth in knowledge and innovation; improvements in governance, social justice and civil rights; and an expanded role of government in the provision of services such as education, health care, welfare, and water and sewerage (Eckersley 2004: 25–42). Comparisons of per capita income and happiness in different countries show that at low income levels, the relationship is strong; above about US$10 000 a year, however, the correlation is close to zero (Diener and Seligman 2004). Across countries, happiness is more closely associated with democratic freedoms than with income. It is also strongly linked to equality, stability and human rights.

When we look at the relationship between income and wellbeing within countries – that is, between individuals or groups – we find population happiness has not increased in recent decades in rich nations (over 50 years in the United States), even though people have become, on average, much richer (Diener et al. 1999; Diener and Seligman 2004; Eckersley 2004: 77–104). We do, however, find that the rich are happier than the poor, especially in poorer countries, but even in rich nations. While it is often said that money can't buy happiness, most surveys suggest happiness grows with increasing income.

The surveys also show, however, that the relationship is strongest at low incomes, where money improves living conditions and alleviates hardship. Beyond these benefits, wealth has symbolic value as a measure of social status, and status affects wellbeing through the social comparisons it defines. So income-related differences in happiness will persist no matter how high average incomes rise as a result of economic growth.

Overall, the research evidence shows that money matters most when it helps us meet basic needs; beyond that the relationship between wealth and wellbeing becomes more complex. This is apparent when we look at the ingredients of personal wellbeing, of which money is one of many, and by no means the most important.

THE ART OF HAPPINESS

We often think of, and measure, wellbeing as happiness or satisfaction with life. This 'subjective wellbeing' is shaped by our genes, our personal circumstances and choices, the social environment in which we live, and the complex ways in which all these things inter-act (Diener et al. 1999; Diener and Seligman 2004; Eckersley 2004: 77–104; Myers 2004). The social sciences, especially sociology, economics and psychology, have greatly improved our understand-ing of wellbeing.

A happy marriage, the company of friends, rewarding work, sufficient money, a good diet, physical activity, sound sleep, engaging leisure and religious or spiritual belief and practice: all these things enhance our wellbeing and their absence diminishes it. Optimism, trust, self-respect and autonomy make us happier. Gratitude and kindness lift our spirits; indeed, giving support can be at least as beneficial as receiving it. Having clear goals that we can work towards, a 'sense of place' and belonging, a coherent and positive view of the world, and the belief that we are part of something bigger than ourselves, also foster wellbeing.

The effects of material conditions on wellbeing are powerfully influenced by perceptions and expectations. Adaptation and social comparison are especially important. We tend to adapt to changes in our situation, whether it's gaining something or losing it. We also assess our position relative to others; comparing favourably makes up happier, comparing unfavourably diminishes us. The gap between our aspirations and our achievements also matters. All in all, wellbeing comes from being connected and engaged, from being suspended in a web of relationships and interests. These give meaning to our lives. We are deeply social beings. The intimacy, belonging and support provided by close personal rela-tionships seem to matter most; isolation exacts the highest price.

Many of the qualities and characteristics associated with well-being are also related to physical health, including longevity (Eckersley 2004: 59–76). Socially isolated people are two to five times more likely to die in a given year than those with strong ties to family, friends and community. Wellbeing itself has a central role in these associations, improving health through direct physiological effects on the immune and neuro-endocrine systems; and by influencing diet, exercise, smoking, drinking and other lifestyle behaviours.

OTHER PERSPECTIVES ON QUALITY OF LIFE

To understand quality of life fully, however, we need to go beyond measures of personal happiness or life satisfaction. Asking people how happy or satisfied they are paints a somewhat rosy picture of life (Eckersley 2004: 77–104). It suggests that most of us are mostly happy most of the time; the average Australian rates his or her happiness or satisfaction at about 75 per cent. If people have not become happier over time, nor do they appear to be unhappier today than in the past.

The reason is that the 'art' of happiness includes the use of various cognitive devices to maintain it, including holding illusory self-beliefs, rationalising our situation and mitigating negative experiences. To a point, at least, we take our situation as a given, and assess our wellbeing within that context. So subjective well-being measures tend to discount broader social conditions; they tell us something about our quality of life, but not everything we need to know to evaluate it. Other perspectives, including trends in some health problems and in public perceptions of quality of life, offer a very different picture of life today. Again, the social sciences are contributing to knowledge in these areas.

Young people's lives reveal most clearly the tenor and tempo of our times. While their health, when measured by life expectancy and mortality, continues to improve, adverse trends in young people's health range across both physical and mental problems, and from relatively minor but common complaints such as chronic tiredness to rare but serious problems such as suicide (Eckersley 2004: 147–69). Between one-fifth and one-third of young people are experiencing significant distress at any one time, with some estimates of the prevalence of a more general malaise reaching 50 per cent. A quarter of Australian children today are overweight or obese, and this proportion is increasing by almost one percentage point a year. Inactivity has also increased (Hoban 2005). These changes place the children at risk of a wide range of health problems later in life, including diabetes, heart disease and cancer.

Illustrating the often sharp contrast between life satisfaction measures and other indicators, a recent study of young Australians found over 80 per cent said they were satisfied with their lives – including lifestyle, work or study, relationships with friends and family, accomplishments and self-perceptions – but that 50 per cent were experiencing one or more problems associated with depression, anxiety, anti-social behaviour and alcohol use (Smart and Sanson 2005).

PUBLIC PERCEPTIONS OF QUALITY OF LIFE

Declining quality of life is also apparent in people's perceptions of life in Australia. Average satisfaction with national conditions rates at about 60 per cent, 15 percentage points below personal satisfaction (Eckersley 2004: 105–25). Asked about trends in quality of life, about twice as many Australians say it is getting worse as say it is getting better. Recent studies, both qualitative and quantitative, show many people are concerned about the materialism, greed and selfishness they believe drive society today, underlie social ills, and threaten their children's future.

We yearn for a better balance in our lives, believing that when it comes to things like individual freedom and material abundance, we don't seem 'to know where to stop' or now have 'too much of a good thing'. Common concerns include: stress, drugs, crime, mistrust, the widening gap between rich and poor, financial pressures, growing job insecurity and work pressures, and, more recently, refugees and terrorism.

For example, sociologist Michael Pusey (2003) found over a half of those surveyed in his Middle Australia Project felt quality of life was falling, with the most common reasons given being, in order: too much greed and consumerism; the breakdown in community and social life; too much pressure on families, parents and marriages; falling living standards; and employers demanding too much. Most people believed family life was changing for the worse, citing the breakdown of traditional values; too much consumerism and pressure to get more money and buy things; a breakdown of communication between family members; and greater isolation of families from extended family networks and the community.

Some studies make quite explicit the tension between concerns about quality of life and the political emphasis on growth (Eckersley 2004: 115–16). One found that 75 per cent of Australians agreed that, 'too much emphasis is put on improving the economy and too little on creating a better society'. Another study found that 83 per cent of 'Australian society is too materialistic, with too much emphasis on money and not enough on the things that really matter'. Another survey revealed that, in contrast to government priorities, 'maintaining a high standard of living' ranked last in a list of 16 critical issues headed by educational access, children and young people's wellbeing, and health care – things many Australians believe are being sacrificed to *increase* the standard of living.

OBJECTIVE MEASURES

While self-reported happiness and public attitudes are important aspects of quality of life, it is important to acknowledge that subjective assessments are, in many instances, supported by objective measures of changes in living conditions, many of which flow, directly and indirectly, from the pursuit of material progress. Thus, the relentless drive for greater economic efficiencies, which are needed to maintain high growth rates, has been accompanied by increasing inequality, sustained high unemployment, the growth in under-employment and overwork, pressures on public services such as health and education, and the geographic concentration of disadvantage, leading to deeper and more entrenched divisions within society (Argy 2003). Increased work pressures and decreased job security not only harm workers, but also threaten the wellbeing of partners and children (Strazdins et al. 2004). This means that the costs to wellbeing can be transmitted from generation to generation. These impacts are discussed in detail in other chapters.

Another 'side-effect' of current patterns of growth is not adequately reflected in subjective measures of happiness and quality of life, but is, nonetheless, important to wellbeing. This is the destruction of the natural environment, of which we are an intrinsic part. However much we seem to be able to address some impacts through increased wealth and technological innovation, the evidence shows we are disrupting planetary systems on a scale that grows ever greater and more pervasive (Steffen et al. 2004). Global warming, for example, is no longer a hypothesis about the future, but a reality of today.

The diminishing returns and rising costs of growth have led to the proposal of a threshold hypothesis, which states that for every society there seems to be a period in which economic growth (as conventionally measured) brings about an improvement in quality of life, but only up to a point – the threshold point – beyond which, if there is more economic growth, quality of life may begin to deteriorate (Eckersley 2004: 32–5). The threshold hypothesis has been supported in recent years by the development of indices, such as the Genuine Progress Indicator, that adjust GDP for a range of social, economic and environmental factors that GDP either ignores or measures inappropriately. These include income distribution; unpaid housework and voluntary work; loss of natural resources; and the costs of unemployment, crime and pollution. These 'GDP analogues' show that trends in GDP and social wellbeing, once moving together, have diverged since about the mid-1970s in all countries for which they have been constructed, including Australia.

The evidence shows that a major flaw in the rationale for 'going for growth' is that it ignores or underestimates the social and environmental costs of growth processes. If, in creating wealth, we do more damage to the fabric of society and the state of the natural environment than we can repair with the extra wealth, it means we are going backwards in terms of quality of life, even while we grow richer. Furthermore, it is doubtful that we can compensate for the costs of growth in this way. The costs are not just material and structural – social inequality or environmental degradation, for example – but also cultural and ethical. Material progress depends on the pursuit of individual and material self-interest that, morally, cannot be quarantined from other areas of our personal and social lives.

MATERIALISM AND INDIVIDUALISM

As we have seen, greed and selfishness figure prominently in people's worries about quality of life. These are closely related to two of the defining characteristics of modern Western culture: materialism and individualism. The research, predominantly in psychology and sociology, tends to validate the concerns. Materialism – the pursuit of money and possessions – seems to breed not happiness but dissatisfaction, depression, anxiety, anger, isolation and alienation (Kasser 2002; Eckersley 2004: 85–96). People for whom 'extrinsic goals' such as fame, fortune and glamour are a priority in life tend to experience more anxiety and depression and lower overall wellbeing – and to be less trusting and caring in their relationships – than people oriented towards 'intrinsic goals' of close relationships, personal growth and self-understanding, and contributing to the community. In short, the more materialistic we are, the poorer our quality of life.

Individualism – placing the individual at the centre of a framework of values, norms and beliefs – is supposed to be about freeing us to live the lives we want. Undoubtedly, loosening social ties can be liberating for individuals, and create more dynamic, diverse and tolerant societies. The full reality of freedom, however, may be very different from this ideal (Eckersley 2004: 85–96). Individualism's downsides are described in different ways: a heightened sense of risk, uncertainty and insecurity; a lack of clear frames of reference; a rise in personal expectations, coupled with a perception that the onus of success lies with the individual, despite the continuing importance of social disadvantage and privilege; and a surfeit or excess of freedom and choice, which is experienced as a threat or tyranny.

One of the effects of these developments is that individualism not only reduces social connectedness and support, but also diminishes personal control, including through confusing autonomy (the ability to act according to our own values and beliefs) with independence (not being reliant on or influenced by others). Emphasising independence can lead to less real autonomy because it encourages a perception that we are separate from others and the environment in which we live, and so from the very things that influence our lives. The more narrowly and separately the self is defined, the greater the likelihood that the social forces acting on us are experienced as external and alien, and so seem beyond out control. This creation of a 'separate self' could be a major dynamic in modern life, impacting on everything from citizenship and social trust, cohesion and engagement, to the intimacy of friendships and the quality of family life.

An important means by which individualism and materialism affect wellbeing is through their influence on values (Eckersley 2004: 49–56). Values provide the framework for deciding what we hold to be important, true, right and good, and so have a central role in defining relationships and meanings. Consistent with what we know about wellbeing, most societies have tended to reinforce values that emphasise social obligations and self-restraint and discourage those that promote self-indulgence and anti-social behaviour. Individualism and materialism reverse universal virtues and vices.

CONSUMERISM AND ITS DISCONTENTS

Materialism and individualism are closely associated – as both cause and effect – with the ever-increasing personal consumption that current patterns of economic growth demand. As this 'consumerism' reaches increasingly beyond the acquisition of things to the enhancement of the person, the goal of marketing becomes not only to make us dissatisfied with what we have, but also with who we are. As it seeks evermore ways to colonise our consciousness, consumerism both fosters – and exploits – the restless, insatiable expectation that there has got to be more to life. And in creating this hunger, consumerism offers its own remedy: more consumption.

This ceaseless consumption is not, then, simply a matter of freedom of choice; it is culturally 'manufactured' by a massive and growing media-marketing complex. For example, big business in the United States spends over a US$1000 billion a year on marketing – about twice what Americans spend annually on education, private and public, from kindergarten through graduate school (Dawson 2003). This spending includes 'macro-marketing', the management of the social environment, particularly public policy, to suit the interests of business.

Together, government policy and corporate practice are distorting personal and social preferences. Psychologists who have studied cults and mind control warn that even the brightest and best of us can be recruited or seduced by social situations and conditions to behave in ways contrary to our values and dispositions; to engage in actions that are immoral, illegal, irrational and self-destructive (Zimbardo 1997; 2002). American psychologist Philip Zimbardo (2002) says that many agents of mind control 'ply their trade daily on all of us behind many faces and fronts'; we need to learn how to resist them and to weaken their dominance.

Our situation amounts to 'cultural fraud': the promotion of cultural images and ideals of 'the good life' that serve the economy, but do not meet human psychological needs, nor reflect the realities of social conditions. To the extent that these images and ideals hold sway over us, they encourage goals and aspirations that are in themselves unhealthy. To the extent that we resist them because they are contrary to our own ethical and social ideals, they are a powerful source of dissonance that is also harmful to health and wellbeing.

Studies and scholarship across a range of fields suggest we are seeing a reaction to this situation (Eckersley 2004: 244–50). The counter-trend is most apparent in the so-called downshifters and cultural creatives: people who are making a comprehensive shift in their worldview, values and way of life, including trading off income for quality of life. Studies suggest that this group now comprises over a quarter of the population in Western nations. American researchers reveal that a quarter of Americans have made a comprehensive shift in their worldview, values and way of life (Ray and Anderson 2000), and surveys suggest that there is a similar number of 'cultural creatives' in Europe and Australia (Hamilton and Mail 2003). Disenchanted with contemporary lifestyles and priorities, they are placing more emphasis in their lives on relationships, communities, spirituality, nature and the environment, and ecological sustainability.

Studies by American researchers Paul Ray and Sherry Ruth Anderson (2000) reveal that a quarter of Americans are 'cultural creatives'. Surveys in European Union countries suggest there are at least as many cultural creatives there. 'They are disenchanted with "owning more stuff", materialism, greed, me-firstism, status display, glaring social inequalities of race and class, society's failure to care adequately for elders, women and children, and the hedonism and cynicism that pass for realism in modern society' (Anonymous 2001: 1–2).

Cultural creatives represent a coalescence of social movements that are not just concerned with influencing government, but with reframing issues in a way that changes how people understand the world. Ray and Anderson say that in the 1960s, less than 5 per cent of the population was making these momentous changes. In just over a generation, that proportion has grown to 26 per cent. 'That may not sound like much in this age of nanoseconds, but on the timescale of whole civilisations, where major developments are measured in centuries, it is shockingly quick' (Anonymous 2001: 1–2).

While Australians haven't yet been measured for their 'cultural creativity', a study by the Australia Institute suggests the proportion of cultural creatives here is likely to be similar to that in the United States and Europe, perhaps even higher (Hamilton and Mail 2003). It found that 23 per cent of Australians aged 30–59 had 'downshifted' in the past ten years; that is, voluntarily made a long-term change in their lifestyle that had resulted in their earning less money. This proportion excludes those who retired, returned to study, set up their own business or left work to have a child. If some of the excluded are included as legitimate downshifters, along with those who have opted for a 'cultural creative' lifestyle from the beginning, the proportion of Australians who are challenging the dominant culture of our times is likely to be substantially higher.

The trend is consistent with the views of American sociologist Ronald Inglehart (2000) who, drawing on surveys of people in the United States and several European nations between 1970 and 2001, found a pronounced shift from 'materialist' to 'post-materialist' values. Post-materialists are still interested in a high material standard of living, but take it for granted and place increasing emphasis on the quality of life. The economic outlook of modern industrial society emphasised economic growth and economic achievement above all, Inglehart says. Post-materialist values 'give priority to environmental protection and cultural issues, even when these goals conflict with maximising economic growth' (Inglehart 2000: 223).

The trend also reflects a development that other sociologists have observed: a new moral autonomy, a more socially responsible and engaged form of individualism. Action is still a form of personal choice and self-expression, but instead of being based on a narrowly defined self-reliance and self-focus, it is framed and shaped by a wider social context. These new orientations create 'something like a cooperative or altruistic individualism', says German sociologist Ulrich Beck (Beck and Beck-Gernsheim 2002:

162). 'Thinking of oneself and living for others at the same time, once considered a contradiction in terms, is revealed as an internal, substantive connection.'

BEYOND GROWTH: TOWARDS SUSTAINABILITY

Postmaterialism is closely associated with the concept of sustainable development, which is increasingly challenging material progress as a framework for making policy decisions. Sustainable development does not accord economic growth 'overriding' priority. Instead, it seeks a better balance and integration of social, environmental and economic goals and objectives to produce a high, equitable and enduring quality of life. A common theme is the perceived need to shift from *quantity* to *quality* in our way of life and our measurements.

We can also characterise the shift from material progress to sustainable development as replacing the outdated industrial metaphor of progress as a pipeline – pump more wealth in one end and more welfare flows out the other – with an ecological metaphor of progress as an evolving ecosystem such as a rainforest – reflecting the reality that the processes which drive social systems are complex, dynamic, diffuse and non-linear.

Sustainable development has been defined in many ways (Eckersley 2004: 234–7). The World Commission on Environment and Development (1987: 8) described it as 'development that meets the needs of the present without compromising the ability of future generations to meet their own needs'. The World Conservation Union, the United Nations Environment Program and the WWF (formerly the World Wide Fund for Nature) have defined it as 'improving the quality of human life while living within the carrying capacity of supporting ecosystems' (1991).

The key challenge of sustainable development has usually been seen as reconciling the requirements of the economy – growth – with the requirements of the environment – sustainability.

However, our growing understanding of the social basis of health and happiness – and so quality of life – can shift this perspective, making an important contribution to working towards sustainability. It provides a means of integrating different priorities by allowing them to be measured against a common goal or benchmark: improving human wellbeing. While wellbeing is not the only consideration here, it is critical to achieving a real political commitment to sustainable development.

PUBLIC POLICY IMPLICATIONS

In shifting from material progress to sustainable development, we need to think less in terms of a 'wealth-producing economy' and more about a 'health-creating society', where health is defined as total wellbeing. We need to pay attention to the content of growth – and the values and priorities it reflects and serves – not just its rate. At present, government policies give priority to the rate, but leave the content largely to the market and consumer choice.

Most economic growth is derived from increased personal consumption, despite the evidence of its personal, social and environmental costs. We need, individually and collectively, to be more discerning about what economic activities we encourage or discourage. While such suggestions are often dismissed as 'social engineering', this criticism ignores the extent to which our lifestyle is already being 'engineered' through marketing, advertising and the mass media, as already discussed.

It is true that recessions and depressions cause hardship, especially through increased unemployment. However, the association between growth and jobs (or other benefits) does not negate the need to examine more broadly and carefully the social effects of growth. Also, we need to bear in mind that the strength of this association is a characteristic of our current economy; we cannot judge possible alternatives by the rules – the internal logic – of the existing system.

Also, to be *against* current patterns of growth is not the same as being *for* failed socialist, centralised, command economies. This common confusion leads to the claim that whatever its faults, capitalism is the best system we have and we should stick to it until someone invents a better one. This claim confuses means and ends, function and meaning, systems and worldviews – how we do something rather than why we do it. Rather than casting the core question in terms of being pro-growth or anti-growth, we need to see that growth itself is not the main game.

Changing our defining idea about how to improve quality of life would have far-reaching implications for public policy. The specifics are beyond the scope of this chapter and my expertise. But in essence the change would involve reducing the proportion of GDP derived from *consumption* undertaken for short-term, personal gratification, and to increase that involving *investment* directed towards broader and longer term social goals. We could choose to redirect economic activity into creating a fairer, cleaner, healthier and safer world. We don't have to keep consuming more in order to generate the wealth to try to fix the problems that consumption gives rise to.

In the face of terrorism, we have not hesitated to direct wealth (and so economic activity) into strengthening defence and national security. The Boxing Day tsunami also saw a large reallocation of resources to help its victims. Confronted with the magnitude and global scale of twenty-first century challenges – population pressures, environmental destruction, economic equity, global governance, technological change – it simply makes no sense to continue to regard these issues as something we can deal with by fiddling at the margins of the economy, the main purpose of which remains to serve, and promote, our increasingly extravagant consumer lifestyle.

American economist Robert Frank (2004) describes this shift in spending as one from *conspicuous* to *inconspicuous* consumption. Conspicuous consumption is like an arms race, an escalation of spending on things like larger houses, better cars and more expensive clothes in order to improve our social status. Inconspicuous goods include shorter commuting, better work conditions, more time with friends and family and more vacations. The list could also be extended to include wider measures of social and environmental quality. Frank says that the evidence suggests wellbeing would be higher in a society with a greater balance of inconspicuous consumption, but that the actual trends have been in the opposite direction.

A wellbeing manifesto, published in 2005 by the Australia Institute, a non-profit public policy research institute, notes that while governments can't legislate to make us happy, many things they do affect our wellbeing (Hamilton et al. 2005). Industrial relations laws can damage or improve the quality of our working lives, government policies can protect the environment or see it defiled, our children's education depends on the quality of schools, tax policies can make the difference between a fair and an unfair society, and the cohesiveness of our communities is affected by city design and transport plans.

The manifesto proposes nine areas in which a government could and should enact policies to improve national wellbeing: improving working conditions; reducing working hours; protecting the environment (including through increased taxation on damaging activities); rethinking education to place more emphasis on wellbeing; investing in early childhood; discouraging materialism (including through greater regulation of advertising); building communities by supporting families, carers and community organisations; reducing inequality and building public infrastructure and services; and improving measures of wellbeing. In reviewing the literature on wellbeing, two leading American researchers, Diener and Seligman (2004) conclude that there are 'distressingly large, measurable slippages' between economic indicators and wellbeing, and urge the establishment of a system of national measures of wellbeing to supplement the economic measures. 'Economic measures have seriously failed to provide a full account of quality of life' (Diener and Seligman 2004: 1–2).

CONCLUSION

This chapter has examined public policy's emphasis on economic growth, and the rationale for this focus, in the light of a wide range of social scientific evidence on quality of life: the nature of subjective wellbeing and the importance of money to wellbeing; some of the key patterns and trends in young people's health; public concerns about quality of life, including the impact of growth; trends in other indicators, including alternatives to GDP; and the effects on wellbeing of cultural qualities that are closely associated with economic growth, notably materialism and individualism.

It might be argued that wealth creation is a legitimate 'overriding aim' of government, but not of a nation, whose priorities will also reflect the goals and interests of other institutions and, of course, individuals. However, the evidence of diminishing returns with rising income demonstrates that, even from a public policy perspective, the focus on high growth as the foundation for raising wellbeing is mistaken. To improve quality of life, we would be better off placing more emphasis on redistributing income, eliminating poverty, and improving community conditions and services.

Quite apart from wealth's limited role in enhancing wellbeing, we have also to take into account the difficulty, if not impossibility, of isolating the requirements for growth (as we pursue it) from a cascade of other, adverse social effects. In essence, money and what it buys constitute only a part of what makes for a high quality of life. And the pursuit of wealth can exact a high cost when it is given too high a priority – nationally or personally – and so crowds out other, more important goals. The need to belong is more important than the need to be rich; meaning matters more than money.

The current worldview framed by material progress and based on self-interested, competitive individualism has created a 'shallow' democracy (where citizenship involves voting every few years for whichever party promises us the best personal deal) and resulted in reduced social cohesion, weaker families and communities, and so diminished quality of life. Challenging this construction is a new worldview framed by sustainable development and based on altruistic, cooperative individualism. This encourages a 'deep' democracy (where citizenship is embodied in all aspects of our lives), leading to greater social cohesion, stronger communities and families, and better quality of life. The former represents a vicious cycle, the latter a virtuous one.

Achieving the transition from material progress to sustainable development as the 'defining idea' of human development requires many specific policy changes, but it also goes beyond this task to redesigning the framework of principles and beliefs within which public policy is decided. The social sciences are playing a pivotal role in this process through their contributions to a better understanding of quality of life and changes in public attitudes and priorities, and the translation of this understanding into better public policy.

12

OPINION FORMATION: PROBLEMS AND PROSPECTS

Ian Marsh[1]

Elsewhere in this volume, Brian Head explores recent changes in governance in Australia. Public, constituency and policy community opinion are critical aspects of this process. Opinion creates the space, for better or worse, within which political leadership is exercised. Ideally, an informed public creates the authority for executive action and may also be the best guide to prudent policy choice. Further, public and/or policy community consent (which does not necessarily mean agreement) can be the ground for flexible and timely policy action. An extensive empirical literature documents the key role of political institutions in these processes (Zaller 1992; Yankelovitch 1992; Page and Shapiro 1992; Reich 1990), and an extensive normative literature argues the case for an informed and engaged public (for example, Pettit 1997; Dryzek 2000; Tocqueville 2003). In a nutshell, an informed and engaged public realises the promise of liberal democracy and fulfils its ideal of citizenship.

This chapter assesses the role and effectiveness of Australia's political institutions in the formation of opinion. It considers the need for strengthened institutional capabilities and explores ways this need might be met. Opinion formation is a process with two dimensions. At one level, the whole ensemble of political institutions creates the framework within which public opinion generally is formed. Here parliamentary rituals such as question time, urgency motions and so forth are critical. In recent years, the media has come to play an increasingly important (and as I will argue a largely negative) role in this social learning. At a second level, opinion on particular issues is formed within particular constituencies or policy communities. Here those who are more or less immediately affected, whether positively or negatively, can be engaged.

These two 'levels' are interrelated. Opinion formation can start at the policy community level and later spill into more general parliamentary and media processes: sometimes these steps occur serially but mostly the links are reciprocal. Opinion formation is also mostly a protracted process. Think of issues like Telstra privatisation, abortion, university funding, gun control and work tests for single mothers. All these have involved detailed action at the level of stakeholder groups, as well as at that of the broader political and media system.

In exploring present and prospective approaches, this chapter first discusses changes in the broader institutional structure. It argues that in recent decades institutional capabilities to mediate the development of opinion have progressively declined. The second section turns to recent policymaking experience, notes the gap between public opinion and policy change, and asks why, in such a context, dramatic change has been possible. The third section explores the emerging agenda and asks if past approaches will continue to sustain policy and political capabilities. The fourth section considers steps that might be taken to build capabilities.

HAS THE CAPACITY TO ENGAGE INTERESTS AND TO BUILD INFORMED OPINION CHANGED?

Three structural changes – the changing role of major party organisations, the pluralisation of social attitudes and the heightened role of the media – have affected the capacity of the political and policymaking system to engage interests, and to stimulate the development of constituency and public opinion.

One important change concerns the standing and influence of party *organisations*. Their roles have waned as the standing and influence of the parliamentary leadership has waxed. A variety of independent developments have combined to produce this outcome. First, party conferences are now largely stage-managed. They are no longer forums for strategic debates. In the case of the Labor Party, its parliamentary leadership often found it expedient to by-pass formal party forums after 1983 (Jaensch 1989). Federal Conference challenged the political leadership twice in the 1980s, but not at all in the 1990s. For its part, the Liberal Party has turned from defence of the status quo to being an advocate of policy change. But its internal processes do not foster open debate. Its conferences are also wholly stage-managed. Differences over policy are interpreted as disloyalty to the current leadership (Brett 2003).

A second change involves the reach of party organisations. Party memberships have collapsed. Labor membership has wavered between 40 000 and 60 000 since 1972, with current membership estimated at fewer than 50 000 (Weller and Young 2000). Liberal Party membership has also collapsed. It is now estimated to be about the same as that of Labor. Combined major party memberships now total less than 1 per cent of the electorate, compared with over 15 per cent in the 20-year period from the late 1940s until the late 1960s.

A third change concerns the ideological division between the parties. Since 1983, both major parties have broadly adopted the neo-liberal economic agenda. The major measures introduced since that time have largely been determined by this wider intellectual framework. Markets have been embraced and political remedies displaced. Citizens have been redefined as consumers. Economic globalisation has been welcomed. The major parties have accepted

Margaret Thatcher's dictum: 'There is no alternative'. Labor has been somewhat more attentive to redistribution and employment issues. The Coalition has been somewhat more vigorous in advocating pro-competitive measures; it has also championed a conservative social agenda. But the rhetorical jousting between the major parties belies high levels of tacit bipartisanship on specific issues.

A fourth change concerns the sources of the political agenda. In the 'golden age' of the two major parties, the party organisations played a prominent role in determining which strategic issues would have priority. But in the post-1960s period these tasks have been taken over by other political organisations. Every wholly new domestic issue on the Australian political agenda in the past 30 or so years was originally championed by a social movement. Think of the impact of the environmental, women's, Indigenous, gay, anti-globalisation, republican and other movements. The major parties have ultimately played critical roles in brokering these issues on to the formal agenda. But the initial aspiration, energy, and motivation started elsewhere. This is a significant development, symptomatic of the new diversification of Australian society.

A related change concerns the role of the major party organisations in linking interest groups to the formal political system. The proliferation of interest groups and the rise of the social movements have overwhelmed previous alignments. Older links – the trade unions with Labor and business with the Liberals – have weakened. In the absence of sharp ideological differences, loyalties have become more fluid. A disinclination to deal with groups has been reinforced in the major parties by the fashionable ideology of public choice theory. This has cast interest groups as selfish and self-serving, and has disputed their representational legitimacy. An example is hostile attitudes to trade unions.

A decline in ability of party organisations to set the political agenda or to link interest groups to the formal political system has diminished the overall strategic policymaking capacities of the formal political system, as has the decline in the ability of party names to influence the formation of public opinion. The major parties no longer sufficiently link the Australian community to the formal political system.

THE MULTIPLICATION OF REPRESENTATIVE POLITICAL ORGANISATIONS

The growing diversity of the Australian community, reflected in the proliferation of interest groups and social movements, is the most significant change in the character of post-war domestic politics. The social movements signify a new diversity in citizen identities (for example, gender, ethnicity and environmentalism). They augment, and sometimes displace, older class-based cleavages. Australia has become a group-based community. The array of organised actors on any issue is large. These groups vary enormously in size, budgets, political skills, organisational sophistication and campaigning capacities. But the major ones are as effectively organised as the major political parties. They have stimulated imitators advocating new issues (for example, euthanasia, legalised heroin or a republic) or defenders of traditional approaches (for example, the shooters party, monarchists, anti-abortion and anti-euthanasia groups).

In consequence, activists no longer have strong allegiances to one or other party. The way that issues are introduced on to the national stage has shifted. Party forums are not the principal arenas for activists. The initiative has moved elsewhere. Public opinion is influenced through public campaigns by activists and through the resultant media attention. This is used to pressure the leadership of the major parties to adopt new agendas. The success of these campaigns has significantly widened the national political debate and raised the importance of public opinion formation. The space between the major parties and the community is now filled by organisations with political capabilities and media skills, and with a demonstrated capacity to shape opinion on particular issues.

THE USE OF MEDIA
CHANNELS BY PARTY LEADERS

From the 1970s, the major parties changed their approach to the development of public opinion. The appointment of a new style of party manager was symptomatic of this change. Professionals in public opinion polling and marketing replaced party loyalists. They promised a new outcome. Direct marketing, polling, media advertising and packaging promised to make dispensable organisational policy development and a large party membership base. Clever marketing, focused on the parliamentary leadership, could, it was imagined, sufficiently compensate for weakened party identifications among electors. Indeed, conferences, large memberships and internal policy development processes came to be seen as constraints: liberation from them allowed the parliamentary leadership to reach out directly to the electorate. Sophisticated marketing techniques seemed capable of delivering the required outcomes in mass opinion formation.

A direct approach to the electorate via the media is clearly one viable option for building public opinion. But there are many constraints. Media requirements for a punchy 'grab' distort presentations. The media have difficulty maintaining attention on an issue without sensationalising developments. The media have commercial interests, which are not necessarily consistent with the development of an informed public opinion. The focus of public debate and major policy announcements on a party's leader implicates his or her prestige in the implementation of whatever has been proposed. This also foreshortens the time available for debate and exchange, limits the scope for developing public and interest group opinion, and turns many issues into futile jousts between governments and oppositions. All these developments limit the formation of an informed public opinion.

Market practices now commonly influence policy development: ministers, departments and political parties attend to focus group and opinion surveys; policy is merchandised by commercial advertising, projecting messages to the public (see the recent campaigns associated with Medicare, domestic violence or the tax system). Instant public responses and unformed opinion are given inappropriate standing. Attention is deflected from actions that might develop better defined strategies and public opinion about them. There is limited scope for actions that might refine and deepen public opinion. Chance or contrived events that can galvanise constituencies for change become much more significant. Otherwise, there needs to be a protracted period of electoral 'softening'. Change in university funding, mooted by former minister David Kemp in 1997, was still only partially settled seven years later. Renewable energy, nursing home funding, welfare change and a host of other issues remain in the too hard basket.

Party leaders, perhaps unintentionally, have turned from leading to following the community. Focus groups and talkback radio, both of which privilege unformed opinion, have acquired an inappropriate level of influence. Save for action based on (mostly unacknowledged) bipartisanship, party leaders are obliged to follow opinion until chance events or a long period of softening up of the electorate allows change.

WHY THEREFORE HAS DRAMATIC POLICY CHANGE BEEN POSSIBLE?

Despite changes to political institutions that have weakened policymaking capabilities, since 1983, Australia's politico-economic strategy has been transformed (for example, Keating 2004; Kelly 1992; Bell 1997; Scharpf and Schmidt 1999). As documented by Quiggin (see Chapter 2), in the name of globalisation, and guided by broadly neo-liberal conceptions of state capacity, the policy frameworks that had guided Australia's industrial and social development for the preceding 80 years have been progressively jettisoned. Protective tariffs no longer isolate the domestic market. Capital controls no longer isolate financial markets. The exchange rate floats freely, its level determined by international financial markets. Capital movements are largely unimpeded. Wage determinations are decentralised and only a minority of Australians are now covered by awards. Some former public utilities have been privatised. Competition policy, covering both government and private actors, has been introduced. Taxation has expanded to include consumption. And social policy has become more targeted, although aggregate spending has been maintained.

This is an exemplary display of both policy and political capacity (for definitions of these terms see Painter and Pierre 2005). How were such outcomes attained? JQ Wilson has defined the broad requirements for policy change on this scale in terms of two basic steps (Wilson 1981). First, there needs to be agreement among intellectual elites about the nature of 'the problem' and about feasible remedies. Second, these approaches must be linked to the needs of political elites. Both steps occurred in Australia. Further, as is clearly documented (for example, Kelly 1992; Pusey 1991), they occurred over roughly the same period and engaged leading members of both major parties and the bureaucratic elite. In other words, at the elite level, there was widespread agreement about the broad terms of economic change. Bipartisanship between the major parties then provided the political base for almost all the changes that were introduced – financial liberalisation, floating of the exchange rate, tariff reductions, shift towards enterprise bargaining, competition policy, privatisation and so on.

Issues that did not attract bipartisan support proved more intractable. Thus Telstra privatisation has still to be achieved in the face of Labor and National party opposition. Similarly, despite the fact that both major parties championed the introduction of a GST, they did not agree at the same time. It was proposed by Treasurer Howard in 1981 and defeated in Cabinet. It was proposed at the 1994 Tax Summit by Treasurer Keating and defeated by business, union and Liberal opposition. It was proposed by Opposition Leader Hewson at the 1993 election but defeated by Prime Minister Keating. It was finally proposed by Prime Minister Howard at the 1999 election and passed into statute in 2000.

What has characterised the policymaking experience of these 22 years? First, despite its decisive role in facilitating change, bipartisanship has mostly been tacit.[2] There were few parliamentary debates where the then opposition spoke out in vigorous support of the government or when it explicitly encouraged its own supporters to accept the broad terms of what the government had enacted. The political incentives inhibiting such action are not hard to discern. But the consequence was an increasing disjunction between rhetoric and parliamentary reality. For example, Bach has recently surveyed the role of the opposition in the Senate (2004). He looked at its usage of procedures to advance its agenda in the six-year period to 2002, through which the government lacked a majority. He concluded:

> The data presented ... would seem to call into question one of the most commonplace assertions about the Australian political system (namely) that (its) essential dynamic is the competition between government and opposition ... These data are consistent with a conception of politics in Canberra operating on two tracks simultaneously. On one track, the government and opposition hammer away at each other ... on the second track a much more cooperative process is taking place with the two parties managing to find common ground on the preponderance of legislative business (Bach 2004: 234).

Second, partly as a consequence of bipartisanship, policy change has been conceived and implemented relatively rapidly. Cabinet took decisions, ministers presented legislation, and change was promulgated. The parliamentary drama was not or only marginally engaged. Alternatively, the Commonwealth and the states reached agreements in private that had far-ranging social consequences. As a result, more general social learning was severely constrained.

Third, and an important qualification to the last point, the Accord played a critical role in building support from the trade union movement, at least to the initial program of change. The inter-sectoral exchanges routinely facilitated by intermediary institutions, like EPAC, or the Australian Manufacturing Council, were another means of building support.

Fourth, economic crisis provided the setting for major policy change. This was symbolised in Treasurer Keating's 'banana republic' metaphor. The crisis arose initially from external sources. In the absence of such a trigger it is much harder to create a sense of urgency. Governments themselves are mostly unwilling to promote a sense of crisis since it reflects on their own competence. Further, international economic league tables contributed to public awareness. If the issues on the policy agenda do not impact via such mediums, it is much harder to generate urgency. Further, even if this could be managed in non-economic areas, a sense of crisis is hard to sustain. More broadly based approaches to policymaking will be essential if Australia is to continue serious policy reform in the absence of continuing crisis.[3]

These features of the policymaking process – principally economic crisis, tacit bipartisanship and largely uncontested change – had unintended consequences that do not foreshadow an unproblematic policymaking future. One consequence is a gap between elite and public opinion. Take Australians' attitudes to globalisation. These were probed in a 2004 Australian Centre for Social Research survey (Gibson et al. 2004). Fifty per cent of those surveyed continue to see globalisation as bad for job security. Sixty-five per cent favour limiting imports to protect the economy, while 42 per cent continue to support restrictions on property purchase by foreigners. Only 56 per cent believe we should pursue closer economic ties with Asia and only 42 per cent want to see strengthened cultural ties. Seventy-four per cent declared that the United States has too much power in world affairs. Finally, 75 per cent believe international companies damage local business.

A consequence of tacit bipartisanship and 'imposed' change has been the decline in confidence of Australians in political institutions. In 1999, 74 per cent of respondents surveyed had no or very little confidence in the federal government (Papadakis 1999).

Eighty-four per cent felt the same about both major parties. Overall, a 30 per cent drop had occurred in confidence in government over the preceding 13 years. In 2000, Ian McAllister showed around one in three voters believed legislators used their public office for financial gain and only one in four believed legislators had a high moral code (McAllister 2000). Belief in legislators' moral standards had declined by two-thirds in two decades. More recent research in 2002 confirms a continuation of this trend showing that since the end of the 1990s federal politicians, business executives and journalists attracted the least respect (Morgan 2002). The public standing of the major parties had equally diminished. Sixty-eight per cent of respondents to the Australian Electoral Survey regarded parties as necessary but 76 per cent indicated they did not think parties care about the views of ordinary people (Jaensch 2003).

Elsewhere, Ian McAllister and John Wanna (2001: 8) suggest 'Australians have become increasingly critical of their political system and its capacity to deliver'. They cite a survey which found 'both parties were on the nose' and findings that indicate Australians' declining confidence in their political system. Convergence between the parties has 'meant choices are not as clear cut as they once seemed' and 'who you vote for seems more important than what you vote for'. In general, 'cynicism is riding high, focused particularly on politicians ... politics is about manipulation ... bipartisan concern for the good of the country is rare' (McAllister and Wanna 2001: 8–11).

These changes in public attitudes are reflected in the standing of the major parties. First preference votes for minor parties in the House of Representatives have doubled from around 10 per cent in the 1970s to around 20 per cent in 1998 and 2001, while the proportion voting for minor parties or independents in the Upper House (Senate) increased to around 25 per cent. The collapse of visceral voter loyalty to one or other of the major parties is evident. Between 1967 and 1997, the number of Australians without a party identification increased from roughly 2 per cent to around 17 per cent. Nearly 60 per cent of the electorate have only weak identification, if any, with one or other of the major parties. The erosion in party identification has diminished the symbolic power of party names. The party 'brand' is no longer sufficient to evoke a loyal response from most voters. This is a significant trend if party names are relied on as a primary cue for citizen attitudes.

In sum, in an era of tacit bipartisanship on economic strategy, and in the absence of a more developed and reciprocal link between elite and popular opinion, many citizens remain unconvinced of the legitimacy of economic change. These people (particularly the actual or imagined losers) are open to populist appeals. This is hardly an auspicious context for addressing complex change in social policy areas where public and policy community attitudes are likely to be critical. Does the emerging policy agenda touch this more complex political terrain?

THE OUTLOOK FOR POLICY AND POLITICAL CAPACITY

In assessing the outlook for policy and political capacity, the emerging policy agenda, and the capacity of ministers to mediate interest integration and broader social learning, are integral.

THE EMERGING POLICY AGENDA

Over the past 22 years the so-called microeconomic reform agenda has been largely implemented. Regulatory structures and arrangements that inhibited the more or less free play of market forces in resource allocation have been removed. This phase is now largely concluded. The emerging agenda consists of a more complex mix of social, environmental, economic and moral questions. This is clear in four recent authoritative strategic assessments. In its review of competition policy, the Productivity Commission foreshadowed much greater attention to arrangements governing health, education and social engagement (Productivity Commission 2005b). The importance of this band of issues was also underlined in Treasurer Costello's statement on population ageing (Costello 2004). The Productivity Commission also flagged the very significant future importance of environmental issues. More recently, the Business Council of Australia has published a comprehensive report on infrastructure (Business Council of Australia 2005; see also Sims 2005). It identified a gap between current levels of provision and future needs, emphasised the importance of governance arrangements, and recommended enhanced collaboration between federal and state governments. Elsewhere, Michael Keating (2004) has added underemployment and skills development to the agenda. He has also noted the emerging gap of around 10 per cent between prospective public outlays and revenue sources. Despite the clear case for public provision, he wonders how arguments for necessary tax increases will be projected to a broader public. Finally, there are also proposals for more ambitious state roles that presuppose enhanced capabilities to build public consent (for example, on economic and industry strategy, see West 2004; Lipsey et al. 2005; on social policy, see Esping-Anderson 2002). Such agendas raise difficult issues of adaptation that will test the capacity of the political system to mobilise consent: a test that it has so far failed lamentably.

This survey of the emerging agenda suggests that, whatever the prudential merit of change, in present institutional contexts, political considerations will likely thwart bipartisanship. In contrast with the past 22 years, and despite the likely continued broad agreement between the major parties about the agenda, and perhaps even about some remedies, tacit bipartisanship is unlikely to be available as the base for policy change.

WHAT CONSTRAINS THE POLITICAL CAPACITY OF THE POLICYMAKING SYSTEM?

The inability of the political system to make even limited bipartisanship transparent is a major constraint on political capacity. If this constraint could be even partially relieved without loss of partisan focus, political capacities would be substantially strengthened. Possible institutional remedies will be considered in the next section.

Three features of the present policymaking system bear upon the capacity of ministers to be wholly responsible for all phases of the policy cycle. First, at the federal level, there is serious executive overload. A very small number of people in the present system determine privately what issues will have standing on the formal political agenda. They are the prime minister, senior ministers and the heads of the major coordinating departments: this group probably numbers no more than ten to fifteen people. They are naturally heavily engaged in day-to-day affairs. This means that the capacity of the system to process issues, particularly in a strategic phase, is weak. The present system concentrates power to a dysfunctional degree in the hands of these key leaders. In practice, this formal power does not translate into real authority, if for no other reason than the inability of these leaders to devote the necessary time to strategic issues.

Second, there is lack of access for interest groups and social movements. They have limited entry points for engaging the attention of the formal system. Individual groups can gain access to argue their case but this has two obvious shortcomings: it is typically on a private, one-on-one basis and such access is highly unbalanced. The lack of a public entry point into the political system for interest groups is a major shortcoming. Outside groups now have no option other than sustained lobbying campaigns to develop public pressure, despite the many grounds for accommodating interests that a more transparent process might disclose. For example, engagement between public officials and interest groups could lead to a broader conception of the relevant issue, and to a transformation of the way it is defined. Or some participants may accept a particular decision that they dislike on the understanding that complementary action will be taken in another area in which they have larger stakes. Others might accept a proposal knowing that the decision will be reviewed later to make sure that outcomes matched expectations. Or the compensation required to induce support on the part of interests negatively affected by proposed changes could become clear. These are the routine tactics of political accommodation, but there are now few forums where these possibilities can be explored in public settings. The journals and newsletters of interest and community groups are important conduits for reaching particular audiences, but there are now no public forums that provide a general platform for publicity.

A third problem with the present formal policymaking system is its inability to create interest coalitions around longer term issues. Such coalitions show that there is broad support for a proposal; and that it serves more than narrow or self-serving interests. Coalitions create momentum and influence the opinions of supporters and sympathisers. Successful campaigns by interest groups point to the power of coalition building. Think of the Australia-wide marches in support of reconciliation, or past collaborative action between the Australian Conservation Foundation and the National Farmers Federation, or between the Australian Council of Social Service (ACOSS) and the Business Coalition for Tax Reform. Except for (now rarely influential) parliamentary committee hearings, there is nowhere for the views of interest groups to be regularly engaged. In the absence of such a capability, the ability to build interest coalitions in support of policy proposals is diminished.

WHAT CAN BE DONE?

More contested issues suggest a need to return to consultative approaches that tacit bipartisanship has allowed elite policymakers to bypass. Recent Australian policymaking experience contains many examples of consultative approaches – and institutions – that could facilitate improved interaction with policy communities (see Head, Chapter 3). Research that defines particular policy 'problems' and that contributes authoritative analysis needs to be institutionalised. This can be located in a focused organisation like the former Bureau of Industry Economics or in a more wide-ranging body like the Productivity Commission. Specialist inquiries can also crystallise key issues and policy options.

The engagement of key stakeholders is an overlapping task. Here mediating bodies like the Economic Planning Advisory Council or the Australian Manufacturing Council illustrate possible durable arrangements. More recent examples of novel approaches to interest engagement include the Innovation Summit, the ACOSS–Business Coalition negotiations on the GST, Minister Nelson's approach to negotiating change in the Higher Education sector and the earlier Ecologically Sustainable Development process (Yencken and Fien 2000). Another set of proposals involves a wider role for new deliberative forums such as consensus conferences, citizens' juries and the like (for example, Fishkin 1995). These latter approaches have attracted widespread academic attention. While such forums may be useful add-ons to existing policymaking structures, they will always be distanced from the structure of power and it is unclear how they might acquire substantive standing.

Earlier discussion suggested three requirements that together point to the desirability of additional approaches. These requirements were: first, a capacity to explore the scope for bipartisanship; second, a capacity to explore the scope for interest integration and coalition building; third, some redirection of initiating capacity at the strategic or agenda entry phase, away from ministers, but still in a primarily political setting.

ENHANCING THE ROLE OF PARLIAMENT AND ITS COMMITTEES

The primary institution that meets these requirements even partially is the committee system of the parliament. The parliament is the only institution capable of achieving a comprehensive, sustained and progressive impact on public, interest group and official opinion. Its committees provide a forum for official, novel, sectional, and deviant or marginal opinions. Bureaucrats, ministers, interest groups and independent experts can appear on an equal footing. Further, through its varied processes and deliberations, parliament can seed the formation of broader public opinion. The theatre of parliament creates dramas that progressively communicate the significance of issues to a broader public. This is now fostered through rituals such as question time and urgency motions that have lost their original purpose. The political drama needs to be refashioned to contribute positively to the development of sectional and public opinion.

Parliament provides the only institutional setting where the scope for an even limited common position between the partisans could be explored and exposed. The capacity to bring into public focus areas of strategic agreement between the major parties, as well as differences, is critical to a renewal of the credibility of political deliberation. Indeed, this might sharpen political debate as contention might focus on precise areas of disagreement, such as differences about specific remedies. As argued elsewhere, in fostering this outcome, parliament could play a particular role at the strategic or agenda entry end of the issue cycle (for example, Marsh and Yencken, 2004; Marsh, 2005).

Committees are the right institutions for routine review of strategic issues; to introduce new issues to the political agenda; and to engage interest groups, parliamentarians, the public service and the broader community in their consideration. But the present system is inappropriately structured and insufficiently focused. The present committees work on a shoestring. The incentives for committee work are weak. Finally, the use of latent parliamentary powers, particularly in the Senate, to gain attention for committee findings and recommendations is hugely underdeveloped. The late Senator David Hamer suggested some time ago that ministers should cease to be drawn from the Senate and that it become a committee House (Hamer 1996). Such steps could be considered if the role of committees were to be significantly upgraded.

STRENGTHENING THE ROLE OF THE
COUNCIL OF AUSTRALIAN GOVERNMENTS (COAG)

In Australia's federal system significant powers and responsibilities rest with the states. No improvements in the machinery of government that aim to develop political competence to deal effectively with long-term strategic issues can ignore the relationship between the Australian government and the states and territories. The peak ministerial council, the Council of Australian Governments (COAG), was established in May 1992 and comprises the prime minister, premiers, territory chief ministers and the president of the Australian Local Government Association. The prime minister of the day chairs COAG. The strategic potential of COAG is not being realised for two main reasons. The first is that COAG meetings do not occur according to a fixed timetable. The second is that the prime minister controls the agenda. Strategic issues that may be of great concern to the states and to the nation may not be recognised. COAG could be used to bring about key nationwide reforms. With COAG as the forum, all the governments can engage in strategic consultations prior to bargaining over detailed matters of implementation. The agreements recently reached at COAG on water policy and the restoration of environmental flows in the Murray–Darling Basin are examples of how cooperation can work. The autonomy of the COAG structure needs to be enhanced if this institution is to contribute as it should to the identification and resolution of longer term policy issues.

CONCLUSION

An enhanced role for the parliament and its committees and a reinvigorated COAG structure may, in conjunction with an array of more familiar approaches, relieve otherwise intractable policymaking pressures. So far as a development of the role of parliamentary committees is concerned, this would not be a wholly novel step. It would renew a role for parliament evident in Australia in the period 1901–1909 (Marsh 1995, especially Chapter 10). The present, familiar, two-party system emerged from that latter date. This system reflected a progressive 'collectivisation' of political action, a process that was mediated at the social level by the mass parties and, at the formal level, by a transfer of power from the legislature to the executive. The contemporary re-emergence of differentiation in social attitudes, and a pluralisation of citizen identities, underwrites the desirability of some reversal of this process. In the absence of visceral citizen identification with one or other of the major parties, political integration and engagement needs to be fostered by other means. This suggests the merit of attention to the institutions and approaches that mediated political integration in the earlier, more individualised period that preceded the emergence of the mass parties.

Reviving the major parties is not the solution. They played strong linkage roles in a very different social environment. Then, Australian society was broadly divided on class lines, and socio-economic class was the principal determinant of political attitudes and loyalties. The encompassing beliefs that animated the major parties were the foundation for their mobilisation of citizens and interest groups. They gave the parties 'energy': direction, scope, motive and 'will'. They endowed political engagement with meaning and purpose. They placed present developments in the flow of history and they made action and change imaginable. These ideologies have been jettisoned and there is scant prospect of their renewal. Australian society is now much more diverse. This is a positive development to which the formal political system needs to adapt.

There are limited numbers of supporters for alternative candidates such as environmentalism or feminism. For its part, the neo-liberal ideology does not recognise any identity broader than that of an individual and a consumer, hardly the foundations for mass mobilisation. If the major parties cannot renew their past linkage and mobilising roles, is there an alternative? The renewal of links between the community and the formal political system requires different approaches: ones that can better align the formal political and policymaking system to the new dynamics of major party competition and to Australia's newly diversified society.

ENDNOTES

1   This chapter draws heavily on analysis and argument I have elaborated elsewhere (Marsh and Yencken 2004; Marsh 2005). I also thank Michael Keating for detailed comments on an earlier draft.

2   Michael Keating has pointed out that bipartisanship also characterised 'The Australian Settlement' of the preceding period. However, in this period there was also explicit disagreement between the major parties about domestic strategy and this provided the fault line around which election campaigning and political mobilisation occurred. The dynamics were thus different from those currently present (for a full discussion see Blyth and Katz 2005).

3   I am indebted to Michael Keating for this entire point.

References

Abelson, DE and Carberry, CM (1997) 'Policy Experts in Presidential Campaigns: A Model of Think Tank Recruitment', *Presidential Studies Quarterly*, 27 (4): 679–97.

Academy of the Social Sciences in Australia (ASSA), (1998) *Challenges for the Social Sciences and Australia*, Volume I, ASSA, Canberra.

Access Economics (2004) *The Cost of Domestic Violence to the Australian Economy: Part 1*, prepared for Office of the Status of Women, Commonwealth of Australia, Canberra.

Adema, W (2001) *Net Social Expenditure*, 2nd edition, Labour Market and Social Policy – Occasional Papers No. 52, OECD, Paris.

Agamben, G (2002) 'Security and Terror', *Theory and Event*, 5(4): 1–2, retrieved from <http://muse.uq.edu.au>.

Allan, C, Loudoun, R and Peetz, D (2005) 'Influences on Work/Non-work Conflict', proceedings of the 19th Annual Conference of the Association of Industrial Relations Academics of Australia and New Zealand (AIRAANZ), 9–11 February, University of Sydney, Sydney.

Alderson, K (2002) Principal Legal Officer. Criminal Law Branch. Attorney-General's Department, *Evidence to Senate Standing Committee for the Scrutiny of Bills*, Parliament of Australia, Canberra, 1 May.

Altman, JC (1991) *Aboriginal Employment Equity by the Year 2000*, Centre for Aboriginal Economic Policy Research, Australian National University, Canberra.

—— (2004) 'Economic Development and Indigenous Australia: Contestations over Property, Institutions and Ideology', *The Australian Journal of Agricultural & Resource Economics*, 48(3): 513–34.

Altman, JC, Biddle, N and Hunter, BH (2004) *Indigenous Socioeconomic Change 1971–2001: A Historical Perspective*, CAEPR Discussion Paper No. 266, Centre for Aboriginal Economic Policy Research, Australian National University, Canberra.

Altman, JC and Hunter, BH (2003) 'Evaluating Indigenous Socioeconomic Outcomes in the Reconciliation Decade, 1991–2001', *Economic Papers*, 22 (4): 1–15.

Altman, JC and Nieuwenhuysen, J (1979) *The Economic Status of Australian Aborigines*, Cambridge University Press, Cambridge.

Altman, JC and Sanders, W (1991) 'Government Initiatives for Aboriginal Employment: Equity, Equality and Policy Realism', in JC Altman (ed.), *Aboriginal Employment Equity by the Year 2000*, Research Monograph No. 2, Centre for Aboriginal Economic Policy Research, Australian National University, Canberra, pp. 1–18.

Anonymous (2001) 'Storming the Mindsets: The Rise of "Cultural Creatives"', *Future News* (newsletter of the Futures Foundation), 6 (2): 1–2. Other details about 'cultural creatives' are available at www.culturalcreatives.org

Argy, F (2003) *Where to From Here? Australian Egalitarianism Under Threat*, Allen & Unwin, Sydney.

Arthurson, K (2001) 'Achieving Social Justice in Estate Regeneration: The Impact of Physical Image Construction', *Housing Studies*, 16(6): 807–26.

—— (2002) 'Creating Inclusive Communities through Balancing Social Mix: Critical Relationship or Tenuous Link?', *Urban Policy and Research*, 20(3): 245–61.

Arthurson, K and Jacobs, K (2004) 'A Critique of the Concept of Social Exclusion and its Utility for Australian Social Housing Policy', *Australian Journal of Social Issues*, 39(1): 25–40.

Atkinson, J (1990) 'Violence Against Aboriginal Women: Reconstitution of Community Law – The Way Forward', *Aboriginal Law Bulletin*, 2(46): 6–9.

Australian Bureau of Statistics, ABS (1973) *The Aboriginal Population, 1971 Census of Population and Housing*, Bulletin Number 9, Reference Number 2.91, ABS, Canberra.

—— (2001a) *Expenditure on Education, Australia*, Catalogue No. 5510.0, ABS, Canberra.

—— (2001b) *Australian Social Trends, 2001*, Catalogue No. 4102.0, ABS, Canberra.

—— (2002a) *Australian Social Trends, 2002*, Catalogue No. 4102.0, ABS, Canberra.

——(2002b) *Australian Economic Indicators Upgrading Household Income Distribution Statistics*, Catalogue No. 1350.0, ABS, Canberra.

—— (2002c) *Government Finance Statistics, Education, Australia*, Catalogue No. 5518.055.001, ABS, Canberra.

—— (2002d) *Education and Training Indicators, Australia, 2002*, Catalogue No. 4230.0, ABS, Canberra.

—— (2003a) *Population Characteristics, Aboriginal and Torres Strait Islander Australians, 2001*, Catalogue No. 4713.0, ABS, Canberra.

—— (2003b) *Census of Population and Housing: Selected Education and Labour Force Characteristics, Australia, 2001*, Catalogue No. 2017.0, ABS, Canberra.

—— (2004a) *Australian Social Trends 2004*, Catalogue No. 4102.0, ABS, Canberra.

—— (2004b) *Census of Population and Housing: Australia's Youth, 2001*, Catalogue No. 2059.0, ABS, Canberra.

—— (2005a) *Ausstats, 'Australian Social Trends' 2000, 2001*, <www.abs.gov.au/Ausstats>.

—— (2005b) *Schools, Australia*, Catalogue No. 4221.0, ABS, Canberra.

—— (2005c) *The Labour Force, Australia*, Catalogue No. 6202.0, ABS, Canberra.

—— (2005d) *Persons Not in the Labour Force*, Australia, Catalogue No. 6220.0, ABS, Canberra.

—— (various) *Labour Force Spreadsheets 1978–2004*, Catalogue No. 6202.0.00.001, ABS, Canberra.

Australian National Audit Office (ANAO) (2004) *Fraud Control in Australian Government Agencies: Better Practice Guide*, ANAO, Canberra.

Australian Social Science Data Archive (2001) 'Australian Election Study 2001', Canberra, Research School of Social Sciences (RSSS), The Australian National University, http://assda.anu.edu.au/codebooks/aes2001/5vars.html

Ayres, I and Braithwaite, J (1992) *Responsive Regulation: Transcending the Deregulation Debate*, Oxford University Press, Oxford.

Bacchi, C (1999) '"Rolling Back the State?" Feminism, Theory and Policy', in Linda Hancock (ed.), *Women, Public Policy and the State*, MacMillan, Melbourne, pp. 54–69.

Bach, S (2004) *Platypus and Parliament: The Australian Senate in Theory and Practice*, Department of the Senate, Canberra.

Bakvis, H and Juillet, L (2004) *The Horizontal Challenge: Line Departments, Central Agencies and Leadership*, Canada School of Public Service, Ottawa.

Banks, G (2003) 'The Good, the Bad and the Ugly: Economic Perspectives on Regulation in Australia', address to the Conference of Economists, Business Symposium, 2 October, Hyatt Hotel, Canberra.

Barak, A (2002) 'Foreword: A Judge on Judging: The Role of a Supreme Court in a Democracy', *Harvard Law Review 16*, 116: 19–162.

Bardach, E (1998) *Getting Agencies to Work Together*, Brookings, Washington.

Barnes, J (1968) 'Australian Aboriginals? Or Aboriginal Australians?', *New Guinea*, 3(1): 43–7.

Barrett, PJ (2004) 'ANAO's Role in Encouraging Better Public Sector Governance', address to Australia and New Zealand School of Government students at the Australian National University, 20 September, ANAO, Canberra.

Barwick, D (1998) *Rebellion at Coranderrk*, Aboriginal History Monograph 5, Aboriginal History Inc, Canberra.

Baumol, W (1967) 'Macroeconomics of Unbalanced Growth: The Anatomy of the Urban Crisis', *American Economic Review*, 57 (3): 415–26.

Baxter, J (2002) 'Patterns of Change and Stability in the Gender Division of Labour in Australia, 1986–1997', *Journal of Sociology*, 38 (4): 399–424.

Beck, U and Beck-Gernsheim, E (2002) *Individualization*, Sage, London.

Becker, GS (1964) *Human Capital: A Theoretical and Empirical Analysis, with Special Reference to Education*, Columbia University Press, New York.

Beddie, BD and Moss, S (1982) 'Some Aspects of Aid to the Civil Power in Australia', *Occasional Monograph No. 2*, Department of Government, Faculty of Military Studies, University of New South Wales, Sydney.

Beer, A, Maude, A and Pritchard, B (2003) *Developing Australia's Regions*, UNSW Press, Sydney.

Bell, S (1997) *Ungoverning the Economy: The Political Economy of Australian Economic Policy*, Oxford University Press, Melbourne.

—— (2002) *Economic Governance and Institutional Dynamics*, Oxford University Press, Melbourne.

Bell, S and Head, BW (1994) *State, Economy and Public Policy in Australia*, Oxford University Press, Melbourne.

Berlin, I (1953/1969) *Four Essays on Liberty*, Oxford University Press, Oxford.

Beveridge, Lord (1955) *Power and influence*, The Beechhurst Press, New York: 3.

Bishop, P and Davis, G (2002) 'Mapping Public Participation in Policy Choices',

Australian Journal of Public Administration, 61 (1): 14–29.

Bittman, M and Pixley, J (1997) *The Double Life of the Family: Myth, Hope and Experience*, Allen & Unwin, Sydney.

Blackshield, AR (1978) 'The Siege of Bowral: The Legal Issues', *Pacific Defence Reporter*, 4 (9): 6–10.

Blunkett, D (2000) 'Influence or Irrelevance: Can Social Science Improve Government?', Secretary of State's ESRC Lecture Speech, 2 February, ESRC and Department for Education and Employment London, retrieved from <http://www.esrc.ac.uk/esrccontent/PublicationsList/4books.infl.html>.

Blyth, M. and Katz, R (2005) 'From Catch-all Politics to Cartelisation: The Political Economy of the Cartel Party', *West European Politics*, 28 (1): 33–60.

Borland, J (2002) 'New Estimates of the Private Rate of Return to University Education in Australia', *Melbourne Institute Working Paper No. 14/02*, Melbourne Institute, University of Melbourne, Melbourne.

Boulden, K (2004) 'The Gender Debates We Have to Have Again', Association of Women Educators National Conference 2004: Sustain the Future, Shape the Future, Lead the Future, 29 September, Australian Education Union, Melbourne.

Braithwaite, J (2002) *Restorative Justice and Responsive Regulation*, Oxford University Press, Oxford.

Braithwaite, V (2003) *Taxing Democracy*, Ashgate, Aldershot.

Brett, J (2003) *Australian Liberals and the Moral Middle Class*, Cambridge University Press, Melbourne.

Bridgman, J and Davis, G (1998) *The Australian Policy Handbook*, Allen & Unwin, Sydney.

Briggs, X (2003) 'Re-shaping the Geography of Opportunity', *Housing Studies*, 18 (6): 915–36.

Brookings Institution (2004) 'Brookings Welfare Reform and Beyond', Initiative Public Forum, 22 September, Massacusetts, Washington, accessed on 4 January 2005, <http://www.brookings.edu/comm/ events/20040922.htm>.

Broom, L and Jones, FL (1973) *A Blanket A Year*, ANU Press, Canberra.

Brown, AJ and Head, BW (2005) 'Choices for Institutional Capacity and Choice in Australia's Integrity Systems', *Australian Journal of Public Administration*, 64(2): 42–7.

Brown, K and Keast, R (2003) 'Citizen–Government Engagement', *Asian Journal of Public Administration*, 25(1): 107–31.

Bulbeck, C (2003) 'Gender Perspectives' in I McAllister, S Dowrick and R Hassan (eds), *Cambridge Handbook of the Social Sciences*, Cambridge University Press, Cambridge, pp.480–97.

Bunyan, T (2005) 'Statewatch Report: The Exceptional and Draconian become the Norm', *Statewatch*, retrieved from <http://www.statewatch.org>.

Burnley I, Murphy P, and Fagan R (1997) *Immigration and Australian Cities*, Federation Press, Sydney.

Business Council of Australia (BCA) (2005) *Infrastructure: Action Plan for Future Prosperity*, March 2005, Melbourne.

Cain, F (1983) *The Origins of Political Surveillance in Australia*, Angus & Robertson, Sydney.

Campbell, I and Burgess, J (2001) 'Casual Employment in Australia and Temporary Employment in Europe: Developing a Cross-national Comparison', *Work, Employment and Society*, 15 (1): 171–84.

Campbell, I and Charlesworth, S (2004) *Key Work and Family Trends in Australia*, Centre for Applied Social Research, RMIT University, Melbourne.

Campbell, K (1981) *Australian Financial System Enquiry – Final Report*, Australian Government Printing Service, Canberra.

Campus Review (2004) 'TAFE Under Pressure', *Campus Review*, 28 July 2004.

Carter, D (2004) 'The Conscience Industry: The Rise and Rise of the Public Intellectual', in D Carter (ed.), *The Ideas Market*, Melbourne University Press, Melbourne, pp. 15–39.

Cass, B (1985) 'Rewards for Women's Work', in J Goodnow and C Pateman (eds), *Women, Social Science and Public Policy*, Allen & Unwin, Sydney, pp. 67–94.

—— (1988) *Income Support for the Unemployed in Australia: Towards a More Active System*, Social Security Review, Canberra.

Castles, FG (1994) 'The Wage Earners' Welfare State Revisited: Refurbishing the Established Model of Australian Social Protection, 1893–93', *Australian Journal of Social Issues*, 29: 120–45.

—— (1996) 'Needs-based Strategies of Social Protection in Australia and New Zealand', in G Esping-Andersen (ed.), *Welfare States in Transition*, Sage, London, pp. 88–115.

—— (2003) *The Future of the Welfare State: Crisis Myths and Crisis Realities*, Oxford University Press, Oxford.

Castles, F and Mitchell, D (1993) 'Worlds of Welfare and Families of Nations', in F Castles (ed.), *Families of Nations*, Dartmouth, Aldershot, pp. 93–128.

Chapman, B. (1997) 'Conceptual Issues and the Australian Experience with Income Contingent Charges for Higher Education', *The Economic Journal*, 107(442): 738–751.

—— (1998) 'Economics and Policy-making: The Case of the Higher Education Contribution Scheme', *Canberra Bulletin of Public Administration*, 90: 120–4.

Charlesworth, H (2003) 'Human Rights in the Wake of Terrorism', *Law Society Journal*, 41(5): 62–4.

Cheshire, P (1999) 'Cities in Competition: Articulating the Gains from Integration', *Urban Studies*, 36(5–6): 843–64.

Chung, D (2002) 'Violence, Control, Romance and Gender Equality: Young Women Negotiating Heterosexuality with a Male Gaze', paper presented at the Expanding our Horizons: Understanding the Complexities of Violence Against Women Conference, 18–22 February, University of Sydney, Sydney.

Clasen, J and Clegg, D (2003) 'Unemployment Protection and Labour Market Reform in France and Great Britain in the 1990s: Solidarity versus Activation', *Journal of Social Policy*, 32(3): 361–81.

Coffey, C (2003) 'Never Too Early to Invest in Children. Early Childhood Education and Care Matter to Business', accessed 12 March 2005 at <http://www.voicesforchildren.ca>.

Colebatch, HK (1998) *Policy*, Oxford University Press, Buckingham.

Commonwealth Grants Commission (CGC) (1995) *Equality in Diversity*, Second edition, Commonwealth Grants Commission, Canberra.

—— (2001) *The Indigenous Funding Inquiry*, Commonwealth Grants Commission, Canberra.

Commonwealth of Australia (1945) *Full Employment in Australia*, Commonwealth Government Printer, Canberra.

—— (1987) *Aboriginal Employment Development Policy Statement*, Australian Government Publishing Service, Canberra.

—— (2001) *Stronger Regions, A Stronger Australia*, Australian Government Publishing Service, Canberra.

—— (1994), *Working Nation. Policies and Programs* (White Paper), AGPS, Canberra.

Community Affairs Reference Committee (2004) *A Hand Up, Not a Hand Out: Renewing the Fight Against Poverty, Report on Poverty and Financial Hardship*, The Senate, Canberra, accessed 15 February 2005, <http://www.aph.gov.au/senate/committee/clac_ctte/completed_inquiries/2002–04/poverty/report/>.

Connell, RW (1995) *Masculinities*, Allen & Unwin, Sydney.

—— (2000) *The Men and the Boys*, Allen & Unwin, Sydney.

Costello, P (2004) *Australia's Demographic Challenges*, The Treasury, Canberra.

Curthoys, A (1992) 'Doing it for Themselves: The Women's Movement Since 1970', in K Saunders and R Evans (eds), *Gender Relations in Australia*, Harcourt Brace Jovanovich, Sydney pp. 425–47.

—— (1998) 'Gender in the Social Sciences in Australia', in Academy of the Social Sciences in Australia (ed.), *Challenges for the Social Sciences in Australia*, vol. 2, Australian Government Publishing, Canberra, pp. 177–216.

Daly, AE (1995) *Aboriginal and Torres Strait Islander People in the Australian Labour Market*, Cat. No. 6253.0, Australian Bureau of Statistics, Canberra.

Daly, K (2000) 'Restorative Justice in Diverse and Unequal Societies', *Law in Context*, 17(1): 167–90.

Dangerfield, G (1935) *The Strange Death of Liberal England*, H Smith and R Hass, London.

Davis, G (1998) 'Policy from the Margins: Reshaping the Australian Broadcasting Corporation', in A Yeatman (ed.), *Activism and the Policy Process*, Allen & Unwin, Sydney, pp. 36–55.

Davis, G and Keating, M (2000) *The Future of Governance*, Allen & Unwin, Sydney.

Dawkins, J (1987) *Higher Education: A Policy Discussion Paper*, Australian Government Publishing Service, Canberra.

Dawson, M (2003) *The Consumer Trap: Big Business Marketing in American Life*, University of Illinois Press, Champaign. Cited in R York (2004) 'Manufacturing the Love of Possession – The Consumer Trap: Big Business Marketing in American Life', *Book Review, Monthly Review*, February.

Deeble, J, Mathers, C, Smith, L, Goss, J, Webb, R, and Smith, V (1998) *Expenditure on Health Services for Aboriginal and Torres Strait Islander People*, Department of Health and Community Services, Canberra.

Delladetsima, P (2003) 'What Prospects for Urban Policy in Europe?', *City*, 7(2): 153–65.

Denham, A and Garnett, M (1999) 'Influence Without Responsibility? Think-tanks in Britain', *Parliamentary Affairs*, 52(1): 46–57.

Denison, EF (1962) *The Sources of Economic Growth in the United States and the Alternatives Before Us*, Committee for Economic Development, New York.

DeParle, J (2004) *American Dream: Three Women, Ten Kids and a Nation's Drive to End Welfare*, Viking Books, New York.

Department of Education, Science and Training (DEST), (2005) *Selected Higher Education Statistics*, accessed 10 April 2005, <http://www.dest.gov.au/ highered/statinfo.htm>.

Department of Employment and Workplace Relations (DEWR), (2004) web page, viewed 15 December 2004, <http://www.dewr.gov.au/news/default.asp>.

Department of Family and Community Services (FaCS), (2003) *Income Support Customers: A Statistical Overview 2001*, Occasional Paper No. 7, FaCS, Canberra.

—— (2003) *Inquiry into Poverty and Financial Hardship in Australia*,

Commonwealth Department of Family and Community Services Submission to the Senate Community Affairs References Committee, Occasional Paper No. 9, FaCS, Canberra.

Dingeldey, I (2004) 'Welfare State Transformation between "Workfare" and an "Enabling" State, Espanet Conference, European Social Policy: Meeting the Needs of a New Europe', Oxford, accessed 17 September 2004, <http://www.apsoc.ox.ac.uk/Espanet/espanetconference/streams/s11.htm>.

Diener, E and Seligman, MEP (2004) 'Beyond Money: Toward an Economy of Wellbeing', *Psychological Science in the Public Interest*, 5(1): 1–31.

Diener, E, Suh, E, Lucas, R and Smith, H (1999) 'Subjective Well-being: Three Decades of Progress', *Psychological Bulletin*, 125(2): 276–302.

Dixon, J (1951) 'Australian Communist Party v Commonwealth', *Commonwealth Law Reports*, 83 CLR 1: 187–8.

Douglas, R (1980) *There's Got to be a Better Way!*, Fourth Estate, Wellington.

Drielsma, P (1997) 'AIDS Policy and Public Health Models: An Australian Analysis', *Australian Journal of Social Issues*, 32(1): 87–99.

Dryzek, J (2000) *Deliberative Democracy and Beyond: Liberals, Critics, Contestations*, Oxford University Press, New York.

Eckersley, R (2004) *Well and Good: How We Feel and Why It Matters*, Text Publishing, Melbourne.

Education Policy Institute (EPI), (2005) 'Global Higher Education Rankings: Affordability and Accessibility in Comparative Perspective', accessed 17 April 2005, <http://www.educationalpolicy.org/>.

Edwards, A (1989) 'The Sex/Gender Distinction: Has it Outlived its Usefulness?', *Australian Feminist Studies*, 10: 1–12.

Edwards, M (2001) *Social Policy, Public Policy: From Problem to Practice*, Allen & Unwin, Sydney.

—— (2003) 'Participatory Governance', *Canberra Bulletin of Public Administration*, 107: 1–6.

—— (2004) *Social Science Research and Public Policy: Narrowing the Divide*, Policy Paper 2, Academy of the Social Sciences in Australia, Canberra.

Eisenstein, H (1996) *Inside Agitators: Australian Femocrats and the State*, Allen & Unwin, Sydney.

Engels, B (2000) 'City Make-Overs', *Urban Policy and Research*, 18: 469–494.

Esping-Andersen, G (1990) *Three Worlds of Welfare Capitalism*, Polity Press, Cambridge.

—— (1999) *Social Foundations of Postindustrial Economies*, Oxford University Press, Oxford.

—— (2002) 'A Child-centred Social Investment Strategy', in G Esping-Andersen (ed.), *Why we need a New Welfare State*, Oxford University Press, Oxford.

—— (2003) 'Why No Socialism Anywhere? A reply to Alex Hicks and Lane Kenworthy', *Socio-Economic Review*, 1(1): 63–70.

Evans, M (1996) 'Public Opinion on Trade Unions in Australia: Continuity and Change', retrieved from <http://www.international-survey.org/wwa_pub/articles/unions.htm>.

Eveline, J (1994) 'The Politics of Advantage', *Australian Feminist Studies*, Special Issue: Women and Citizenship, 19: 129–54.

Fincher, R and Wulff, M (1998) 'The Locations of Poverty and Disadvantage', in R Fincher and J Nieuwenhuysen (eds), *Australian Poverty Then and Now*, Melbourne University Press, Melbourne, pp. 144–64.

Fink RA (1965) 'The Contemporary Situation of Change among Part-Aborigines of Western Australia', in RM Berndt and CH Berndt (eds), *Aboriginal Man in Australia*, Angus & Robertson, Sydney, pp. 419–34.

Fischer, F (1990) *Technocracy and the Politics of Expertise*, Sage, New York.
—— (1993) 'Citizen Participation and the Democratization of Policy Expertise', *Policy Sciences*, 26(3): 165–87.
Fishkin, J (1995) *The Voice of the People: Public Opinion and Democracy*, Yale University Press, New Haven.
Fisk, EK (1985) *The Aboriginal Economy in Town and Country*, Allen & Unwin, Sydney.
Frank, RH (2004) 'How Not to Buy Happiness', *Daedalus*, 133(2): 69–79.
Friedmann, J (2001) 'Intercity Networks in a Globalizing Era', in A Scott (ed.), *Global City-Regions*, Oxford University Press, Oxford, pp. 119–36.
Friedman, M (1962) *Capitalism and Freedom*, University of Chicago Press, Chicago.
—— (1968) The Role of Monetary Policy, *American Economic Review*, 68(1): 1–17.
Friedman, T (1999) *The Lexus and the Olive Tree: Understanding Globalization*, Farrar Strauss Giroux, New York.
Gale F (1972) *Urban Aborigines*, ANU Press, Canberra.
Gibson, R, Wilson, S, Denemark, D, Meagher, G and Western, M (2004) *The Australian Survey of Social Attitudes 2003*, Australian Social Science Data Archive, Centre for Social Research, Australian National University, Canberra.
Gibson-Graham, JK (1994) 'Reflections on Regions, the White Paper and a New Class Politics of Distribution', *Australian Geographer*, 25(2): 148–52.
Giddens, A (1999) *The Third Way: The Renewal of Social Democracy*, Blackwell, London.
Gilbert, R and Gilbert, P (1998) *Masculinity Goes to School*, Allen & Unwin, Sydney.
Gillies, M (2005) 'Measure for Measure', *Higher Education Australian*, 23 March, p. 43.
Gleeson, B (2003) 'Learning about Regionalism from Europe', *Australian Geographical Studies*, 41(3): 221–36.
Gleeson, B and Low, N (2000) *Australian Urban Planning*, Allen & Unwin, Sydney.
Goldie, J, Douglas, B and Furnass, B (2005) *In Search of Sustainability*, CSIRO Publishing, Melbourne.
Goodall, H and Huggins, J (1992) 'Aboriginal Women are Everywhere: Contemporary Struggles', in K Saunders and R Evans (eds), *Gender Relations in Australia*, Harcourt Brace Jovanovich, Sydney.
Goodin, RE (1988) *Reasons for Welfare*, Princeton University Press, Princeton.
Goodnow, J and Pateman, C (1985) 'Preface', in J Goodnow and C Pateman (eds), *Social Science and Public Policy*, Allen & Unwin, Sydney, pp. vi–vii.
Grabosky, PN (1995) 'Using Non-government Resources to Foster Regulatory Compliance', *Governance*, 8(4): 527–50.
—— (1997) 'Inside the Pyramid: Towards a Conceptual Framework for the Analysis of Regulatory Systems', *International Journal of the Sociology of Law*, 25(3): 195–201.
Grattan, M (2000) 'Off with the Black Hat, on with the White', *Sydney Morning Herald*, 17 April, p. 2.
Hamer, D (1996) 'Towards a Viable Senate', in JR Disney and JR Nethercote (eds), *The House on Capital Hill: Parliament, Politics and Power in the National Capital*, Federation Press, Canberra, pp. 63–80.
Hamilton, C and Mail, E (2003) *Downshifting in Australia: A Sea-change in the Pursuit of Happiness*, Discussion Paper No. 50, The Australia Institute, Canberra.

Hamilton, C, Eckersley, R and Denniss, R (2005) *A Manifesto for Wellbeing*, The Australia Institute, Canberra, retrieved from <www.wellbeingmanifesto.net >.

Hancock, Linda (1999) 'Women's Policy Interests in the Market State', in L Hancock (ed.), *Women, Public Policy and the State*, Macmillan, Melbourne, pp. 3–19.

Hanlon, M (2004) 'There's no Time like the Present', *Spectator*, 7 August.

Hanushek, E (1986) 'The Economics of Schooling: Production and Efficiency in Public Schools', *Journal of Economic Literature*, 24: 1141–77.

Harding, A, Lloyd, R, and Warren, N (2004) 'Income Distribution and Redistribution: The Impact of Selected Government Benefits and Taxes in Australia in 2001–02', paper prepared for the 28th General Conference of The International Association for Research in Income and Wealth, 22–28 August, Cork, Ireland.

Harris, A (2004) *Future Girl: Young Women in the Twenty-first Century,* Routledge, New York and London.

Harris, M (2004) 'From Australian Courts to Aboriginal Courts in Australia', *Current Issues in Criminal Justice*, 16 (1): 26–40.

Harvey, D (1989) 'From Managerialism to Entrepreneurialism: The Transformation in Urban Governance in Late Capitalism', *Geografiska Annaler*, 71B(1): 3–17.

Haslam, C and Bryman, A (1994) 'Social Scientists and the Media: An Overview', in C Haslam and A Bryman (eds), *Social Scientists Meet the Media*, Routledge, London, pp. 186–211.

Hawke, RJL and Howe, B (1990) *Towards a Fairer Australia: Social Justice Strategy Statement 1990–91*, Australian Government Publishing Service, Canberra.

Hayek, FA (1960) *The Constitution of Liberty*, Routledge & Kegan Paul, London.

Head, BW (1997) 'Corporatism', in D Woodward, A Parkin and J Summers (eds), *Government, Politics, Power and Policy in Australia*, 6th edition, Longman, Melbourne, pp. 333–55.

—— (1999) 'The Changing Role of the Public Service: Improving Service Delivery', *Canberra Bulletin of Public Administration*, 94: 1–3.

Head, BW and Ryan, N (2004) 'Can Co-Governance Work?', *Society and Economy*, 26(2–3): 361–82.

Henderson, D (1995) 'The Revival of Economic Liberalism: Australia in an International Perspective', *Australian Economic Review*, 28(1): 59–85.

—— (1998) *The Changing Fortunes of Economic Liberalism: Yesterday, Today and Tomorrow*, Institute of Economic Affairs, London.

Henry, K (2004) *Enhancing Freedom, Generating Opportunities – Challenges for Governments, Chances for Citizens*, address to Institute of Public Administration, 20 July, Victorian Division, Victoria.

Henton, D (2001) 'Lessons from Silicon Valley', in A Scott (ed.), *Global City-Regions: Trends, Theory, Policy*, Oxford University Press, Oxford, pp. 391–400.

Hewson, J and Fischer, T (1992) *Fightback! Fairness and Jobs*, Panther Publishing and Printing, Canberra.

Hicks, A and Kenworthy, L (2004) 'Varieties of Welfare Capitalism', *Socio-Economic Review*, 1(1): 27–61.

Hindess, B (2004) *Corruption and Democracy in Australia*, Report No. 3, Democratic Audit of Australia Project, Research School of Social Sciences, Australian National University, Canberra.

Hirsch, F (1976) *Social Limits to Growth*, Harvard University Press, Cambridge.

Hirschman, A O (1996) 'Two Hundred Years of Reactionary Rhetoric: The

Futility Thesis', in P Barker (ed.), *Living As Equals*, Oxford University Press, Oxford, pp. 59–83.

Hoban, R (2005) 'The "Bubble Wrap" Generation', *VicHealth Letter*, No. 24, Summer, pp. 8–13.

Hocking, J (1993) *Beyond Terrorism: The Development of the Australian Security State*, Allen & Unwin, Sydney.

—— (2001) 'Robert Menzies "Fundamental Authoritarianism": The 1951 Referendum', in P Strangio and P Love (eds), *Arguing the Cold War*, Vulgar Press, Melbourne, pp. 47–59.

—— (2004a) 'Protecting Democracy by Preserving Justice: "Even for the Feared and the Hated"', *The University of New South Wales Law Journal*, Thematic Issue: Counter-terrorism Laws, 27(2): 319–38.

—— (2004b) *Terror Laws: ASIO, Counter-terrorism and the Threat to Democracy*, UNSW Press, Sydney.

Howard, J (1998) 'Address to the World Economic Forum Dinner', Melbourne, 16 March, Press Office of the Prime Minister, Parliament House, Canberra.

—— (2004) 'Getting the Big Things Right: Goals and Responsibilities in a Fourth Term', address to Enterprise Forum Lunch, Adelaide, 8 July, News Room, Office of the Prime Minister, Parliament House, Canberra.

Human Rights and Equal Opportunity Commission (HREOC) (2002) *A Time to Value. Proposal for a National Paid Maternity Leave Scheme*, HREOC, Sydney.

—— (2004) 'Women, Work and Equity Speeches Online', HREOC, Sydney, retrieved from <http://www.hreoc.gov.au/sex_discrimination/index.html>.

Hunter, BH (2004) *Indigenous Australians in the Contemporary Labour Market*, Cat. no. 2052.0, Australian Bureau of Statistics, Canberra.

Inglehart, R (2000) 'Globalisation and Postmodern Values', *Washington Quarterly*, 23(1): 215–28.

Innes, JE and Booher, D (2003) *The Impact of Collaborative Planning on Governance Capacity*, Working Paper 2003/03, Institute of Urban and Regional Development, University of California, Berkeley.

International Development Program (IDP Australia) (2005) *Statistical Data on Australia's Exports of Education Services*, accessed 7 March 2005, <http://www.idp.com/marketingandresearch/research/statistics/default.asp>.

International Labour Organisation (ILO) (2004) *Working Time and Worker Preferences in Industrialized Countries: Finding the Balance*, ILO, Geneva.

Jackson, W (2003) 'Achieving Inter-agency Collaboration in Policy Development', *Canberra Bulletin of Public Administration*, 109: 20–26.

Jaensch, D (1989) *The Hawke–Keating Hijack: The ALP in Transition*, Allen & Unwin, Sydney.

—— (2003) 'Australia's Political Parties' [unpublished mimeo], Democratic Audit of Australia, Research School of Social Sciences, Australian National University, Canberra.

Jaumotte, F (2004) *Female Labour Force Participation: Past Trends and Main Determinants in OECD Countries OECD*, Economics Department, OECD, Paris.

Jonas, W (2004) *Social Justice Report 2003*, Human Rights and Equal Opportunity Commission, Sydney.

Jones, R (1994) *The Housing Needs of Indigenous Australians, 1991*, Centre for Aboriginal Economic Policy Research, Australian National University, Canberra.

Jordan, A (1989) 'Of Good Character and Deserving of a Pension. Moral and Racial Provisions in Australian Social Security', *Reports and Proceedings*, Social Welfare Research Centre, University of New South Wales, Sydney.

Karmel, P, Committee Chair (1973) *Schools in Australia: Report of the Interim Committee for the Commonwealth Schools Commission*, Australian Government Publishing Service, Canberra.

Kasser, T (2002) *The High Price of Materialism*, MIT Press, Cambridge and Massachusetts.

Keane, J (2002) 'Whatever Happened to Democracy?', public lecture delivered to the Institute for Public Policy Research, 27 March, London.

Keating, P (1999) 'The Labour Government 1983–1996', speech given at the University of New South Wales, 19 March, Sydney, retrieved from <http://www.keating.org.au>.

Keating, M (1993), 'The Influence of Economists', in S King and P Lloyd (eds), *Economic Rationalism. Dead End or Way Forward?*, Allen & Unwin, Sydney, pp. 57–81.

—— (2004) *Who Rules? How Government Retains Control in a Privatised Economy*, Federation Press, Sydney.

Keating, M and Mitchell, D (2000) 'Security and Equity in a Changing Society: Social Policy', in G Davis and M Keating (eds), *The Future of Governance: Policy Choices*, Allen & Unwin, Sydney, pp. 122–52.

Kelley, J and Sikora, J (2002) 'Australian Public Opinion on Privatisation, 1986–2002', *Growth*, No. 50: 54–8.

Kelly, P (1992) *The End of Certainty: The Story of the 1980s*, Allen & Unwin, Sydney.

Kemp, D (1988) 'Liberalism and Conservatism in Australia since 1944', in B Head and J Walter (eds), *Intellectual Movements and Australian Society*, Oxford University Press, Melbourne, pp. 322–62.

Kenway, J, Willis, S, Blackmore, J and Rennie, L (1997) *Answering Back: Girls, Boys and Feminism in Schools*, Allen & Unwin, Sydney.

Kernaghan, K (1993) 'Partnership and Public Administration', *Canadian Public Administration*, 36(1): 57–76.

Kettl, DF (ed.) (2002), *Environmental Governance: A Report on the Next Generation of Environmental Policy*, Brookings, Washington DC.

Keynes, JM (1936) *The General Theory of Employment, Interest and Money*, MacMillan, London.

Kiker, BF (1966) 'The Historical Roots of Human Capital', *Journal of Political Economy*, 74(5): 481–99.

Kim, W (2001) 'Repositioning of City–Regions: Korea after the Crisis', in A Scott (ed.), *Global City–Regions: Trends, Theory, Policy*, Oxford University Press, Oxford, pp. 263–81.

King, A (1998) 'Income Poverty Since the Early 1970s', in R Fincher and J Nieuwenhuysen (eds), *Australian Poverty, Then and Now*, Melbourne University Press, Melbourne, pp. 71–102.

Kuttner, R (2004) 'The Torturers Among Us: Legalese Can't Protect the Bush Administration from its Crimes', *The American Prospect Online*, 14 June, retrieved from <http://www.prospect.org>.

Lake, M (1999) *Getting Equal: The History of Australian Feminism*, Allen & Unwin, Sydney.

Lasswell, H (1951) 'The Policy Orientation', in D Lerner and H Lasswell (eds), *The Policy Sciences: Recent Developments in Scope and Method*, Stanford University Press, California, pp. 3–15.

Lee, HP, Hanks, P and Moribito, V (1995) *National Security*, Law Book Company, Sydney.

Leigh, A (2003) 'Randomised Policy Trials', *Agenda: A Journal of Policy Analysis and Reform*, 10(4): 341–54.

—— (2004) *Optimal Design of Earned Income Tax Credits: Evidence from a British Natural Experiment*, Research School of Social Sciences, Australian National University, accessed 6 April 2005, <http://www.Andrewleigh.com>.

Lepsius, O (2004) 'Liberty, Security and Terrorism: The Legal Position in Germany', *German Law Journal*, 5(5): 435–54.

Lindbeck, A (1997), 'The Swedish Experiment', *Journal of Economic Literature*, 35(3): 1273–319.

Lipsey RG, Carlaw, K and Bekar, C (forthcoming) *Economic Transformations: General Purpose Technologies and Long-term Growth*, Oxford University Press, Oxford.

Lomborg, B (2001) *The Skeptical Environmentalist: Measuring the Real State of the World*, Cambridge University Press, Cambridge.

Lovering, J (1999) 'Theory Led by Policy: The Inadequacies of the "New" Regionalism', *International Journal of Urban and Regional Research*, 23: 379–95.

Lustgarten, L (2004) 'National Security, Terrorism and Constitutional Balance', *The Political Quarterly*, 75(1): 4–16.

Luxembourg Income Study (LIS), (2004) web page, viewed 15 December, <http://www.lisproject.org>.

McAllister, I (2000) 'Keeping them Honest: Public and Elite Perceptions of Ethical Conduct Amongst Australian Legislators', *Political Studies*, 48(1): 22–47.

McAllister, I and Wanna, J (2001) 'Citizens' Expectations and Perceptions of Governance', in G Davis and P Weller (eds), *Are You Being Served?*, Allen & Unwin, Sydney, pp. 7–35.

McCain, M and Fraser Mustard, J (2002) *The Early Years Study: Three Years On*, The Founders Network of the Canadian Institute for Advanced Research, Toronto.

McClure, P (2000) *Participation Support for a More Equitable Society: Final Report of the Reference Group on Welfare Reform*, accessed 15 February 2005, <http://www.facs.gov.au/internet/facsinternet.nsf/aboutfacs/programs/esp-welfare_reform_final.htm>.

McCredden, L (2004), 'Writing Authority in Australia', in D Carter (ed.), *The Ideas Market*, Melbourne University Press, Melbourne, pp. 80–94.

McCulloch, J (2000) *Blue Army: Paramilitary Policing in Australia*, Melbourne University Press, Melbourne.

McDonald, P (2001a) 'Theory Pertaining to Low Fertility', presented at the International Union for the Scientific Study of Population Working Group on Low Fertility, International Perspectives on Low Fertility: Trends, Theories and Policies, 21–23 March, Tokyo.

—— (2001b) 'Work–Family Policies are the Right Approach to the Prevention of Very Low Fertility', *People and Place*, 9(3): 17–27.

—— (2002) 'Issues in Child Care Policy in Australia', *Demography and Sociology Program*, Research School of Social Sciences, Australian National University, Canberra.

McGuire, L (2003) 'Benchmarking Community Services', *Journal of Contemporary Issues in Business and Government*, 9(2): 63–74.

McNally, N (2004) 'Illegal Imprisonment at Guantanamo Bay', *Law Society Journal*, 42: 78–82.

MacKinnon, D, Cumbers A and Chapman, K (2002) 'Learning, Innovation and Regional Development: A Critical Appraisal of Recent Debates', *Progress in Human Geography*, 26(3): 293–311.

Maddison, A (2001) *The World Economy: A Millennial Perspective*,

Development Centre of the Organisation for Economic Cooperation and Development, Paris.

Maher, C, Whitelaw, J, McAllister, A, Francis, R, Palmer, J, Chee, E and Taylor, P (1992) *Mobility and Locational Disadvantage within Australian Cities*, Australian Government Publishing Service, Canberra.

Management Advisory Committee (MAC), (2004) *Connecting Government: Whole of Government Responses to Australia's Priority Challenges*, Commonwealth Government, Canberra.

Mandell, MP (ed.), (2001) *Getting Results through Collaboration: Networks and Network Structures for Public Policy and Management*, Quorum Books, Westport.

Mann, M (1988) *States, War and History*, Blackwell, Oxford.

Marchetti, E and Daly, K (2004) 'Indigenous Courts and Justice Practices in Australia', *Trends and Issues*, No. 277, Australian Institute of Criminology, Canberra.

Marginson, S (1997) *Educating Australia: Government, Economy and Citizen since 1960*, Cambridge University Press, Cambridge.

—— (2005) *Dynamics of National and Global Competition in Higher Education* [in press].

Marmot, MG (2004) 'Evidence-based Policy or Policy-based Evidence?', *British Journal of Medicine*, 328: 906–7.

Marsh, I (1995) *Beyond the Two-party System*, Cambridge University Press, Melbourne.

—— (2005) 'Neo-liberalism and the Decline of Democratic Governance: A Problem of Institutional Design', *Political Studies*, 53(1): 22–44.

Marsh, I and Yencken, D (2004) *Into the Future: The Neglect of the Long Term in Australian Politics*, Australian Collaboration/Black Inc, Melbourne.

Marshall, TH (1949) 'Citizenship and Social Class', Marshall Lectures, Cambridge. Reprinted in TH Marshall (1963) *Sociology at the Crossroads*, Heinemann, London, pp. 67–127.

Martin, DF and Finlayson, JD (1996) 'Linking Accountability and Self-determination in Aboriginal Organisations', *CAEPR Discussion Paper 116*, Centre for Aboriginal Economic Policy Research, Australian National University, Canberra.

Martin, L, Committee Chair (1964) *Tertiary Education in Australia*, Volume 1, Australian Universities Commission, Melbourne.

Martin, V. (1984), *Australian Financial System Report of the Review Group (Martin Review Committee Report)*, Australian Government Printing Service, Canberra.

Masters, G (2005) 'Raising the Question: Are We World Class?', *Education Review*, 16 February, p. 8.

Meegan, R and Mitchell, A (2001) 'It's Not Community Round Here, It's Neighbourhood', *Urban Studies*, 38: 2167–94.

Melbourne Institute (2004) 'Household Income and Labour Dynamics (HILDA)' web page, viewed 15 February <http://www.melbourneinstitute.com/hilda>.

Metin, A. (1977) *Socialism without Doctrine* (originally published as *Le Socialisme Sans Doctrines in Paris, 1902*), Alternative Publishing Cooperative, Sydney.

Meyer, BD and Rosenbaum, DT (2001) 'Welfare, the Earned Income Tax Credit, and the Labor Supply of Single Mothers', *The Quarterly Journal of Economics*, 116(3), 1064–114.

Miers, D (2001) *An International Review of Restorative Justice*, Crime Reduction Research Series Paper 10, UK Home Office, London.

Miller, M (1985) *Report of the Committee of Review of Aboriginal Employment and Training Programs*, Australian Government Publishing Service, Canberra.

Morgan, R (2002) Roy Morgan Research web page, <http://www.roymorgan.com.au>.

Myers, DG (2004) 'Happiness', excerpted from *Psychology*, 7th edition, Worth Publishers, New York.

National Committee of Vocational Education Research (NCVER), (2004a) 'Students and Courses', accessed 31 March 2005, <http://www.ncver.edu.au /statistic/ index.html>.

—— (2004b) 'Financial Information', accessed 31 March 2005, <http://www.ncver.edu.au/ statistic/index.html>.

National Crime Prevention (1999) *Pathways to Prevention: Developmental & Early Intervention Approaches to Crime in Australia*, Full Report, National Crime Prevention, Attorney-General's Department, Canberra.

Nelson, B, Commonwealth Minister for Education, Science and Training (2003) *Our Universities: Backing Australia's Future*, DEST, accessed 18 December 2004, <www.dest.gov.au/highered/index1.htm>.

Neutze, M, Sanders, W and Jones, G (1999) *Public Expenditure on Services for Aboriginal People: Education, Employment, Health and Housing*, Discussion Paper No. 24, The Australia Institute, Canberra.

North, DC (1990) *Institutions, Institutional Change and Economic Performance*, Cambridge University Press, Cambridge.

Norton, A (2004) 'The Politics of Protection: Public Opinion can Favour Liberalising Trade', *Policy*, 20(2): 10–15.

Oakley, S (2004) 'Politics of Recollection', *Urban Policy and Research*, 22(3): 299–314.

O'Connor, J (1973) *The Fiscal Crisis of the State*, St. Martin's Press, New York.

Organisation for Economic Co-operation and Development (OECD), (1989) *Labour Market Policies for the 1990s*, OECD, Paris.

—— (1990) *Employment Outlook*, OECD, Paris.

—— (1999) *Convention on Combating Bribery of Foreign Public Officials*, OECD, Paris.

—— (2001) *The Well-being of Nations: The Role of Human and Social Capital*, OECD, Paris.

—— (2004a) *Employment Outlook*, OECD, Paris.

—— (2004b) *Benefits and Wages: OECD Indicators*, OECD, Paris.

—— (2004c) *Education at a Glance*, OECD, Paris.

Orchard, L (1995) 'National Urban Policy in the 1990s', in P Troy (ed.), *Australian Cities*, Cambridge University Press, Melbourne, pp. 65–86.

Office for Women (2004) 'Violence Against Women: Australia Says No', Office for Women, Canberra, retrieved from <http://www.australiasaysno.gov.au/ booklet/viewBooklet/index.htm>.

Osborne, D and Gaebler, TA (1992) *Reinventing Government: How the Entrepreneurial Spirit is Transforming the Public Sector*, Addison-Wesley, Reading, Massachusetts.

Ostendorf, W, Musterd, S and De Vos, S (2001) 'Social Mix and the Neighbourhood Effect', *Housing Studies*, 16(3): 371–80.

Page, B and Shapiro, RY (1992) *The Rational Public: Fifty Years of Trends in Americans' Policy Preferences*, University of Chicago Press, Chicago.

Painter, M (1998) *Collaborative Federalism: Economic Reform in Australia in the 1990s*, Cambridge University Press, Melbourne.

Painter, M and Pierre, J (2005) *Challenges to State Policy Capacity: Global*

Trends and Comparative Perspectives, Palgrave Macmillan, London.

Papadakis, E (1999) 'Constituents of Confidence and Mistrust in Australian Institutions', *Australian Journal of Political Science*, 34(1): 75–93.

Peel, M (1995) *Good Times, Hard Times*, Melbourne University Press, Melbourne.

—— (2003) *The Lowest Rung*, Cambridge University Press, Melbourne.

Pettit, P (1997) *Republicanism: A Theory of Freedom and Government*, The Clarendon Press, Oxford.

Pfau-Effinger, B (2004) *Development of Culture, Welfare States and Women's Employment in Europe*, Ashgate, Aldershot.

Phillips, LM (2000) *Flirting with Danger: Young Women's Reflections on Sexuality and Domination*, New York University Press, New York.

Pierson, C and Castles, F (2001) *Australian Antecedents of the Third Way*, Joint Sessions of the European Consortium for Political Research, Grenoble.

Plant, R (2003) 'Citizenship and Social Security', *Fiscal Studies*, 24(2): 153–66.

Pocock, B (2003) *The Work/Life Collision. What Work is Doing to Australians and What to do About it*, Federation Press, Sydney.

Pocock, B (2005a) 'Who's a Worker Now? And What Does it Mean for Australian Politics?', keynote address to The 19th Annual Conference of the Association of Industrial Relations Academics of Australia and New Zealand (AIRAANZ), 10 February, University of Sydney, Sydney.

—— (2005b) 'Work/Life "Balance" in Australia: Limited Progress, Dim Prospects', *Asia Pacific Journal of Human Resources*, forthcoming.

Pocock, B and Clarke, J (2004) *Time Over Money, What Young Australians Think About Their Parents' Work, Time Guilt and Their Own Consumption*, Discussion Paper No. 61, The Australia Institute, Canberra.

Pocock, B, van Wanrooy, B, Strazzari, S and Bridge, K (2001) *Fifty Families: What Unreasonable Hours are Doing to Australians, Their Families and Their Communities*, Australian Council of Trade Unions, Melbourne.

Power, M (2003) 'Evaluating the Audit Explosion', *Law and Policy*, 25(3): 185–202.

Preston, N and Sampford, C (2002) *Encouraging Ethics and Challenging Corruption*, Federation Press, Sydney.

Preston T and 't Hart, P (1999), 'Understanding and Evaluating Bureaucratic Politics: The Nexus Between Political Leaders and Advisory Systems', *Political Psychology*, 20(1): 49–98.

Probert, B (2002) '"Grateful Slaves" or "Self-made Women": A Matter of Choice or Policy?', *Australian Feminist Studies*, 17(37): 7–17.

Probert, B and Macdonald, F (1999) 'Young Women: Poles of Experience in Work and Parenting', in Dusseldorp Skills Forum (ed.), *Australia's Young Adults: The Deepening Divide*, Dusseldorp Skills Forum, Sydney, pp. 135–57.

Productivity Commission (1998) *Impact of Competition Policy Reforms on Rural and Regional Australia – Inquiry Report No. 8*, Australian Government Printing Service, Canberra.

—— (2003) *Overcoming Indigenous Disadvantage: Key Indicators 2003*, Productivity Commission, Canberra.

—— (2005a) *Report on Government Services*, Productivity Commission, Canberra.

—— (2005b) *Review of National Competition Policy Reforms*, Report No. 33, Productivity Commission, Canberra.

Pusey, M (1991) *Economic Rationalism in Canberra: A Nation-building State Changes Its Mind*, Cambridge University Press, Cambridge.

—— (2003) *The Experience of Middle Australia: The Dark Side of Economic Reform*, Cambridge University Press, Cambridge.

Putnam, RD (1993) *Making Democracy Work: Civic Traditions in Modern Italy*, Princeton University Press, Princeton.

—— (2000) *Bowling Alone: The Collapse and Revival of American Community*, Simon & Schuster, New York.

Quiggin, J (1987) 'White Trash of Asia?', *Current Affairs Bulletin*, 64(2): 18–25.

—— (1997), 'Economic Rationalism', *Crossings*, 2(1): 3–12.

—— (1998) 'Social Democracy and Market Reform in Australia and New Zealand', *Oxford Review of Economic Policy*, 14(1): 76–95.

—— (2005) 'Hayek and Pinochet: One More Time', retrieved from <http://john-quiggin.com/index.php/archives/2005/02/25/hayek-&-pinochet-one-more-time>.

Raco, M (1999) 'Competition, Collaboration and the New Industrial Districts', *Urban Studies*, 36: 951–68.

Ray, PH and Anderson, RS (2000) *The Cultural Creatives: How 50 Million People are Changing the World*, Harmony Books, New York.

Reaburn, N (1978) 'The Legal Implications in Counter Terrorist Operations', *Pacific Defence Reporter*, 4(10): 34–36.

Rector, R (2004) 'Lifting Up the People', *National Review*, 56(22): 58–60.

Reddel, T (2002) 'Beyond Participation, Hierarchies, Management and Markets', *Australian Journal of Public Administration*, 61(1): 50–63.

Reddel, T and Woolcock, G (2004) 'From Consultation to Participatory Governance?', *Australian Journal of Public Administration*, 63(3): 75–87.

Reed, R, Allen, M, Castleman, T and Couthard, T (2003) '"I Mean You Want to be There for Them": Young Australian Professionals Negotiating Careers in a Gendered World', *Australian Journal of Labour Economics*, 6(4): 519–36.

Reich, R (1990) *The Power of Public Ideas*, Harvard University Press, Harvard.

Rhodes, RAW (1997) *Understanding Governance*, Open University Press, Maidenhead.

—— (2003) 'What is New About Governance and Why Does it Matter?', in J Hayward and A Menon (eds), *Governing Europe*, Oxford University Press, Oxford, pp. 61–73.

Ring, IT and Brown, N (2002) 'Indigenous Health: Chronically Inadequate Responses to Damning Statistics', *Medical Journal of Australia*, 177(11): 629–31.

Robertson, Boni (1999) *The Aboriginal and Torres Strait Islander Women's Taskforce on Violence Report*, Department of Aboriginal and Torres Strait Islander Policy and Development, Brisbane.

Rowley, CD (1970) *Outcasts in White Australia*, ANU Press, Canberra.

Rowse, T (1998) 'The Modesty of the State: Hasluck and the Anthropological Critics of Assimilation', in K Saunders and CT Stannage (eds), *Paul Hasluck in Australian History*, University of Queensland Press, Brisbane, pp. 119–32.

—— (2001) 'Democratic Systems are an Alien thing to Aboriginal Culture', in M Sawer and G Zappala (eds), *Speaking for the People*, Melbourne University Press, Melbourne, pp. 103–33.

—— (2002a) *Indigenous Futures: Choice and Development for Aboriginal and Islander Australia*, UNSW Press, Sydney.

—— (2002b) *Nugget Coombs: A Reforming Life*, Cambridge University Press, Melbourne.

Ruming, K, Mee, K and McGuirk, P (2004) 'Questioning the Rhetoric of Social Mix', *Australian Geographical Studies*, 42(2): 234–48.

Salinger, JD (2004) *The Catcher in the Rye*, Penguin Books, London.

Sanders, W (1991) 'Destined to Fail: The Hawke Government's Pursuit of Statistical Equality in Employment and Income Status between Aboriginal and Other Australians by the Year 2000 (or, A Cautionary Tale Involving the New Managerialism and Social Justice Strategies)', *Australian Aboriginal Studies*, 1991/2: 13–18.

Sassen, S (1991) *The Global City*, Princeton University Press, Princeton.

Saunders, P (UNSW), (2002) *The Ends and Means of Welfare: Coping with Economic and Social Change in Australia*, Cambridge University Press, Cambridge.

Saunders, P (CIS), (2004a) *Australia's Welfare Habit and How to Kick It*, Duffy & Snellgrove, Sydney.

—— (2004b) *Lies, Damned Lies and the Senate Poverty Inquiry Report*, Issues and Analysis No. 46, Centre for Independent Studies, Sydney.

Sawer, M (1990) *Sisters in Suits: Women and Public Policy in Australia*, Allen & Unwin, Sydney.

—— (1993) 'Reclaiming Social Liberalism: The Women's Movement and the State', in R Howe (ed.), *Women and the State: Australian Perspectives*, Special edition of *Journal of Australian Studies*, Bundoora, La Trobe University Press in association with the Centre for Australian Studies, Deakin University and the Ideas for Australia Program.

—— (1999) 'The Watchers Within: Women and the Australian State', in L Hancock (ed.), *Women, Public Policy and the State*, Macmillan, Melbourne, pp. 36–53.

—— (2002) 'In Safe Hands? Women in the 2001 Election', in J Warhurst and M Simms (eds), *2001: The Centenary Election*, University of Queensland Press, St Lucia, pp. 253–259.

—— (2004a) 'Populism and Public Choice in Australia and Canada: Turning Equality-seekers into "Special Interests"', in M Sawer and B Hindess (eds), *Us and Them: Anti-Elitism in Australia*, API Network, Curtin University of Technology, Perth, pp. 33–55.

—— (2004b) *The Ethical State? Social Liberalism in Australia*, Melbourne University Press, Melbourne.

—— (2005) 'Mums and Dads of Australia', forthcoming in M Simms and J Warhurst (eds), *Mortgage Nation: The 2004 Election*, API-Network, Perth.

Schapper, HP (1970) *Aboriginal Advancement to Integration*, ANU Press, Canberra.

Scharpf, F and Schmidt, V (1999) *Welfare and Work in the Open Economy*, Oxford University Press, Oxford.

Schmidt, V (2000) 'Values and Discourse in the Politics of Adjustment', in FW Scharpf and VA Schmidt (eds), *Welfare and Work in the Open Economy. Vol. 1: From Vulnerability to Competitiveness*, Oxford University Press, Oxford, pp. 229–309.

Schor, J (1998) *The Overspent American: Why We Want What We Don't Need*, Basic Books, New York.

Schwab, RG (1998) *Educational "Failure" and Educational "Success" in an Aboriginal Community*, Discussion Paper 161, Centre for Aboriginal Economic Policy Research, Australian National University, Canberra.

Scott, A, Agnew, A, Soja, E and Storper, M (2001) 'Global City–Regions', in A Scott (ed.), *Global City–Regions*, Oxford University Press, Oxford, pp. 11–30.

Scott, C. (2003) 'Speaking Softly Without Big Sticks: Meta-Regulation and Public Sector Audit', *Law and Policy*, 25(3): 203–19.

Scutt, J (1985) *Poor Nation of the Pacific: Australia's Future*, Allen & Unwin, Sydney.

Self, P (2005) 'Alternative Urban Policies', in P Troy (ed.), *Australian Cities*, Cambridge University Press, Melbourne, pp. 246–64.

Sen, AK (1999) *Development as Freedom*, Anchor Books, New York.

Shergold, P (2004) *Connecting Government: Whole-of-Government Responses to Australia's Priority Challenges, Management Advisory Committee*, Report 4, Australian Government Publishing Service, Canberra.

Sims, R (2005) *Repairing and Restoring Australia's Infrastructure*, Port Jackson Partners, Sydney.

Smart, D and Sanson, A (2005) 'What is Life Like for Young Australians Today and How Well are They Faring?', *Family Matters*, 70: 46–53.

Smyth, P (1998) 'Remaking the Australian Way: The Keynesian Compromise', in P Smyth and B Cass (eds), *Contesting the Australian Way: States, Markets and Civil Society*, Cambridge University Press, Melbourne, pp. 81–93.

Spiller, M (2000) *The Capital Cities and Australia's Future*, Property Council of Australia, Sydney.

Standing, G (2002) *Beyond Paternalism: Basic Security as Equality*, Verso, New York.

Stanner, WEH (1970) 'Foreword', in HP Schapper (ed.), *Aboriginal Advancement to Integration*, ANU Press, Canberra, pp. vii–ix.

—— (1972) 'Howitt, Alfred William (1830–1980)', *Australian Dictionary of Biography 1851–1890*, D-J, 4: 432–5.

Steffen, W, Sanderson, A, Tyson, P, Jäger, J, Matson, P, Moore III, B, Oldfield, F, Richardson, K, Schellnhuber, H-J, Turner II, BL and Wasson, R (2004) *Global Change and the Earth System: A Planet Under Pressure*, IGBP Global Change Series, Springer-Verlag, Berlin Heidelburg New York.

Stewart, J and Jones, G (2003) *Renegotiating the Environment: The Power of Politics*, Federation Press, Sydney.

Strang, H (2001) *Restorative Justice Programs in Australia: A Report to the Criminology Research Council*, Research School of Social Sciences, Australian National University, Canberra.

Strazdins, L, Korda, RJ, Lim, LL-Y, Broom, DH, D'Souza, RM (2004) 'Around-the-clock: Parent Work Schedules and Children's Wellbeing in a 24-h Economy', *Social Science and Medicine*, 59: 1517–27.

Stretton, H (1970) *Ideas for Australian Cities*, Georgian House, Melbourne.

Summers, A (2003) *The End of Equality: Work, Babies and Women's Choices in 21st Century Australia*, Random House Australia, Sydney.

Swift, J (1729/1953) 'A Modest Proposal', in H Davis (ed.), *The Prose Works of Jonathan Swift*, Volume 12, Basil Blackwell, Oxford, pp. 109–18.

Taylor, J (1993a) *The Relative Economic Status of Indigenous Australians, 1986–91*, Centre for Aboriginal Economic Policy Research, Australian National University, Canberra.

—— (1993b) *Regional Change in the Economic Status of Indigenous Australians, 1986–91*, Centre for Aboriginal Economic Policy Research, Australian National University, Canberra.

Taylor, J and Altman, JC (1997) *The Job Ahead: Escalating Economic Costs of Indigenous Employment Disparity*, ATSIC Office of Public Affairs, Canberra.

Teese, R and Polesel, J (2003) *Undemocratic Schooling: Equity and Quality in Mass Secondary Education in Australia*, Melbourne University Press, Melbourne.

The Taskforce on Higher Education and Society (2000) *Higher Education in Developing Countries: Peril and Promise*, World Bank, Washington.

The Treasury (2004) *Policy Advice and Treasury's Wellbeing Framework*, The Treasury, Canberra.

Tiesdell, S and Allmendinger, P (2001) 'Neighbourhood Regeneration and New Labour's Third Way', *Environment & Planning C: Government & Policy*, 19: 903–26.

Tocqueville, A (2003) *Democracy in America*, Harvey Mansfield jnr and Delba Winthrop (eds), University of Chicago Press, Chicago.

Todd, T and Eveline, J (2004) *Report on the Review of the Gender Pay Gap in Western Australia*, prepared for the Minister for Consumer and Employment Protection, School of Economics and Commerce, University of Western Australia, Crawley, retrieved from <http://www.tlcwa.org.au/wa_ir/files/Report_Gender_Pay_Gap.pdf>.

Travers, P (1991) 'Salami Tactics and the Australian Welfare State', in M Adler, C Bell, J Clasen and A Sinfield (eds), *The Sociology of Social Security*, Edinburgh University Press, Edinburgh, pp. 95–109.

Uhr, J (2004) 'Terra Infirma? Parliament's Uncertain Role in the "War on Terror"', *The University of New South Wales Law Journal*, Thematic Issue: Counter-terrorism Laws, 27(2): 339–51.

Uitermark, J (2003) '"Social Mixing" and the Management of Disadvantaged Neighbourhoods: The Dutch Policy of Urban Remixing Revisited', *Urban Studies*, 40(3): 531–49.

United Nations Development Programme (UNDP), (1997) *Reconceptualising Governance*, Discussion Paper 2, UNDP, New York.

United Nations Educational, Social and Cultural Organisation (UNESCO), (1968) *Readings in the Economics of Education*, UNESCO, Paris.

United Nations High Commissioner for Refugees (UNHCR), (2002) *Report of the United Nations High Commissioner for Human Rights to the World Conference on Human Rights,* 4 UN Doc E/CN.4/2002/18.

Victorian Government (2002) *Melbourne 2030: Planning for Sustainable Growth*, Department of Infrastructure, Melbourne.

—— (2003) *Manufacturing Policy: Agenda for New Manufacturing*, Victorian Government Printer, Melbourne.

—— (2004) 'Victoria: Leading the Way', *Economic Statement*, April 2004, Victorian Government Printer, Melbourne.

Walter, J (2004) 'Elites, Politics and Publics', in M Sawer and B Hindess (eds), *Us and Them: Anti-elitism in Australia*, API Network, Curtin University of Technology, Perth, pp. 203–24.

Watson, I, Buchanan, J, Campbell, I and Briggs, C (2003) *Fragmented Futures: New Challenges in Working Life*, Federation Press, Sydney.

Weiss, C (1986) 'Research and Policy-making: A Limited Partnership', in F Heller (ed.), *The Use and Abuse of Social Science*, Sage, London, pp. 214–35.

Weiss, L (1998) *The Myth of the Powerless State: Governing the Economy in a Global Era*, Polity Press, Cambridge.

Weller, P and Young, L, (2000) 'Political Parties and the Party System: Challenges for Effective Governing', in M Keating, J Wanna and P Weller (eds), *Institutions on the Edge*, Allen & Unwin, Sydney pp.156–77.

West, J (2004) 'Financing Innovation: Markets and the Structure of Risk', *Growth 53*, Committee for Economic Development of Australia, Melbourne, pp. 12–34.

Western, J (1998) 'Sociology', in Academy of the Social Sciences in Australia (ed.), *Challenges for the Social Sciences in Australia*, Australian Government Publishing Services, Canberra, pp. 223–31.

White, R (2003) 'Communities, Conferences and Restorative Social Justice', *Criminal Justice*, 3(2): 139–60.

Whitehouse, G (2004) 'Pay Equity – 20 Years of Change and Continuity, Human

Rights and Equal Opportunity Commission', Sydney, retrieved from <http://www.hreoc.gov.au/sex_discrimination/index.html>.

Wigmans, G (2001) 'Contingent Governance and the Enabling City', *City*, 5(2): 203–23.

Williams, T (2000) 'Richer by Degrees', *The Advertiser*, 13 June, p. 13.

Williamson, J (1990) 'What Washington Means by Policy Reform', in J Williamson (ed.), *Latin American Adjustment: How Much Has Happened?*, Institute for International Economics, Washington, pp. 7–33.

Wilson, JQ (1981) 'Policy Intellectuals and Public Policy', *Public Interest*, 64: 31–47.

Wilson, S and Breusch, T (2003) 'Taxes and Social Spending: The Shifting Demands of the Australian Public', *Australian Journal of Social Issues*, 38(1): 39–56.

Wilson, W (1987) *The Truly Disadvantaged*, Bantam Books, New York.

Winchester, H (1999) 'Lone Fathers and the Scales of Justice: Renegotiation of Masculinity after Divorce', *Journal of Interdisciplinary Gender Studies*, 4(2): 81–98.

Wolf, A (2002) *Does Education Matter? Myths about Education and Economic Growth*, Penguin, London.

Wooden, M and Warren, D (2003) 'The Characteristics of Casual and Fixed Term Employment: Evidence from the HILDA Survey', *Working Paper No. 15/03*, Melbourne Institute, University of Melbourne.

World Commission on Environment and Development (1987) *Our Common Future*, Oxford University Press, Oxford.

World Conservation Union (IUCN), United Nations Environment Program, World Wide Fund for Nature (1991) *Caring for the Earth: A Strategy for Sustainable Living*, IUCN, Gland, Switzerland.

Yankelovitch, D (1992) *Coming to Public Judgment*, Syracuse University Press, New York.

Yeatman, A (1998) *Activism and the Policy Process*, Allen & Unwin, Sydney.

Yencken, D and Fien, J (2000) 'Songlines and the Gondwanan Inheritance', in D Yencken, J Fien and H Sykes (eds), *Environment, Education and Society in the Asia Pacific*, Routledge, London, pp. 145–7.

Yeoh, B (1999) 'Global/globalizing Cities', *Progress in Human Geography*, 23(4): 607–16.

Young, K, Ashby, D, Boaz, A and Grayson, L (2002) 'Social Science and the Evidence-based Policy Movement', *Social Policy and Society*, 1(3): 215–24.

Zaller, J (1992) *The Nature of Origins of Mass Opinion*, Cambridge University Press, Cambridge.

Zimbardo, P (1997) 'What Messages are Behind Today's Cults?', *APA Monitor*, 28(5): 14.

—— (2002) 'Mind Control: Psychological Reality or Mindless Rhetoric?', *APA Monitor*, 33(10): 5.

INDEX